Baby

Baby

Joseph A. Stirt, M.D.

NEW HORIZON PRESS
Far Hills, N.J. 07931

Library of Congress Catalog Card Number: 92-060566

Joseph A. Stirt, M.D.
Baby
ISBN 0-88282-111-3
New Horizon Press

"Therefore the Judgement of the intellect is,
at best, only the half of truth,
and must if it be honest, also
come to an understanding
of its inadequacy."

Carl Jung

Author's Note

These are my actual experiences. The personalities, events, actions, and conversations portrayed within the story have been reconstructed from my diary and records. In addition I have utilized letters, personal papers, and the memories of participants. In an effort to safeguard the privacy of certain individuals, I have changed their names, and in some cases, altered otherwise identifying characteristics and chronology. Events involving the characters happened as described; only minor details have been altered.

Introduction

Life plays many tricks on us; surprises and ironies never cease. I entered the world of modern medicine naively, as a twenty-two-year-old medical student. Four years of medical school at UCLA, one of the great citadels of state-of-the-art, cutting edge medical progress have left me confused. I know an awful lot about a bunch of rare diseases, like systemic lupus erythematosus, dermatomyositis, and polycystic kidney disease, but next to nothing about how to take care of a patient with more mundane problems.

I have spent nine years since medical school applying all the slowly acquired wizardry and knowledge I can muster to people with disease, the sick, my patients. I started as an intern at Los Angeles County-University of Southern California Medical Center, a large county hospital which almost exclusively treated indigent patients, then spent two years in practice in Los Angeles as a part-time general practitioner. After that it was three years of specialized training as an anesthesiologist at UCLA, and finally three-plus years as a medical faculty member at UCLA and the University of Virginia, where I brought to bear every test known to man when indicated, and at times, when not.

Along with my medical education came a pervasive, underlying attitude which gradually led me to think of people not as patients with diseases but as the diseases themselves. "I'll work up the hypertensive, because I've already had an alcoholic."

Like many of my fellow physicians, I believe in the tests and machines which have largely supplanted, instead of supported, personal contact in the practice of medicine. In fact, that I rarely showed emotion seemed to me a superior trait for the practice of medicine. Until the story about to unfold occurred, I sought to be the cool, consummate physician-scientist.

Even now I don't side with those who simply decry modern medical technology as an expensive, unnecessary adjunct to "good, old-fashioned medicine." As you will see in the narrative to follow, the ending of this story doubtless would have been far different without the application of much of the recently acquired scientific knowledge so relentlessly applied to the care of my family.

But, as first my wife Judith and then my infant daughter bore the brunt of "big science," I saw that modern medicine often flays its victims, both patient and family, physically, emotionally and financially.

I learned, as I became "the next of kin" instead of the attending physician, it looks a lot different from the sharp end of the needle.

It Begins . . .

Judy is due November 19. We haven't spent a day or night of her pregnancy apart—so far. Everything has gone smoothly or so it seemed until today when our obstetrician, Dr. Jasmeen, who comes from Sri Lanka, tells us in his clipped British accent that "it would be a good idea to do an ultrasound—since by my examination the baby seems small for dates."

I nod as he explains to us the value of the ultrasound, a seemingly innocuous test which utilizes sound waves beyond the audible human hearing threshold to make a sort of radar image on the screen. I nod again as he elegantly gestures and continues, "By measuring the B-P diameter (bi-parietal diameter—the distance from one side of the head to the other, ear to ear) now should the pregnancy last longer than forty weeks I'll be able to tell, by the rate of head growth, whether the pregnancy indeed is past due, or whether the dates were a week or two off and the gestation can safely continue a bit longer," he smiles graciously inviting my confidence.

My smile back, though, comes a bit more slowly, more warily. It is mixed with a twinge of alarm. His words make sense to me. However, my concern is with risks.

As a physician, one thing you definitely know more about

1

than anyone else is the risk of any medical procedure. When I, the physician, want to do a test, feel it's necessary and beneficial to my patient, I expect my patient to accede because, after all, our interests coincide, don't they? Aren't both of us interested in as rapid a recovery and resolution of the problem as possible?

On the surface, yes. But one of us, the patient, bears a far more difficult burden than I, the orchestrator of investigations. Both immediately, as with the constipation and pain involved in clearing from the bowel the residue of a barium enema, and far into the future, silently carrying the results of potential gene mutations induced in ova and testicles subjected to the intense x-ray barrage needed for a bowel examination, my patient carries the load. I go home each night and sleep well. Or did.

So, when the ultrasound examination is scheduled, rather than ask our obstetrician, whom I respect immensely whether or not there are any risks attached, for either Judy or the baby, I decide to do some investigation on my own.

Now, getting up-to-date scientific information is an art. It goes far beyond looking up a book in a card catalog and going to the proper shelf to find it. You start by looking up the subject you're interested in, say, "Ultrasound," in the *Index Medicus*, a publication issued yearly and updated monthly by the National Library of Medicine. Under ultrasound you find subheadings such as "adverse effects," "diagnostic use," "instrumentation," and "methods." This year alone, sixteen hundred articles have been published about various aspects of ultrasound.

Despite the lengthy process, I like to find things out for myself, in as much detail as I want. I have difficulty accepting what someone else says as the final, definitive word on a subject. It's an old habit, lifelong, which has always caused me problems in relationships and continues to do so in my marriage. Ask my wife. It drives her crazy.

But it is why I feel that asking our obstetrician can't possibly be as informative as finding out about ultrasound myself. I dutifully spend hour after hour in the biomedical library going through the past ten years' data on ultrasound examinations during pregnancy.

My emotions, as I sift through the literature, are mixed. Overwhelming determination to find out everything I can mixed with fear and anger. Fear that something out of the ordinary has to be done and anger that it has to be Judy and me. Millions of other people get pregnant and have children without any problem—why us? Then in the next moment, I shrug and think, why not us?

Weighing the risks, which have not been shown conclusively to exist at all in man, but are simply laboratory results obtained from effects on growing cells in test tubes, against the potential benefits our obstetrician has pointed out, I come to the conclusion it might be harmful and it might not. With this weighty finding stuck firmly in my mind, I decide to get Judy's opinion. I haven't said a word to her about my research, figuring that if there is nothing risky I won't have worried her unnecessarily.

This habit of withholding information is another trait which causes us both grief, as Judy feels it's a form of lying, my keeping things from her "for her own good." While this is a practice very prevalent among physicians, who often feel as if they are the only ones capable of deciding whether or not a patient or family should be given information, lest the layman not be able to cope with it, or "take it the wrong way," in my case it is behavior which existed long before I entertained any thoughts of medical school.

Despite my doubts, we decide to go ahead, but as the time draws near for Judy's ultrasound examination, a procedure which for most people would be like having a dental check-up, but which for me has already resulted in hours of dusting off seldom-used volumes in the biomedical library and reading each one, I am still vacillating and approach our obstetrician in the hospital hallway (a "curbside consult," it's called) to ask him about possible adverse effects.

"You've asked the right man," he says smiling again.

This time my face sets seriously, I don't even try to match his upbeat look. "Only days ago I went to a national symposium on the evaluation of ultrasound as an aid to parental diagnosis. They neatly summarized information too new to have been written up in any medical journal. Essentially, Dr. Stirt, my conclusion as to the safety of the procedure," he scratches his chin in a professorial manner, "based on the newest information is that the procedure is without known risk."

Reassured for the moment I tell him of my concerns and independent investigation. His eyebrows raise. Obviously I have surprised and, I would bet, irritated him to some extent.

Why irritation? I know the feeling when someone, layman or other physician, questions my judgment. "How can they possibly say anything relevant?" I wonder to myself. They don't really *know*. Reluctantly, I have come to the conclusion over the years that the reason it's so annoying to me is because *I* don't really know everything, and my own doubts make me aware of the shallow, superficial nature of all that I call state-of-the-art science, almost all to be discarded piecemeal over the coming years as new concepts emerge.

In my mind, I still harbor a small bit of anxiety about ultrasound. You just never know. Perhaps adverse effects of the test will take years to surface, maybe decades. Witness the World War II shipyard workers who innocently slept in piles of asbestos, and now, forty years later, die painful, choking deaths of lung cancer.

I sigh. A physician makes a bad patient. A physician and a nurse about to have a child are worse. An anesthesiologist and a former neurosurgical intensive care unit nurse are an absolutely horrendous pair. We know too much; we've seen too many things; we've done too many painful things to too many people. That evening I say to my wife, "This obstetrician is a brave man to take us on. Personally, I'd leave town."

She smiles and says, "I would've left long ago."

THURSDAY, AUGUST 18, 10:00 A.M.

The ultrasound exam shows no abnormalities, but does confirm the baby is small. Amazingly we can see the baby's heart, spine, head . . . I ask Dr. Jasmeen not to tell us the sex of the child. I like surprises—although it's easy to tell at this point six months into the pregnancy. The obstetrician gives us a photo of the ultrasound picture—our first baby picture!

For weeks after we leave the office, I look intermittently at this photo. For me it is very moving, almost like a cubist painting, the halves of the scalp appear to overlap one another, the lower portion of the body separated from the head by a half-inch black band of exposed negative. "This is my baby," I murmur to myself over and over. "What a great looking kid!"

SUNDAY, OCTOBER 9, 8:00 A.M.

I'm scheduled to present a paper in Atlanta tomorrow. We talk about whether or not Judy should go: she is due in six weeks. I think the time is a little too close for comfort. She reluctantly agrees; the thought of rushing to a hospital in Atlanta, and being attended during the delivery by a whole host of strangers, doesn't appeal to either of us. On the other hand, we don't like being separated for any reason, and especially not now. Judy is scared: partly because of the pain she anticipates, and partly because of the unknown.

There's no way around the meeting, though. I have to present the paper. So I'm now in the air, on my way to Atlanta. I'll be back Wednesday.

MONDAY, OCTOBER 10, 10:00 P.M.

The presentation went well. I'm watching Monday night football as I write. Judy's fine, no problems. She misses me and I her. Tomorrow I'll attend a few exhibits, go running and have dinner with an old friend from Los Angeles.

TUESDAY, OCTOBER 11, 4:20 A.M.

Ring. I am suddenly woken up, wondering if I've left a wake-up call by mistake, or if I've forgotten to turn off the alarm setting on the clock. Murmuring curses I realize it's the phone. The one day I can sleep late, with no obligations or appointments, and some idiot has to go and ring my room by mistake.

Fumbling with the receiver, I pick it up.

"What is it, what is it?" I moan. "What," until I hear my wife say, "Joe, it's me, Judy." Instantaneously I sober up. An old intern's maxim, never yet proved wrong, is "The phone doesn't ever ring at 4:00 A.M. with good news."

"There's water leaking down my legs—what should I do?"

"Call the obstetrician," I say trying to keep my voice calm. Knowing all this is happening too soon. The baby is too small.

Judy objects, "It's too early in the morning, I don't want to wake him up."

"Call him—that's why he's an obstetrician." Kind of bizarre logic, now that I think about it. I mean, I don't suppose he went into obstetrics so he could get 4:00 A.M. phone calls.

"I'll wait until 6:30," says Judy.

"I'm coming home as soon as I can," I mumble and tiredly slide out of bed. Slowly feelings of excitement and dread grow within me. Excitement because we're actually going to have a baby, dread because it's six weeks premature and small. I know the incidence of problems, both minor and serious, is directly related to infant size and maturity. I also know it is the second abnormal event to occur, the first being the small size of the child necessitating an ultrasound examination at six months.

TUESDAY, OCTOBER 11, 11:30 A.M.

I spend the next seven hours making endless phone calls, waiting in lines, superimposed on worrying about what is happening to Judy. Finally I get a plane reservation.

At Washington-National Airport en route to my final plane change, I call the hospital and ask to speak to my wife. "She's sleeping now; they've started her on a mag drip," the monotone voice of one of the obstetrical floor nurses tells me. A "mag drip" is shorthand for an intravenous infusion of magnesium sulfate, which relaxes the uterine muscle and prevents it from contracting and laboring to expel the baby as it naturally would. But why was Judy on one? Why not let her have the baby, as labor almost always begins soon after rupture of the membranes (breaking the bag of water), as had occurred with Judy.

My last experience with the conduct of labor occurred eight years ago during my month of obstetrics in my internship. I recall that the risk of intrauterine infection, called amnionitis (inflammation of the amniotic sac), steadily increases, with increasing hazards to both mother and child, once the bag has ruptured. Why are they taking a chance? I turn the question over and over in my mind, agonizing, as the plane heads back home.

TUESDAY, OCTOBER 11, 4:00 P.M.

Exhausted and drained, I get to the hospital. My apprehension has grown to unmanageable proportions; I anticipate the worst.

It doesn't happen. Judy's groggy, dopey, as the magnesium also affects the brain and central nervous system and most other organ systems to one degree or another, but she's alive.

Looking at her, my heart quickens. I'm scared. I didn't plan on this surge of emotion within me. I am embarrassed by the fact that I don't do well when Judy's in the hospital.

She had a kidney infection a year ago and spent five days hospitalized. Despite my attempts to evaluate the situation cooly, rationally, it nearly drove me crazy.

I chat with her, hold her hand, hug and kiss her.

Then I page our obstetrician. After what seems a lengthy wait, but is only twenty minutes or so, he comes upstairs and explains to me what is happening.

It seems things have changed in the decade since I rotated through obstetrics. Although infection is a hazard once the membranes have ruptured, it has become apparent since 1978 that hyaline membrane disease, also known as respiratory distress syndrome of the newborn, is more prevalent in premature babies who are delivered immediately after rupture of the membranes than in those infants whose delivery is delayed one to two days. Somehow, for unknown reasons, the lining of the infant's lungs begins to mature once the membranes have burst, providing some protection against this dreaded disease.

Despite this he and I know respiratory distress syndrome continues to be a problem for preemies. It still kills babies. Unable to absorb sufficient oxygen through their immature lungs, premature infants with the disease must be aggressively managed with ventilatory support and supplemental oxygen, often leading to numerous permanent, damaging effects even if the child survives. Because of this, Judy's treatment now seems quite appropriate to me, even optimal, I guess.

I drive home at 11:00 P.M. at Judy's urging to get her teddy bear, her reassurances that she'll be fine echoing in my head. She's now asleep, the magnesium having knocked her out. I feel no shame or embarrassment at fetching her childhood toy. When I brought the bear to her hospital room that other time, she hid it at first under the blankets, but certain objects have more power over us than we'd like to admit. As a dying priest said to Andre Malraux, when asked what a lifetime of hearing confession had taught him, "There is no such thing as an adult."

Once there I muse about whether my going to Atlanta and being away from Judy has any relationship to her ruptured membranes. This is the sort of thinking that most physicians feel is unscientific speculation, even crazy. How could they be related?

One part of me wants to agree, but another reminds me that the cause of the beginning of labor remains a deeper mystery now than ever in the past. Some signal from the mother or fetus causes biochemical and physical changes in the amniotic sac; it thins down and subsequently ruptures. This is all we know.

So, when I consider seven and a half months of rhythmic cycles of brain neurotransmitters in Judy's head, rising and falling each day, knowing each morning that that night we'll be in bed together, arms around one another, and then think about the odd fact that after one night away from her, the first one in her entire pregnancy, the membranes break and labor begins, I have to wonder, how much of a relationship is there between her mood, being alone, and her body's response?

Judy thinks this sort of thinking too mechanistic and scientific, while my colleagues to whom I tentatively mention my thoughts think them weird and unjustified, very speculative and unscientific. Two worlds, I suppose, two very different places. Do I belong fully in either one?

WEDNESDAY, OCTOBER 12, 7:00 A.M.

When I reach the hospital I find Judy perspiring, semi-conscious. I worry about this as I stare at her, pale, tossing on the hospital bed, but what can I do? A tall blond nurse with Barbie doll features has been with her all night, watching her response to the magnesium. "I'm Alice," she smiles, "the night nurse." I ask her how Judy's been. What kind of night she's had. She smiles again, "We're doing fine, Dr. Stirt," and nods reassuringly. A meter is strapped to Judy's abdomen to measure the frequency, intensity, and length of her contractions. They had increased in strength and length during the night, so the magnesium infusion had been accelerated. To make certain Judy doesn't become toxic from the stuff, white-coated technicians looking ghoul-like come in occasionally to take blood from her arm to measure her magnesium level.

Knowing how frightened she is of needles and blood being drawn (ironic, in that she's probably drawn as much blood and subjected as many people to injections as the most experienced of technicians) I tell her how sad I am they have to keep hurting her.

She says cloudily, "Oh, that wasn't so bad. But the thing that hurt me was my chest."

"Chest?" I reply, agitatedly. When I'd asked the nurse who watched Judy what kind of night she had, she'd said nothing about chest pain. Magnesium can depress the heart, among its other side effects; had Judy had angina pectoris, a failure of heart muscle to obtain sufficient oxygen to function, because her heart was so weakened by the magnesium? Inside I go berserk. Are they going to give her a heart attack with their wonderful new labor management theory? Fuck the baby, I think, I need Judy.

Trying to keep my voice steady, I ask Alice about Judy's chest pain. "Oh, yes," she says her blue eyes widening, "she had some sharp pain about 2:00 A.M. over her precordium (heart area) and we got an EKG but it was normal. Her mag level was in the toxic range, we slowed down the drip."

My heart beats even faster. So Judy had had symptoms severe enough to cause alarm. I grimace, because no one does an electrocardiogram at 2:00 A.M. for the hell of it. It takes effort, and at that hour effort is at a premium. There is only one conclusion, Judy has become toxic from the magnesium. Cause and effect. Anger rises within me, I clench my fists, but say nothing.

What is equally hard to take is the realization that, once again, I wasn't with her when the problem occurred. There she was, writhing in pain, frightened, groggy, alone, as I slept peacefully. No way of knowing she was in trouble. My God, I think, can I afford to leave her for an instant? Why is it that now twice something serious has happened each time I've been elsewhere? Guilt clutches at me. For all my insight into what is really happening, what good am I actually doing?

"I was really scared," Judy says in a small, hoarse voice, "it hurt like someone was stabbing me with a knife, all over my chest and down my left arm. I was crying and biting my pillow." I feel hollow. That is it. I swear to myself I am not leaving her alone again, no matter what. If I have to sleep in her room, I'll do it.

Summoning Dr. Jasmeen, our obstetrician, I ask him what his game plan is. He brings his hands together, looking like he is meditating out loud, "I had hoped to halt her labor, which has been intensifying, requiring the increased amount of magnesium that led to her overdose and chest pain, but," he pauses and my heart skips a beat, "her labor is progressing anyway. Ideally," he continues, "we'd halt her contractions, then put her in a room for one to two weeks," (Weeks?, agitatedly I think; what about infection, which increases dramatically after membrane rupture?) "to let the fetus mature a bit more. Its lungs are immature by L/S ratio." [A test to determine the ration of lecithin (L) to sphingomyelin (S) in the amniotic fluid, the relative levels of which fairly accurately predict the risk of respiratory distress syndrome after birth.] He pauses again, pulling on his earlobe thoughtfully, "Leaving the baby undelivered for a week or two would give it a chance to mature," he says, his voice fading off. I look away. All I can foresee is a week or two of further complications and unforeseen events. I mumble, "Why us? Why?" He is silent.

1 P.M. Dr. Jasmeen performs a sterile pelvic examination on Judy, sterile to minimize the risk of infection to the now exposed baby and amniotic sac. "Her cervix is now dilated to three centimeters diameter," he says. My eyes are focused on Judy. Her contractions are growing more intense.

The nurse interrupts, "Her white cell count is now 20,000 cells per cubic millimeter," she says matter of factly. My face reddens. I feel like smacking her. Normal is 5,000–

10,000. Elevation means infection. Judy also now has a fever of 101 degrees, another indication that infection is beginning.

"Let's begin intravenous antibiotics," Jasmeen says.

"Remember," I interrupt, "Judy has a history of a severe allergic reaction to sulfa drugs. In fact she is very reactive in general." He nods but doesn't respond.

After he leaves, I pace the floor nervously. Will she have another reaction to antibiotics and really get messed up?

On top of all this, I begin to have difficulties with Judy's day nurse, Ella Fromm, a buxom, fiftyish woman who has adopted an attitude not uncommon in obstetrical nursing these days: the father had better listen to her because she is running the show. I overhear her saying to another nurse, "If he keeps questioning my judgment and saying things like that to his wife, I'm going to kick him out of the room."

I bite my lip. Of course, it is impossible for such a thing to happen unless I am physically removed, and what a scene I'll make then. I can see the headline, Attending Physician Forcibly Removed From Wife's Bedside, and the story to follow bringing out how it occurred in his own hospital during a difficult labor. I almost hope for a confrontation. Anything to let them know how I am feeling.

During the next few hours what provokes me most are our Nurse Fromm's constant reassurances that things are "Going fine." "Bullshit." I keep mumbling almost loud enough for her to hear. I've worked in hospitals long enough, and so has my wife, to know differently. I look over at Judy. She is so groggy, tired and miserable she is in no condition to question anyone's judgment, which is part of the reason so much happens to patients while they're sick that later seems incomprehensible—tests and procedures assented to because everyone else involved seems forceful and certain about their benefits and the patient and family don't know things are going terribly.

But I know. My wife is infected—she has an elevated temperature; she feels hot and sweaty, she has shaking chills, her white blood cell count is elevated, she is on antibiotics.

The infection is undoubtedly seated in the amniotic sac around the baby: amnionitis.

The implications are ominous. The transition from a localized infection to generalized septicemia, an infection in the blood stream which potentially could seed any other area of Judy's body and which leads, occasionally, to irreversible shock, could be imminent.

They perform an ultrasound examination. I stand by helplessly. I am no longer thinking about the risks of ultrasound. There are more horrendous risks on the horizon.

"The baby is small, I estimate four to four and one-half pounds," Jasmeen announces. "Its lungs are immature by L/S ratio. Only thirty-three hours have elapsed since the membranes ruptured, it's not nearly as long as I had hoped to delay the delivery."

We both look over at Judy. Her contractions are much more frequent now, painful, more intense, lasting longer, and regular: labor is underway. Her cervix is dilating in spite of the mag, which is being infused at the maximum possible rate allowing for Judy's magnesium toxicity and chest pain last night.

Judy is frightened: the magnesium has made her groggy and weakened her extraocular (eye) muscles to the point where she has double vision, she's exhausted since she's gotten almost no sleep, the pain of her contractions makes her call out. Moreover she's hot, sweaty, chilled, thirsty, sick to her stomach (the mag also causes nausea), and not allowed anything to drink for fear of more nausea and vomiting, and possibly inhaling the vomit should general anesthesia be required for a Caesarean section.

"Please don't leave, Joe, please." She bites her pillow and squeezes my hand with each contraction; several injections of Demerol, a powerful narcotic, have failed to ease her pain. "Help me!" she calls out.

Finally my need to comfort her overwhelms my usual reticence and my attempt to appear the calm, emotionally controlled physician.

Flushing slightly, I get in bed with her, much to the obvious displeasure of her nurse, who glares at me. I am apprehensive, then thrilled. "You're going to have our baby, Judy,
it's going to be today," I say soothingly.

"But they're trying to stop me from having it."

"It's not working. The baby wants to come and no one
can stop it."

Nurse Fromm looks angry. "Dr. Stirt, really!" she says
frowning. But I don't care. It really is happening. No matter
what anyone tries or says or does or wishes, the baby is coming.

WEDNESDAY, OCTOBER 12, 1:30 P.M.

Dr. Jasmeen comes in, examines the recordings of Judy's contractions, and walks out of the room, beckoning me to follow.

He confirms my own deductions. "I think we're going to
go ahead and let Judy have the baby." Jasmeen pauses, his
eyes fastened on an invisible spot on the ceiling. "She seems
to be getting mildly septic."

Involuntarily I shiver. "The infection from the amniotic
sac is spreading into the rest of Judy's body?"

He nods, "We're going to 'pit' her."

"Pit" refers to Pitocin, or oxytocin, a hormone which
enhances uterine contractility. Normally produced by the pi-
tuitary gland, it is synthesized for use as an adjuvant to labor.
Putting a woman on a "pit drip," or "pitting" her, is an artificial way of speeding up the natural process of labor and delivery.

Unfortunately, "pit" is used far more frequently for the
convenience of the obstetrician and nursing team than the
benefit of the mother. But in cases like Judy's, it offers a way
of accelerating labor which when prolonged is potentially
harmful to the mother or fetus.

Still I know if the rate of the infusion is turned up too
rapidly the intensity and frequency of uterine contractions
increases so quickly, labor can turn into a nightmare of pain.

I have always likened a pit drip to cracking a whip, driving and flogging on the uterus until finally it yields its contents.

Along with the "pit drip" comes internal fetal monitors, tiny electrodes attached by needles placed in the baby's scalp as it comes down the birth canal. These will yield information on the baby's heart rate in response to uterine contractions, a very useful indicator of fetal condition during the birth process.

I am aware of all this and keep running over it in my mind. As if the knowledge of what will be happening will calm and reassure me. It doesn't.

A few minutes later the attention of everyone in this room—nurse, doctor, husband, patient—is directed towards these icons of data for information about how things are going. If one of the machines goes on the fritz, attention is immediately directed to getting it working again as quickly as possible. Judy, the laboring patient, recedes into the corner of our collective consciousness, just as her bed is pushed into the corner of the room, the holy center being occupied by the machines, the monitors.

Though like everyone else, I watch the gauges intently, actually I'm not very impressed by them. Unfortunately, like so many things in medicine and in life, I know this device is prone to all sorts of failures. Information may be incorrect, it can be improperly interpreted, or the electrode itself may stop working as it comes loose during a particularly strong contraction, when its presence would be most helpful.

Moreover, even if it works properly, I can't get enthusiastic about the sound, paper and machinery; I've seen too many disasters precipitated by attention to and belief in devices instead of the patient they were built to serve. My pulse quickens. This time the patient is Judy, my wife, and our child.

Trying to get some distance, some perspective, I walk downstairs to the operating room area, where the chief of OB (obstetric) anesthesia is working. "It's time for anesthesia," I tell him. Current practice in obstetrical anesthesia is to place a thin catheter in a laboring patient's epidural space, a "potential" space just adjacent to the spinal canal, and inject small amounts of anesthetic drugs into this catheter, providing anesthesia to only the areas experiencing labor pain.

It sounds wonderful, but often isn't. The needle used to place the catheter in the back is large, and occasionally penetrates the membrane surrounding the spinal cord, leading to leaks of cerebrospinal fluid, the clear liquid which bathes and supports the spinal cord, causing severe headaches as the brain falls against the skull, unsupported by its customary liquid cushion.

The anesthetic can be accidentally placed in the spinal canal, producing total anesthesia of the lower portion of the body instead of the selective analgesia which allows a woman to push on command even though pain sensation is diminished. The drug can enter the bloodstream, which may produce signs and symptoms of toxicity up to and including nausea, vomiting, seizures, and, rarely, cardiac arrest. So, although routine, a "labor epidural" can, like any medical maneuver, turn quickly into a "thrash" ("thrash," an in-house medical term for what happens when things go wrong in a hurry, was chosen perhaps because the scene resembles nothing more than a combination of violent argument and a barroom brawl, with frantic activity, shouting, confusion, and, occasionally a good outcome).

I've previously asked Jason Rawlings, our OB anesthesiologist, if he'll take care of Judy's anesthetic, and he's agreed to do it. Judy and I have been to only one Lamaze class, and a given individual's response to the pain of labor is unpredictable. I want to be prepared. Judy has flat out said she wants no needles stuck in her back, period, but things have a way of changing. One thing anesthesiology in particular has taught me, which applies as well outside of medicine, is that more often than not what you hope will happen doesn't, but what you know usually doesn't happen does. Sometimes I think the secret of life is learning to discard the wish and anticipate the reality, a mundane and meager point of view, I admit.

Jason okays Judy's epidural, now that she is being "pitted." Though we both know obstetricians and anesthesiologists have carried on a raging battle for years about whether or not an epidural anesthesia slows down labor.

He meets me upstairs a few minutes later, and we watch as several hard contractions hit Judy. Writhing in the bed she sobbingly agrees to the epidural.

"Will it hurt?" she asks me.

"A little, for a second," I say.

"I want you to do it," she pleads.

I shake my head, "No, Judy, I can't."

There is no way I am going to take care of her obstetrical anesthesia. Besides being out of touch with the subspecialty and not having actually done a labor epidural anesthetic since my residency, I know my judgment when it comes to Judy will be totally distorted.

"A doctor who treats himself has fool for a patient," physicians say knowingly, and this extends to our own families and friends. You tend to do the easiest, least painful thing when it comes to someone you know, instead of doing what's right. You delay ordering the tests you should get, waiting instead for more symptoms, more definite evidence.

When personal feelings instead of medical knowledge affect my treatment, that is wrong. If this happens because I know someone and don't want to hurt them, that is wrong too. So I choose not to care for those I love, but to hopefully find someone who cares almost as much but really won't agonize over doing something temporarily unpleasant but ultimately potentially beneficial.

Despite my rationalizations I breathe a sigh of relief when the needle goes in smoothly.

Judy visibly relaxes once the catheter is in place and the first dose of anesthesia goes in even though her contractions continue. Though I've seen this happen hundreds of times, I'm still a little amazed at the fact that anesthetics actually work.

For the next hour and a half Judy sits propped up in bed,

while I, half sitting on a stool next to her bed, watch, listen and talk.

"Do you realize," I say to her, "we're having the last hours we'll ever have alone together without worrying about anyone else? At least until I'm fifty-three and you're forty-four?" A great sense of irrevocable change overwhelms me. I can't alter the course of events now no matter how I feel.

Suddenly Judy turns to me: "I don't want it, please, I'm scared." I look at her surprised at the confession. She has lost her inhibitions, vestiges of growing up a convent school girl in colonial British Jamaica. The teddy bear has come out from under the blankets into her arms and crying, she hides her head under my green scrub shirt.

"I'm scared, and it still hurts," she says. Everyone else in the room wears a look that says Oh, Christ, grow up, will you, but what do I care?

I bend toward her and awkwardly kiss her hair, then her face. We become silent for a while.

At 3:30 P.M. the obstetrician examines Judy once again. "Time to have your baby, Judy," he says. We move from the cramped, cluttered labor room into the delivery room across the hall (sounds like a truck loading and mail service) where Judy is transferred to the delivery bed, her feet placed in stirrups, hand grips for her to push against lay at her sides.

For the next hour Judy pushes and pushes, a combination of fear and determination. I feel horribly responsible for helping put her in this position. At that moment, I think if we could just call it quits and say, "Forget it," and make the whole scene vanish, returning home, Judy never having been pregnant, we would.

At 4:15 P.M. the obstetrician says, "A few more pushes and the baby will be out." Then I see the baby's head. "Hey there's a lot of dark hair," I say amazedly. For the first time, I really feel that there is a baby, not just an ultrasound picture.

At 4:30 P.M. Dr. Jasmeen says, "One big push," and an absolutely blood-curdling scream comes out of Judy. I think she is dying or dead. My heart palpitates so loudly I'm afraid everyone in the room can hear it.

Neither Judy nor I look up at the mirror placed strategically at the juncture of wall and ceiling to allow a laboring mother to watch the baby's head slowly descend and emerge from the birth canal. So when at 4:41 there is a baby in the obstetrician's hands, a tiny, red, mashed-up looking thing, crying and wiggling, we can't believe it. Judy is frightened and me, I feel like fainting.

With a mixture of awe and trepidation, I look over at the baby and unlock Judy's vise-like grip from my hand. Suddenly, it passes through my mind that maybe it's some kind of trick. Neither of us actually saw it happen. A very well-run hoax though, if that's what it is, quite convincing. Especially when I look at the child's feet. Judy has big feet and toes peculiarly flexible and mobile, and the baby's feet are like miniatures of hers.

Unable to stop myself from trembling, I unsteadily walk over to the bassinet where the pediatricians from the intensive care unit are busy drying off the baby, assessing her color and tone and strength. Any time a premature or small baby is expected, the risk of complications immediately after birth is greater than normal. Such children have immature nervous systems, and are much more prone to irregularities of heartbeat and breathing. Thus, it is routine in any hospital caring for mothers expected to deliver prematurely to have a pediatrician available for resuscitation if needed. A few moments of oxygen deprivation at birth can yield a lifetime of brain damage and mental retardation; frightening thought.

Studying the baby intently, I breathe a sigh of relief, mixed with pride. Our baby seems fine, vigorous, crying, good color. I want to shout, It's a girl! But my usual reticence restrains me.

I watch the physicians begin the Apgar test, rating the baby on a scale of 0 to 10, on color, muscle tone, heart rate, respiratory movement, and reflex irritability. This score, given at one and five minutes after birth, becomes the basis for explaining why an infant does well or poorly. Again, I feel shaky.

A score of zero or one indicates a moribund child, needing vigorous resuscitation; a perfect ten heralds little chance of problems. Scores in the eight to ten range indicate a good prognosis. As they call out the scores and our baby's are rated eight and nine, I sigh happily. I know that rarely do infants in such condition develop problems. Instantaneously all my worries about her prematurity and small size evaporate and I feel the tears in my eyes spill out. Despite my attempts to appear calm, it is all too much. Science and all my medical training goes to hell.

I bring the child over to Judy who stares, smiles and promptly closes her eyes.

"I just want to rest," she says in a self-satisfied voice.

I pick up the baby. "Daughter," I say slowly, the very word seems powerful. I am pleased it is a girl; I would rather have a girl than a boy if I could have chosen. Women have always been easier for me to get along with than men.

I look at her more closely. I don't mind her squashed face, the nose pressed to one side, her misshapen head, or anything about her. She's mine. I check her hands. Judy's ultra-flexible fingers, that can bend backwards a bit at each joint. She weighs 4 pounds, 7 ounces.

I bend down toward Judy, our child in my arms, "Baby looks great!" I say.

"How the hell does someone have an eight pound baby?" Judy asks me. "That little thing almost killed me." I couldn't imagine myself. "Do you like it?" Judy inquires.

"I love her," I reply. "She's great. A little girl." Judy looks at me, smiles, and falls asleep.

I turn to Dr. Jasmeen, "How long will Judy and the baby have to stay in the hospital?" I ask.

He strokes his chin. "Judy will probably stay two days, the baby two to five days for observation, to see how she feeds, then home." I am unhappy about the news. I want everybody out of the hospital as fast as possible. Terrible things happen in hospitals, I believed back then. I was right.

WEDNESDAY, OCTOBER 12, 5:00 P.M.

Resident's admitting note.

Neonatal Intermediate Nursery [NIN].

Chief complaint: Prematurity.

History and Present Illness: Patient is a 2030 gram product of estimated gestational age 34–35 weeks born to 26 year old white female, gravid 1 para 0.

Pregnancy unremarkable with exception of premature rupture of membranes 36 hours prior to delivery. Mom presented to hospital several hours later, sterile pelvic done, $MgSO_4$ [magnesium] started. Mom denied fever, chills. Initial WBC of mom-15,000 with 82 segs, 3 bands, 11 lymphs, 4 monos. Mom broke through $MgSO_4$ and patient delivered by normal spontaneous vaginal delivery at 1641 on 10/12/83. Delivery uncomplicated. Apgars 8/9. Patient in no distress at time of delivery.

Physical exam: slight cyanosis of fingers and toes, otherwise unremarkable.

Blood cultures sent.

Plan:

1. Blood cultures;

2. Ampicillin 100 mg/kg/day every 12 hours, gentamycin 2.5 mg/kg/day every 8 hours;

3. IV at keep vein open rate;

4. Feeding: 10 cc sterile H_2O [15 cc is a tablespoon], then breast milk every 3 hours;

5. Dextrostix.

I glance at the chart. This is a standard admission assessment in today's university hospital. I look at the description of Judy's labor and delivery frowning. It's totally unrelated to what happened. But in medical terms the description is accurate. Of course, the tension, fear, uncertainty, loneliness, chills, fever, delirium, double vision, chest pain and electrocardiogram have all vanished. The wrenching pain of the contractions and labor, the blood-curdling scream as the baby emerged, gone into thin air. Reading such a description, the person disappears. Our faulty memory does the rest.

The major concern at this point is infection. Blood cultures, samples of the baby's blood taken with as sterile a technique as possible from the umbilical cord, are sent to the laboratory to see if any bacteria are present. The baby had been exposed to germs inside the uterus for thirty-six hours. This has to be a concern—especially in view of Judy's infection. Judy's white blood cell count is slightly above normal. The infection could well have spread to the baby.

Judy had been placed on antibiotics already, prior to the baby's birth, so it is possible enough drug had reached the baby even before birth via the placenta to suppress signs of infection without eradicating it. Thus, the blood cultures might be negative, but the baby could still be infected. To guard against this possibility, the baby is started on antibiotics.

The drugs chosen, ampicillin and gentamycin are broad spectrum antibiotics that will kill almost any bacteria. Routinely, each hospital places infants felt to be "at risk" on antibiotic regimens peculiar to that given institution. The choice of treatment depends on the experience and bias of the chief of the neonatal intensive care unit. Treatments vary markedly in drugs, doses, and lengths. No obvious superiority of one over another has yet emerged. Not realizing how idiosyncratic this treatment, as well as almost all current therapy, really is can lead the layman to think things are really as good as they can be, optimal, the best. Optimal perhaps, but one of many choices would be more accurate.

I stare at the baby's incubator, peering in. An IV (an intravenous infusion line) has been inserted in the baby's arm. Feeding with water is begun first, to see how she tolerates oral intake and to make certain food ends up in her stomach rather than her lungs. Breast milk, as Judy planned to breast feed the baby, would come next. Dextrostix, a quick chemical test of urinary sugar, would indirectly assess whether or not the baby's blood sugar was in the normal range.

"It is a lot of medical paraphernalia for a small baby to contend with," I murmur, "I'm sorry you have to go though all this."

WEDNESDAY, OCTOBER 12, 5:30 P.M.

Nurse's note, NIN.

Admitted to NIN per arms of resident. A small infant weighing 2030 grams, appeared pink with slight grunting respirations at rate of 49/min accompanied by slight subcostal retractions. IV started, antibiotics begun IV, erythromycin ointment to eyes (prophylaxis). Hooked up to cardiac monitor, placed in isolette. Both parents came in to hold.

Assessment: Prematurity with possible sepsis.

Plan: Monitor vital signs, dextrostix; antibiotics and feeding as ordered. Watch closely for signs of sepsis; allow parents to come in and hold infant. Mom wants to breast feed; will pump breast for now.

Slowly I read the words. Then I turn to stare at our newborn baby. So it has come to this. Electrodes have been pasted to her tiny chest. Little skin is visible. Encased in a warmed plastic box which isolates her from the sights and sounds of the artificial, fluorescent world she lives in, our daughter will spend her first night on earth. Damn it, why us? Why her? Thousands of children are born here every year, yet

I stand here watching ours amidst the cacophony and twenty-four hour light of the neonatal intermediate unit. I take a deep breath and try to reassure myself. Oh well, it's only for a couple of days, then we'll be on our way out of this zoo.

WEDNESDAY, OCTOBER 12, 6:30 P.M.

> **Resident's note.**
>
> In no acute distress, physical examination normal. Anticipate prematurity-related problems.

Looking at these words I ask myself did he really anticipate problems? Probably not, but he has to write it down anyway. You have to write something down to justify the auditors' questions regarding why an apparently healthy baby is receiving special observation in an expensive monitoring area.

Still things are looking pretty good. I hurry to Judy's room to tell her.

WEDNESDAY, OCTOBER 12, 8:30 P.M.

> **Head nurse's note, NIN.**
>
> Labor and Delivery Summary.
> Observations/comments: Slight grunting, subcostal retractions with acrocyanosis. Slightly labored respirations. NG [naso-

gastric] tube inserted left nostril, tube feeding started. So far tolerated well. Weak grasp, weak bite, no suck elicited.
Overall assessment: Preemie 35 weeks with slight respiratory distress.
Parental profile: Parental response to infant's hospitalization: grieving appropriately. Parental understanding of hospitalization: very good medical background.

I hold the chart so tightly my knuckles redden. Frustration gnaws at me. Only two hours ago everything seemed to be going well. Now the baby's respirations are becoming abnormal. I look closely at her. She is small, weak, and too premature to suck and be able to eat, so they have inserted an NG tube (a small, flexible plastic tube which is placed into the nose and goes down into the stomach) and begun tube feedings. I shake my head. It isn't just her prematurity that is making her weak. Some of the magnesium which Judy had received was transferred through the placenta and umbilical cord to the baby, making her weaker. Hopefully, this will pass out of her system, as well as Judy's, over the next few days.

I sigh heavily. One unknown in obstetrics is how much effect any drug, no matter how seemingly benign, has on the fetus, developmentally in utero, in the process of labor and delivery, immediately following birth and over the long term. The recent discovery that babies born to heroin-addicted mothers, for example, have withdrawal symptoms immediately after birth and physical separation from the mother makes the connection vivid.

WEDNESDAY, OCTOBER 12, 9:00 P.M.

Doctor's orders.

Condition: Stable
Feeds: 1st feed 10 cc sterile water, then 10 cc breast milk,
then advance to 25 cc every 3 hours as tolerated.

WEDNESDAY, OCTOBER 12, 9:30 P.M.

Doctor's orders.

Feed: 10% Dextrose in water 25 cc via NGT, when dextrostix
is stable, use Enfamil #20, 25 cc q 3 hours for feedings.

A lot happens in hospitals now that didn't happen a few
years ago. Progress is what we call it. At this point Judy is
hospitalized and receiving intravenous antibiotics because of
infection. The baby is hospitalized and receiving intravenous
antibiotics to ward off possible infection. Formula has been
ordered for the baby, to be dripped into her stomach via tube
because she is too weak to feed herself.

Judy is so tired and groggy there is no way she can
breast-feed the baby even if the baby could feed, which she is
too weak to do. A breast pump to extract Judy's milk is out of
the question at this point, far too strenuous. So, to give the

baby food, artificial formula is chosen. Neither Judy, asleep, nor I knew that this had been undertaken, but we'd have certainly thought it the right thing to do. Is it?

Not too long ago, and in some hospitals even now, feedings of premature infants were and are undertaken very deliberately. After all, for many, many years babies were born prematurely, often at home, where no options for tube feedings with formula existed. A baby was delivered when labor began, without drugs or delay, and simply rested for a day or two until it felt like eating. No harm in it. But now, we can override the natural flow of events, and so it is that young Caroline Anne Stirt has her first meal.

WEDNESDAY, OCTOBER 12, 10:00 P.M.

I return home. Judy's asleep, the baby's in the NIN, for closer observation than she'd be getting in the newborn nursery where healthy full-term babies go. Judy's mother calls. She's been planning for months to come visit us to help us over the first few weeks. Say what people do about in-laws, Judy's parents are great. I am all for her mom coming and staying as long as she likes.

I tell Norma, Judy's mother, the baby has come. She is thrilled. "Can you come up sooner, Grandma?" I ask, teasingly.

"I'll try, Joe. Let me talk to my boss and maybe I can come up Friday."

With all that's happening I want her here as soon as possible. I'm a physician, a scientist, what do I know from babies? "The baby needs you," I say. "She's saying 'Grandma, where's Grandma?' I can tell."

"Oh, Joe, I feel her calling me, I do," Norma says excitedly. Jamaica puts a sense of the unreal and magical into a person, I think. I've sensed it about Judy since I've known her, this cloistered belief in magic, ghosts, dreams, and demons called "duppies." The island is peppered with them, descendents of voodoo and "obeah," Jamaican black magic. "I'll come as soon as I can."

"I'll tell Judy. She'll be glad." I feel strong and high. What a great thing, this child. A strange sense of amazement and wonder fills me. I've been to medical school, studied development, delivered babies, and still it is truly incomprehensible. How did it happen, I wonder? The nature of life is much more mysterious than ever.

THURSDAY, OCTOBER 13, 8:00 A.M.

I wake up alone, and walk around the house. Silence. Never again, I think. Dressed, I go to the hospital. Judy is awake. "How does it feel, mom?" I ask her. She smiles, pleased.

"Are you happy, Joe? Do you like her?"

"Crazy about her. And you. Let's go see her."

I help Judy out of bed. Yesterday she'd sat in a wheelchair when we'd gone over to the NIN to see and hold Carrie. She'd been too tired and sore to stand up. I bring the wheelchair to her bedside now, but she shakes her head and says "No, I can walk."

"Are you sure? You don't look that strong."

"I'm tough." She smiles and grimaces, then, holding my arm, pulls herself up and leans heavily against my shoulder. "Let's go."

Slowly we move down the hall to the NIN. There is Carrie, sleeping in her isolette.

"Can we hold her?" I ask. For the first time I experience the irritation and anger of being parents of an unhealthy baby, or, at least, a child needing special care. Funny how I am asking if I can hold my own child. Here I am, a physician, in my own hospital, as a rule doing as I wish unbeholden to anyone, but now I am hesitant, and passive. Being a patient or a parent of a patient is a great leveler.

We wait for ten minutes, looking at her inside her box, until a nurse is free to come over and help slowly disentangle the four electrode wires connecting our baby to the EKG monitor, the NG tube taped to her nose, a syringe of formula attached to the end of the tube, the intravenous tubing in her left hand. Our little baby is barely visible under it all.

Judy and I sit there amidst the other babies, nurses, beeps and alarms, and odd technicians, parents, and physicians.

"Let's just take her home," Judy whispers to me miserably.

My agony matches her own, but I cover it with my usually rational approach, "We can't, Judy. She's not even able to eat yet."

"I don't like it. They're acting like she's sick. There's nothing wrong with her, she's just teeny. She can wait a couple days to eat. Babies do that."

"I don't know," I say. The ultimate conflict. A physician expects his orders to be followed. Total patient compliance, no matter how questionable to an impartial outside observer, is always viewed as a part of being a good patient. The unspoken threat is, of course, "If you don't go along with what we recommend, we can't be responsible for what happens."

Of course, the irony is that if you do go along and play the role, and untoward events occur, "Well, that's life, we can't be certain it will work as we hope, and complications and unexpected events do occur. Sorry about that. Here's what we'll do next . . ."

Now Judy is counseling sedition and mutiny. Leave the hospital, take the baby home AMA (against medical advice)? When, occasionally, a patient does leave AMA, we physicians sagely smile and shake our heads, knowing much better, and feel sorry for the fool as well as angry that our obvious wisdom has been tossed aside and disregarded by someone who really doesn't know much but certainly should've known that doctors know best. It would be interesting to really find out, considering the mind-set of patients who do go AMA, exactly how they do once they leave the hospital.

Still I know for me to take the baby home AMA would

unleash a torrent of conflicts, both personal and professional. What if the baby does get sick, and has to come back? Facing the same team of physicians I'd snubbed would be difficult and embarrassing, especially since some were also members of my own department. Going AMA is a bit like nuclear deterrence—the option is there, but, once exercised, there is no pulling back—the damage is done. What about just being at work? At my hospital a small-town atmosphere prevails—everyone knows everyone's business. It would be difficult explaining why I'd done what I'd done to my colleagues, most of whom would never even consider so radical a move. It would be just as difficult not explaining. I'd only worked there three months, and had no close friends or even good acquaintances among members of my department. This would truly isolate me forever.

Another problem to be considered is that really this hospital is the only game in town. We'd come from Los Angeles, where many hospitals would have been capable of taking expert care of our baby should she need it. Here, there is only one, and we are already there.

Trying to be calm and analytical, I tell Judy all this, and she retorts, "What do you care about—the baby or the impression you make on everyone? Who cares what anyone else thinks? They're not the ones with a little baby in a box!"

Now I really feel miserable. For the first time we both experience the unnatural strain and tension a hospitalized baby puts on a relationship. "We're not taking her home," I say more decisively than I feel. "She's only going to stay here another day or so, until she gets strong enough to eat, then we'll go home."

Funny, this reminds me of my mother's words to me and my brother twenty-five years earlier, in May, 1958, when, running wild and frequently brought home by the police, she was unable to care for us and placed us in a children's home.

"It's just for the summer. You'll come back home in the fall, before school," she had said. All summer we counted the days until Labor Day, when we'd be going home. Then we found out it wasn't going to happen. We never did get home. Now I was saying the same things, giving reassurances I hoped were true but which somehow rang hollow. I knew how easy it was to say words that appeased, but in the end betrayed.

For hours Judy and I sit, huddled in a corner of the NIN, just to be near the baby. Every once in a while we talk to her, to each other, but mostly we sit there silently, thinking. Finally, we go back to Judy's room, which fortunately is unoccupied except for her. All the rooms on the obstetrics floor are double rooms, but because of the trauma of Carrie's birth and condition we'd asked our obstetrician to find Judy one she could have alone.

Now Judy tries to extract some breast milk using the hospital's breast pump, a device looking much like an early 1900's physics experiment, and sounding much like one also. As if it was an omen of the emptiness we both feel nothing happens. No milk. Disappointed we sit and watch the machine's suction cup, looking for a drop or two, but none comes.

Of course, we both know the rational reason. Judy is still weak and sleepy from the magnesium. The tension, anger, and stress made trying to relax, as we are told to do, impossible. So now we sit here, victims of technology once again, the machine vibrating on, while the baby receives formula, which we had been advised prior to her birth is not nearly as good for her as breast milk, "With all the immunoglobulins (proteins which build resistance to infection)."

Judy begins to cry. I feel like joining her. Everything is wrong. We'd pictured ourselves sitting in Judy's room, the baby in her arms, sucking at her breast, me holding her hand, an idyllic family. Instead, we sit alone, depressed, and as always these days, with the noise of a machine in the background.

We spend Thursday going back and forth between the NIN and Judy's room. On one trip back to her room, we notice a suitcase on the other bed. Surprised, we look at each other, wondering what it means. Within minutes an obviously expectant mother, husband, relatives and friends flock into the room. We exchange greetings with them, and walk out into the hallway.

"It looks like you've got a roommate," I say.

"They never told me anything about someone else coming into the room," Judy answers, her upper lip begins quivering.

"Well, it's happening. I guess we'll just have to live with it."

"Oh, God," Judy says, her face agonized. "I can't stand listening to all that happy talk. Everyone smiling, laughing and carrying on when I feel like shit."

"Maybe we can move to another room," I offer and go looking for the head nurse. I find her making out charts at the floor desk.

"Someone's just taken the other spot in Judy's room," I pause. She doesn't look up. "With all that's happening to our baby, it's rough," I explain, expecting sympathy. "Any chance of Judy moving to another unoccupied room?"

"No, that's the only open bed we have now," she replies curtly, ruffling her papers.

I go back and tell Judy.

"I'm leaving," she announces.

Judy begins packing her suitcase, jamming things in. I quickly go off to find our obstetrician to smooth things over. No need to check out AMA, I think. I'll have him discharge her early, and no feathers will be ruffled. Judy could care less, but I have to work here, after all. Dr. Jasmeen is getting a cup of coffee in the cafeteria. Trying to look unruffled I stand next to him in line and tap him on the shoulder.

"Doctor," I begin hesitantly. "They've put another patient in with Judy." He nods noncommittally. "Because of everything," I pause, "she really wants to leave."

Again the noncommittal nod. "Well," he says, "there's really no need for her to stay here any longer. Although I would have let her so she could see the baby more easily."

"I think she really needs to go home," I interrupt.

"Just as well, just as well," he waves me off.

Sighing, I go to find Emma Carter the head nurse, feeling somewhat like a bagman, carrying messages around the hospital. Emma stands like a battle sergeant at her floor station. "Yes, Dr. Stirts," she says starchily.

"My wife Judy is checking out, our obstetrician's discharging her," I offer tentatively, hesitantly.

She bristles, probably because she found out from me instead of Jasmeen. Even though hospitals exist to serve their customers, a.k.a. patients, the customer is not always right. Maybe not ever. "Now, Dr. Stirts," she says, annoyance plain in her voice. "Is there some problem, is anything wrong, is there anything I can do to make your wife stay?" I try to protest but she doesn't give me an opportunity. "Well," she says, turning away, "something must have changed in a hurry; someone's nose is out of joint."

I just don't have the energy for an argument or discussion about something which is already a *fait accompli*. Obviously, Judy was fine until someone moved into her room totally out of the blue. No one came by to ask how she felt about it, or even let her know it would be happening. Yet these issues seem to not even occur to the people running the ward. In fact, they have never occurred to me before Judy had been hospitalized. Before this, I hadn't given much thought to the mechanistic way hospitals function. In fact it was well suited to my own ministrations. Now I think of little else.

On the way back I go by to see the baby. More notes are clipped to her chart. I stop to read them.

THURSDAY, OCTOBER 13, 5:05 *P.M.*

Third year medical student note.

Baby girl Stirt appears to be breathing with less distress and is being fed by mother.

Sepsis workup: Blood cultures negative × 1 day. Antibiotics continuing.

Bilirubin 5.9. Meconium stools large × 3, guiac negative.

Respiratory: chest x-rays show bilateral hilar infiltrates, clouded costal margins. Breath sounds equal and clear.

Feedings: Enfamil 25 cc P.O. every 3 hours via NG.

Plan: Chest x-ray in A.M.

  Antibiotics at least 3 days if cultures negative.

  Watch respiratory status.

Thursday, October 13, 5:15 P.M.

Pediatric resident addendum to above note.

Weight today 2060 grams (up 30 grams)

In via NG, since birth (24 hours): Dextrose 10% in water, 50 cc; Enfamil 135 cc

In via IV, since birth: Dextrose 10% in water, 119 cc

Total fluids in, since birth: 304 cc

Total out since birth: 129 cc urine, 5 meconium stools

Impression: premature neonate;

  Rule out sepsis—36 hours ruptured membranes;

Plan: Advance feedings and environment as tolerated

  Blood cultures pending;

Repeat chest x-ray tomorrow;
Watch resp. status.

Again I experience relief. At one day old, the baby seems to be all right. Not great, but all right. She is breathing more easily, indicating that the possibility of respiratory distress syndrome, which had led to the attempts to delay Judy's delivery as much as possible, is diminishing. There is a discordant note however, the chest x-ray shows hilar infiltrates and clouded costal margins, which means there are shadows near the middle (hilar) and out toward the ribs (costal margins). These shadows often indicate infection, although chest x-rays have an odd way of not correlating well with a patient's clinical course when lung infection ("pneumonia") is present.

Very often the chest x-ray will appear terrible, full of haziness, cloudiness, and opacities, and yet a patient will have absolutely no visible signs or symptoms of distress (a symptom is a problem reported by a patient, a sign is noted by a physician on examination). Physical examination often is entirely benign in such patients—no indication, without the telltale x-ray, that anything is amiss. Conversely, quite often a patient with obvious distress and evidence of acute lung infection will have a clear x-ray.

So, even though Carrie has no evident respiratory distress and her lungs seem fine on physical examination, the chest x-ray picture differs. This would be closely watched, both by repeated x-rays and observation. In the meantime, she is receiving the broad spectrum antibiotics.

The third short note clipped to the board is a bit more alarming. I bend closer to examine it. It was written twenty-five minutes later than the first:

Thursday, October 13, 5:30 P.M.

Radiology report.

This picture is most consistent with pneumonia, or an aspiration syndrome.

"Damn!" I murmur, I'm beginning to wish I didn't know so much but there is nothing I can do. Once a physician, always a physician; and the fact that for the first time in my life feeling miserable about the skills and attitude it has taken me a lifetime to cultivate doesn't make me feel better or change. Now I reflect that radiologists rarely make diagnoses. The farthest they're willing to go is "consistent with." It's just part of the specialty. They don't see the whole patient, only shadows on a lighted box in a dark room, with a few explanatory comments attached to the x-ray request sheet. On the one hand, this makes them cautious, as they don't have all the information available about a given patient, have never seen or examined the patient. On the other hand, they are thus very capable of being objective. A radiologist sees concrete things, and uses standard criteria to correlate what he sees with various diagnoses. Still, I don't like the fact that he thinks Carrie's x-ray best fits the classic pictures of pneumonia or an aspiration syndrome, rather than some of the other less serious possibilities.

Aspiration syndrome, also known as aspiration pneumonia, is a feared entity. It is the result of either passive regurgitation or active vomiting of stomach and intestinal contents which instead of leaving the body are inhaled or pass into the lungs. The material causes a tremendous inflammatory response in the lungs, rendering them unable to oxygenate the blood properly, and often is the final insult in a debilitated patient, leading to death.

I look at the baby. Even though I say nothing, my mind screams. My heart constricts. Carrie has a nasogastric tube in place, from her nose into her stomach, because she is too weak to feed herself. Formula is being dripped into her stomach via the tube. Carrie's weakness means that if any formula were to back up around the tube and pass up through her esophagus to the back of her throat, she probably would have difficulty coughing it up and preventing it from entering her lungs. Nevertheless, her history and overall clinical picture is most likely one of infection: the exposure for thirty-six hours after rupture of the membranes, Judy's amnionitis.

The calculation of Carrie's intake and output is now critical. A baby will compensate for its own intake and output but not when intravenous feeding is involved. Hence, it is important to make certain she isn't "flooded" with a combination of oral and intravenous fluids to a point that she literally overflows. When this occurs, it occurs in the lungs, since the blood vessels there are most permeable. "Pulmonary edema" is the medical term for this oversupply of fluid. It shows up on chest x-rays as infiltrates and shadows, and clinically by producing shortness of breath and wet sounds when the lungs are listened to with a stethoscope. Carrie doesn't appear to have this problem—at least not yet.

She also has no evidence of sepsis, that is, disseminated infection throughout her body detectable by growth of bacteria from her bloodstream in cultures. This is the meaning of "Blood cultures negative × 1 day." Nothing is growing. This would appear incontrovertibly good, but I know it isn't necessarily so.

Only after you've drawn blood for culture can you understand why a negative blood culture isn't the final answer. Many patients who die of overwhelming sepsis never have positive blood cultures until far along in the course of their illness. The reason: "seeding," or showering of bacteria into the bloodstream from an infected organ or focus, doesn't occur continuously, but is sporadic. Thus, drawing blood randomly has only a small chance of catching a patient in the course of active bacterial entry into the bloodstream.

Medical dogma currently states that the fever and chills which commonly accompany the clinical course of systemic infection are indicators of active showering of organisms into the bloodstream, but even when blood for culture is hurriedly drawn from a shaking, chilled patient, quite often the results yield no definitive organism.

So, news of Carrie's negative blood culture doesn't make me feel reassured. I've heard it too many times before, and seen the worst occur in spite of it. Part of the ritual and mystery of medicine is demonstrated by this adoration, as it were, of the blood culture results. Each morning the intern calls the bacteriology laboratory, gets the report ("No growth at twenty-four hours") dutifully repeats it on rounds ("Blood cultures are still negative at twenty-four hours"), and enters it in his progress note on the chart.

The term "progress note," like so many medical phrases, · is amusing if considered for a moment. Quite often, it describes not progress, if progress is considered to be movement forward or improvement, but, rather, deterioration. There is something bizarre about reading a series of "progress" notes detailing a patient's gradual decompensation and eventual death. In certain cultures and religions of the East, however, where death is considered liberation, no incongruity would exist. Perhaps our euphemistic term reveals more about our own attitudes than we'd like to acknowledge.

Then I ask myself, a bit annoyed, what, by the way, is a note by the third year medical student doing on Carrie's chart? I already know the answer. One of the functions of a university teaching hospital is to give medical students, nursing students, students from every medically related discipline, a chance to "learn by doing." The classic catechism of the big teaching hospital is "See one, do one, teach one." Unfortunately for you as a patient at a university hospital, you're the "one."

Whether being the object of an unsure, frightened medical student's first attempts at inserting an intravenous catheter, or the victim of a series of unsuccessful attempts at a spinal tap, someone has to be the patient. A lot more in the way of physical pain and suffering goes on at such a hospital than would necessarily have to occur. But it's absolutely necessary in a larger sense.

With this in mind, the third year student's note on the chart followed by the pediatric resident's is expected, I suppose. But not for my child! "Let them learn on someone else's child," I mumble. "Carrie is no teaching case. I want her cared for only by the best residents and staff. No rookies need apply." I hurry over to tell them and stop short. Only raised eyebrows would follow my announcement. Despite wishing I didn't, I still care about those raised eyebrows.

THURSDAY, OCTOBER 13, 9:00 P.M.

I decide not to tell Judy of Carrie's possible difficulties. I want to spare her the conjecture. Nothing is certain. Moreover, there is nothing either one of us can do but wait. When I go to her room, Judy is objecting to being made to sit in a wheelchair for the trip out to the parking lot. "I've been walking all day," she explains.

Judy Sheremour, the coffee-skinned head nurse who has been called in, scoffs, "You know it's our policy. The hospital is liable until you're out of the building."

Again, why bother to fight? We wait for fifteen minutes for someone to find a wheelchair, but this is obviously very low on the list of nursing priorities right then. Finally, I go out and search the hospital, finding one in a corridor two floors above. Without a word I take it into an elevator and down to Judy's room. On the way out we stop to peer into

Carrie's bassinet. She is sleeping quietly. We smile at each other.

The nurse and I escort Judy out to the parking area, where she gets in the car. A few minutes later, waiting for a stoplight to turn green, I look over at Judy who's silently crying, tears rolling down her face.

"I didn't want it to be like this," she gasps. "What about the poor little baby? I wanted all of us to go home together."

There isn't anything to say.

Judy was a tough, compassionate, experienced neurosurgical intensive care unit nurse when I'd met her. She'd seen and treated the worst, children and young adults who'd gone from healthy, vital individuals to paralyzed, quadriplegic, brain damaged, comatose bodies in minutes after an automobile accident. She'd seen the families, disbelief in their faces, file silently into the intensive care unit, standing at the bedside gazing at their lifeless children and been able to carry on without breaking down.

Like me, though, now she reacts differently. Our own child is at risk. Even though Carrie had only been our child for one day, and is really more the hospital's child than ours, what with the few hours we'd had with her under the intense fluorescent lights, sitting in the midst of a cramped observation unit, the baby attached by innumerable wires and tubes to her machines, we already had a sense of profound loss.

We both fear the distance the baby's illness is creating between her and ourselves. Now we are going home alone, with little idea of when she would join us.

"When can the baby come home?" asks Judy tearfully.

"I suppose when she can eat," I say without conviction.

Judy gulps for air. "I want to take her home tomorrow. Nobody's doing anything at the hospital we can't do." She pauses and looks at me anguished. "If they want her tube fed, we can do it just as well."

Judy has a point. She certainly could take good care of her own baby, and nothing special is being done for her beyond the tube feeding. Yes, she is getting intravenous antibiotics, but these are prophylactic, part of a regimen on which all premature infants are placed to forestall infection with common organisms. Of course, placing every premature newborn infant in the hospital on antibiotics created resistance to these drugs and made infection by other, less easily treatable organisms, more likely, but that is the trade-off.

But although I nod, Carrie's chest x-ray has me worried. It had first been ordered, but not urgently, at 5:00 P.M. on October 12th, right after birth, but the x-ray had not been officially requested until the morning of October 13th, and had not been obtained until 3:00 P.M. that day. By then, Carrie's overall clinical respiratory status seemed better.

Still, what bothers me is that it isn't normal. Added to Carrie's inability to feed herself, and the fact that she is on IVs and in the hospital for what seems to me to be an indeterminate period of time, Carrie's condition is becoming frightening. Unpredictable things happen in hospitals, few of them good. Our obstetrician had said the baby would be hospitalized two or three days but she isn't getting any better. In fact she is worse, at least on x-ray, and I see no chance of her coming home tomorrow, on day two. Despite this, I try to be upbeat for Judy.

"Judy, let's see how she looks tomorrow. If she can eat, maybe we'll take her. I don't want us taking her unless she's stable. She could need special care. It's just too much at home."

We both know everything is ten times harder at home than in the hospital. You always need something which would be immediately at hand in the hospital but is unavailable at home. Also, I don't want to make waves. What if the baby gets worse, or has to come back to the hospital? I don't like the chest x-ray result, although clinically she seems fine. "We'd better wait until tomorrow," I repeat.

"What about Gypsy?" asks Judy. "Can we get her?" We'd gotten a golden retriever puppy only weeks before, and I'd taken her to the kennel, figuring housetraining a puppy on top of everything else that is going on is too much.

I shake my head, "Judy let's leave her in the kennel until the baby comes home. It's gonna be just too much, running back and forth to the hospital and cleaning up dog shit and piss every time we come back home."

"But we're going to get the baby tomorrow," says Judy emphatically, her widening eyes fixed on me. "So why not just get the puppy now?" I avert mine and look away.

"We'll see tomorrow," I say. I am too drained to worry about the dog.

"It's really pretty terrible isn't it?" says Judy softly. "Here we are, baby's room is all ready, but baby's in the hospital, and the puppy's in a kennel. I hate the whole thing."

I do too. I feel helpless, empty, and useless, but tell myself, at least I have Judy. We order a pizza, eat a few pieces, go to bed, and just lay there, looking at the walls and holding each other.

At 11:00 P.M. I call the observation unit. "How's Carrie?" I ask, introducing myself as her father. A few moments elapse and the nurse caring for Carrie comes to the phone.

"She's doing fine," she says. "Sleeping quietly."

"Thanks," I say with a sigh of relief.

"How is she?" asks Judy.

"Fine, sleeping quietly. Let's go to sleep too. We'll see her first thing tomorrow morning."

FRIDAY, OCTOBER 14, 8:45 A.M.

The telephone rings. It is the hospital.

"Dr. Stirt?"

"Yes, speaking."

"Hi, this is Caroline's resident. I don't want you to be alarmed or anything, but Caroline's had a difficult night; so we're moving her over from the observation unit to the intensive care unit. We're not sure what's happening with her, but just to be on the safe side, we're putting her in the unit so we can keep a closer eye on her."

"What changed?" I say, my voice cracking. Judy stares at me, frightened.

"Well, we noticed that about 3:00 A.M. she wasn't eating [eating? taking food down her tube?] as well as she had been. We checked her tube and it was in the right place, so we stopped feeding her since she seemed to be spitting up a lot of her food. Also, her belly seems to be getting a little distended, and generally she's just a little more irritable than she was."

"Anything else?"

"Well, she seems to have some blood in her stool that wasn't there earlier, so we think something's going on in her belly; we're just not sure what."

"What are the possibilities?"

"Well, the most likely possibility is necrotizing enterocolitis [NEC]. She's got a lot of air in the wall of her intestine which is pretty indicative of NEC."

"All right, we'll be right in."

"Don't rush or anything, she's holding her own, but I thought you'd want to know where we stand."

"Yes, thank you for alerting me as to her condition." The words, words as a physician I had used dozens of times come out without my gauging their effect on Judy.

"What's wrong?" she asks anxiously, pulling on my arm.

I stare at her for a moment.

"Well, the baby's not doing so good." I pause. "She was o.k. until 3:00 A.M. or so, then she stopped keeping her food down, and since then her belly's swelling up and she's got some blood in her stool, and she seems more fussy and irritable, so they're moving her to the ICU."

Judy starts crying, and so do I.

"What should we do?"

"I think we better go over there," I say, frustration creeping into my voice. "There isn't much we can do but at least we can be there." Judy nods and silently we pull on our clothes. The worst thing imaginable to both of us has happened. Our baby is now in intensive care.

For the average person, "intensive care" carries a spec-

ter of machines, tubes, wires and the like, beeping and
alarms. For Judy, who essentially lived in an intensive care
unit for five years as a nurse, and myself, having cared for
scores of patients in such units, it means something much
more ominous.

We both know behind the knowledgeable, overwhelming
technological facade medicine threw up, in such a unit lies
the unknown. A hospitalized patient, no matter how ill, is
always better off if he or she can be managed on the ward or
floor, without the seeming wizardry of intensive care. Intensive care remains a fallback, a last redoubt if things go sour,
or, as we say, a patient starts to "circle the drain."

An intensive care unit represents everything modern
medicine has to offer. The machinery and technology are
state-of-the-art, and take the place of human contact and concern. A patient who can't talk because a breathing tube in his
windpipe prevents it, whose respirations are controlled by a
machine, whose every heartbeat is recorded on a screen,
whose urinary output is channeled via a tube into a bag, who
doesn't eat but receives all intake via tubes in the arms and
chest, becomes less human, somehow, and more an extension
of the machinery serving him. If indeed, it's not the other way
around, the patient serving the machinery as its object and
raison d'etre.

If you don't improve in an intensive care unit, there's no
where else to go. When they go downhill, the only place patients in the hospital ICU end up in is the morgue.

The whole professional atmosphere of an ICU reflects
the sense that it's a "last resort," although not like any other
resort you'd ever go to. Such units, no matter how modern,
are always crowded, as new equipment always takes up more
space than was provided by the designers, and very, very
noisy. The lights are on twenty-four hours a day, and bright,
to make certain no dial setting or change is missed in the
shadows.

The medications used are those of the final stand, and
their nicknames reflect this. For example, patients in an ICU

often receive dopamine, a drug used to stimulate a failing heart and make it work more efficiently. Only, dopamine isn't the name used by the nurses in the ICU, who know how commonly dopamine is one of the drugs resorted to just before a patient's demise. The realistic ICU nurse's name for dopamine is "no-hope-amine." Similarly with a drug used to treat potentially lethal fungal infections. The drug often causes worse problems than the infection, and instead of amphotericin it is called "ampho-terrible."

These are the sorts of things Judy and I fear when we learn that Carrie is being moved to ICU.

I feel very distant from everything as I finish dressing and we get into the car.

Perhaps it is my way of dealing with Carrie or perhaps it's simply occasioned by the fact that we haven't had a chance to get to know each other at all, her in her plastic box, me on the outside looking in.

Judy sits huddled in the corner of the car, saying nothing, her face an agonized mask.

What disturbs me most as we drive to the hospital is the future, more than the present. The baby has no past, really, but is all future. Unlike an adult, whose development has been well defined, the baby represents potential, and the newborn intensive care unit represents potential disaster.

No matter about the glowing statistics emanating from pediatric intensivists about increased survival rates after intensive care in ever younger and tinier premature infants. Many survivors, if not most, have lifelong deficits, whether minor or major. The thought of Carrie blind, brain-damaged, or undergoing an unending series of operations, on multiple medications, and never able to live as we pictured a healthy child doing, is agonizing. This is the picture I now see in my mind. And it is horrifying. I've seen too many of those "survivors."

FRIDAY, OCTOBER 14, 10:00 A.M.

Arriving at the hospital we go directly to the ICU. It's tiny and brightly lit. Hordes of physicians, nurses, secretaries, clerks, and technicians mill about. Slowly we walk down the central corridor looking for Carrie's room. On our left is a huge blackboard with names on it, and next to the names, tests to be ordered and performed that day. "Stirt" is written about halfway down a list of twelve names. Next to the name is a lot of writing.

As we scan it, the beginning of a dawning awareness on our part occurs. Many objective indicators exist of how our baby, or any patient, for that matter, is actually doing in the ICU. I term this one the "Test Sign." Simply compare the number of lab tests and procedures ordered on a given day with the previous day's testing, and you'll know instantly whether things are getting better or not.

We finally find her room, actually an alcove which she shares with two other sick infants. We read the signs about washing our hands well for five minutes, put on our gowns and stand outside her room, dreading going in.

Finally we clasp each other's hand and step across the dreaded threshold. At first we can't see our baby, or even her area. It is surrounded by a crowd of blue-gowned people— her doctors and nurses. Here is my first conscious awareness of yet another sign of Carrie's course. This is the "Body Sign." Just count the number of people around the bed, compare it to the usual number, and draw your own conclusion about how the patient's doing. Looking around, even without a previous day's crowd to compare this one to, I know the situation is desperate.

Suddenly I think of how it felt to be a resident or medical student on a service and have a patient turn sour or be admitted as an emergency and die before treatment and how depressing or interesting it was depending on your degree of fatigue, clinical responsibility, and inclination toward that particular specialty.

I had a terrible attitude in medical school and as an intern I hated it, and simply endured each day. On certain services, for example, surgery, the workload even as a medical student was arduously high with little sleep. We performed examinations, did tests, went to surgery where we tried to stay awake learning on a retractor, totally oblivious to the operation being performed until a tapping sound on the retractor indicated we should bear down harder.

I hadn't minded pediatrics. Pediatrics was a "soft" rotation, in that the interns and residents did all the work and as medical students we essentially followed along, watched and listened. I recall my time in the neonatal ICU as a medical student. I'd stand at the periphery of a crowd much like the one around Carrie's bed, and listen to the arguments about what the diagnosis was, what tests to order, what antibiotics to put the baby on, and the rest. I was interested in the intellectual exercise, amazed at the flimsy basis of most decisions ("In my experience" or "I read a paper last month . . .").

The laughing, supercilious barbs about the prognosis if this test were positive stopped as the parents hesitatingly came into the ICU, with its intimidating aura and technosupremacy. But like the physicians making the decisions and debating the merits and demerits of a particular course of action, I really didn't lose any sleep over the child or the parents. After rounds we all put on our game faces and went to breakfast, where the repartee resumed.

Yet, I can't see any other way of coping with the constant degree of tension and crisis that accompanies modern intensive care medicine. To expect doctors and nurses to grieve over sick patients as they treat them would render them powerless to help in the long run, as it would be like treating your own family. All judgment lost, all objectivity abandoned, who could perform a painful test when a less painful one might be almost as good? Who could sleep at night, or not fall apart emotionally with grief in every non-working moment?

Now, standing outside the group, looking in, I feel a longing and envy to be among them, to be looking at this baby as just another unfortunate patient with disease instead of my own child.

As Judy and I inch towards the bassinet doctors and nurses begin to introduce themselves. I try to respond and so does Judy. We know we'd better get used to this bunch. They are our only hope of our baby surviving.

Then we look down and see Carrie. It is horrible, worse then I could have imagined. Her eighteen inch long body is covered with electrodes, tubes, transducers, and wires. Lethargic and spread-eagle, she is blindfolded. Bright lights are beaming down on her naked body. Her belly is hard and swollen like a melon, red and shiny, dwarfing the rest of her. She looks like a refugee from an underdeveloped country. I reach down to hold her tiny hand, and squeeze it. She wiggles her fingers a little, but otherwise lies perfectly dead still.

Judy stands next to me shaking. We are both silent, agonized, not knowing what to do or say. A nurse comes over and says, "I need to draw some blood, could you please wait outside for a few minutes?"

Still not saying a word, we walk out into the corridor, our eyes downcast. Finally I turn to Judy, "She's finished," I say slowly. "Look at her."

Fighting back tears, Judy shakes her head. "I really don't believe this is happening, I really don't."

I have the same feeling. It is too much to assimilate. But I have to talk, to try to grasp the reality of this situation, bad as it is.

"Judy, that's as bad as I've ever seen a baby look. Did you see her belly?" I clench my fists as I think of the pain and discomfort her little brain is experiencing, her first exposure to the world not filled with warm and loving hands as we'd hoped, but instead no physical contact, no food, and only pain.

"I can't believe a baby can be normal after something like this. No way. How can you experience nothing but machines, light, and noise, with no sense of belonging to anyone, and still develop properly?"

This is our fear, as much as anything else, that we will eventually leave the hospital all right, but with a baby who is permanently stunted in one way or another. No words or reassurances can help, because we'd both seen far too much, far too many children like Carrie sent to chronic care facilities for the rest of their aborted, painful lives.

Healthy babies are the rule elsewhere, but here in the ICU everyone is sick, very sick. Yet for most people, all this is something they'd only heard about. "Why us?" I think once again. Judy had watched everything she'd done during the pregnancy, taken no medication, and yet here we are destroyed.

Hearing soft cries from Carrie's bed, we duck back inside. One nurse is holding Carrie down as another jabs at her heel with a sharpened lance to get blood. Instinctively we shiver. A small baby has such tiny veins it's the only way to quickly obtain a sample. But it hurts, it hurts like the devil. I'd had it done in medical school in our hematology course, and my fingertip, where my partner had stuck me, was sore for a week afterward.

"How," I whisper to Judy, "can Carrie ever let anyone touch her again without crying and withdrawing, when the only human contact she is likely to get from now on consists of this?" Judy shakes her head miserably wincing, wanting to do something, anything. I lean towards Judy, "Let's find a doctor who can help us talk to the resident in charge of Carrie." We find one down the hall. He points us in the right direction. Once we find the resident we look for a quiet place to sit but can't find one in the ICU. We settle for the anteroom of the resident's sleep room, a six by eight foot cubbyhole filled with chairs, a desk, backpacks, coats, books, and debris, the garbage can overflowing with meals hurriedly half consumed and then abandoned for some emergency.

I introduce myself and Judy, and he does likewise. His name is Bill Young. It turns out we'd gone to the same medi-

cal school, UCLA, although he'd graduated two years ahead
of me. We talked about the oddity of that, two UCLA grads
meeting in a neonatal ICU in Charlottesville, Virginia.

"Let me go get Carrie's chart," he offers. I nod apprecia-
tively.

A few minutes later Bill comes back chart in hand.
Quickly reading through the contents he says, "The baby was
doing fine until 3:00 A.M., that's when the nurse on duty noted
a change—her formula wasn't being digested."

Nurse's note.

At 3:00 A.M. noted spitting up yellow secretions, checked NG tube
in case down too far. Reinserted tube and checked placement—
in place. Aspirated, obtained 5 cc yellow fluid/solid material. Infant continued to spit up and drool. Fussing and irritable, frequent crying. Held 7:00 A.M. feeding and reported situation to
resident. Stooled small amount; bloody-brown seedy, mucousy
material that was positive for blood on testing. NG tube placed
on suction.

"Bloody material appeared in her stool," he goes on.
"The baby's neurological status had changed. All in all, something probably centering in her gastrointestinal system had
occurred," he pauses, "and she was deteriorating."

I look at Judy. She is crying silently. Bill Young looks
grim. Nothing is more sobering than caring for small infants
and realizing how rapidly they can fall apart. A small baby
can go from apparently well to moribund in hours. There is
almost no reserve in an infant, no fat or energy stores, no

ability to withstand environmental stresses such as temperature changes—in this respect they are almost like cold-blooded animals, responding directly to their environment. Thus, the need for close control and observation of temperature, intake and output.

"Joe, look at this," he says fingering another entry, "it will give you a more complete picture." We both huddle over the chart.

Nurse's transfer note to ICU.

Vital signs stable, abdominal girth 29 centimeters, increasing, tender, distended. Stools grossly bloody. Child lethargic, intermittent grunting with labored respirations. Vomiting yellow, stone-like substance. Noted to be apneic and dusky for 30 second periods. Chest and abdominal x-rays done, sepsis work-up done. On intermittent suctioning. Transfer to ICU.

"And this," he points to still another notation.

Radiologist's report.

Two day old female with abdominal distention and bloody stools.

Portable chest x-ray 0815 hours: comparison 10/13/84. The lungs are much clearer than on the previous exam with minimal infiltrate remaining at the right lung base. The heart size remains within normal limits.

The bowel gas pattern is abnormal with both dilated loops of bowel and numerous areas of a frothy appearance of the bowel itself. In addition, pneumatosis of the bowel [air within the intestinal wall itself] is noted in multiple locations, most prominently in the right lower quadrant and left upper quadrant. An N-G tube terminates in the stomach.

Impression: (1) Chest improved in appearance with residual infiltrate remaining at the right lung base; (2) Abnormal bowel gas pattern as described above with pneumatosis in the bowel wall.

"All consistent with necrotizing enterocolitis," Bill states.

I ask him, "What exactly is 'NEC?' "

"Well," Bill says, "it's a very uncommon disease, which has no known cause, although a lot of people believe it's an infection of the bowel from an organism no one has been able to isolate. It occurs most often in premature babies, and comes on suddenly, like it did with Carrie."

"Does it have anything to do with getting formula as opposed to breast feeding?" Judy interrupts. I know this is on her mind because Judy has been very decisive during her pregnancy about doing what is best for the baby and, even here we have now been thwarted by events beyond our control.

I watch her agony and feel as if it is my own. If it turns out that formula fed babies are more likely to get NEC than those who are breast fed, I know Judy will never forgive herself, will always blame herself for not being able to produce the milk that would have prevented Carrie's illness.

I breathe a sigh of relief when he says, "No, breast fed babies are as likely to get it as bottle babies." Later, I found out this wasn't always believed to be so, and there is still some doubt about it. In fact, much of the way Carrie has been managed to this point, although considered optimal care in many major medical centers, might have been considerably different in other hospitals. But who could know, and, anyway, here we are.

"What's the course of the disease?" I ask. Young looks somber.

"It's totally unpredictable. There's no specific treatment for the disease, since we really don't know what we're treating. Basically, it's supportive treatment: close monitoring, treating what symptoms occur. Sometimes the disease resolves quickly, and in other kids it goes on a while. It's impossible to tell how Carrie's going to do, but she's obviously a very sick little girl.

"We're going to insert an arterial line [a catheter placed in an artery to measure blood pressure directly and obtain blood samples for analysis of oxygen, carbon dioxide, and various blood constituents without requiring repeated sticks, as we'd seen being done earlier]. We'd also like to get a bone marrow biopsy, since her white count's so low."

I wince, a bone marrow biopsy is a dreadful procedure. I've seen them done in medical school. A large, sharp needle is forcibly driven into the sternum (breastbone), hip, or shinbone, pushed and twisted down into the marrow, and a syringe is then used to suck out samples of marrow. Laboratory analysis of these samples provides a picture of what kind of blood cell formation is going on, as all blood cells are formed and developed in the marrow and released into the peripheral circulation when mature. Occasionally, in a child, the force exerted on the needle breaks the fragile shinbone.

The question to be answered in Carrie's case is, is her bone marrow suppressed due to the infection and, if so, how badly? If her marrow is indicative of poor blood cell formation, this would provide grounds for giving her blood transfusions, for her body will have no other way of getting enough white cells (which fight infection), red cells (which carry oxygen), or platelets (small cells which prevent bleeding by helping blood clot as needed).

Specifically, she would receive white cells, a constituent of whole blood which fights off infection. This is really important because if her white count drops too low, she will be highly vulnerable to overwhelming infection from almost any organism. This vulnerability to infection is the reason patients with leukemia or other cancers who are receiving chemotherapy are kept in isolation, as the chemicals used to kill the cancer cells are not specific and also damage healthy cells especially blood cell precursors in the bone marrow.

I don't bother asking about whether or not she will get anesthesia for the bone marrow procedure, since I know that even in adults local anesthetic is totally inadequate, and in a baby the needle used to put in local anesthetic only causes more pain. It is like sticking a baby's heel for blood. You have to do it, so you do it, and you simply endure the enraged screaming all around you, hating yourself and the child.

That is one of the reasons I didn't go into pediatrics. I don't have the toughness to keep causing babies to cry "for their own good."

"Well, if she needs the bone marrow, I guess you might as well do it, and the arterial line and whatever else she needs, don't you think so, Judy?" Shakily, I turn towards her. Judy nods. She looks hollow, empty, and resigned. I feel the same way.

We thank Bill, and go back to see Carrie. By now she has more tubes emerging from her body, as the arterial line had been placed in her while we were talking to Dr. Young. Wearily I shake my head. Judy stares straight ahead with her level gray-green eyes tear filled. This procedure, like everything else in medicine, carries risks. Sometimes the rest of the blood vessels carrying blood to the hand fail to take over when the main vessel is occluded by the catheter used for this procedure. In such cases, gangrene of the thumb and index finger occur, and occasionally the whole hand has to be amputated—not a common occurrence, but a recognized complication of arterial cannulation. I know, because I put them in all the time for patients undergoing surgery. In fact, I'd written a paper about the subject several years earlier, for which I've reviewed the world's literature on complications; so the reports and pictures of dead fingers and hands are quite real to me.

No one but a physician, and especially an anesthesiologist, would react the way I do to the catheter now lying in Carrie's radial artery, just short of her left thumb. No one would see so many possibilities for disaster, but I could, and do. I doubt any of the pediatricians who'd decided to insert that catheter saw the procedure the same way. Lucky for them, unlucky for me.

For the rest of the morning Judy and I walk about without direction. Finally I become radicalized and say to her, "Enough is enough. I've been dumbly acceding to every statement about the baby's course and treatment."

"I know," she says, "but we have to do something, please, Joe," Judy's voice breaks.

I nod. Through the haze, her words strike a cord. Frustration turns to anger, then to depression and pain. "Carrie's doctors are no better or worse than me, and they are making these decisions based on the same mixture of intuition, experience, and half-truths expressed as scientific fact in the medical literature, as I do in my own work. Judy, this is our child, I'm going to find out everything I can about what's wrong with her.

"Our baby's care, and her life, really depend on how others interpret the 'facts.' At least, I can put in my two cents worth." Of course, I know that from the pediatrician's point of view, nothing could be worse. A physician may have doubts about the course he chooses, but he expects to hear about these doubts from his peers, not his patients or their parents. I'm the same way. "I'm going to the biomedical library and read," I announce.

For the next several days that's exactly what I do, until I feel almost as knowledgeable on NEC as my baby's doctors are. After all, an attending physician has a special area of interest that almost certainly does not include the disease you

or your child has; the odds are way against it. In fact, Bill
Young who initially attended our baby was involved in research on respiration, and probably had once known much
more about NEC, during the course of his training, than he
now did. He may have cared for a case or two during his
training, but that was years ago.

The "house staff" in a teaching hospital, the interns and
residents, are in even worse shape when it comes to expertise.
They lack both experience, obviously, and information, and
have very little time to get information, considering the demands placed on them by a whole roster of babies, each as
sick as ours.

The residents don't have the luxury of hours to spend in
a library looking up the latest articles and studies about NEC,
and even if they did, they don't have the scientific background
required to interpret them, and do anything but believe the
conclusions.

My baby is one of many her physicians are caring for
simultaneously. While Carrie occupies all of my and Judy's
thoughts, she represents only a small part of her physicians'
concerns. They aren't losing sleep over her, we are.

With this in mind I learn all I can about NEC. I learn it is
the most common acquired gastrointestinal emergency in the
neonatal intensive care unit, occurring in 2000 to 4000 infants a year in the United States. Considering the 3,500,000
babies born annually, this is a minuscule number. It is a rare
disease. I look around the library as I read this, bitterly. "Why
Carrie? If so few babies get it, why the hell does it have to be
her?"

I read on. The disease seems to be getting more common
with the advent of modern neonatal intensive care and saving
of small birth weight infants who once would have died soon
after birth. NEC was once thought to be due to underdeveloped immune protection in the immature gastrointestinal
tract, hence the belief that breast milk, with its high content
of immune system proteins, might prevent NEC. More recent

studies showing equal incidences of NEC in breast fed and bottle fed babies have cast doubt on that theory.

The disease is much more common in low birth weight and premature infants, and being of a probable infectious origin, would be more likely to occur in babies at higher risk for infection, as Carrie is since she'd stayed in-utero for thirty-six hours after Judy's water broke, until Judy herself became infected.

Then I read something chilling. The disease has been seen to occur in clustered epidemics. This suggests that Carrie has possibly gotten it from someone or something in the environment. Combined with her thirty-six hours of exposure in-utero prior to her birth, this leads me to one conclusion: it wasn't at all inevitable that Carrie would get NEC. She's been unlucky, a victim of time, place, and circumstance, and to some extent it is our fault, Judy's and mine.

If we'd gone to another obstetrician at another hospital, perhaps he might have delivered Carrie immediately, not being up-to-date on the latest in neonatal research, and none of this would have happened. Perhaps just being in this hospital, and this delivery room and neonatal observation unit, has exposed Carrie to some infectious organism she'd not have gotten elsewhere. Judy and I have already spent endless hours on the "what ifs" and "whys" of Carrie's birth. The discussions only add to our frustration and go nowhere.

Now I learn that some centers purposely avoid feeding low birth weight infants anything for several days, on the theory that it's the load of food presented to the underdeveloped gut that precipitates NEC. Certainly, many babies don't take anything but water for several days until breast milk begins to flow, and no harm is done to them.

All this only adds to my feelings of guilt. Judy and I are responsible for having Carrie, and for having her here, and now she is a victim of our decisions, paying a price in pain and agony we'd never be able to forget. We can't shrug and walk away, because with every visit we make we are reminded vividly of what we've created. This is the other side of parenthood, one that relatively few people experience, thank goodness.

FRIDAY, OCTOBER 14, 12:30 P.M.

Judy and I eat our lunch in silence in the hospital cafeteria. It is becoming increasingly difficult to make small talk. Words hang in the air between us, sentences go unfinished. Whether we are with Carrie or away from her, she is all we think about.

By the time we make our way back to intensive care, the sparks of my anger at myself and the chain of events that has transpired to put Carrie in the unit ignites. There in the ICU, across the room from her, is another premature baby with NEC. I find out the child has been delivered by our obstetrician in this hospital yesterday, the day after Carrie was born. "Is there something in this hospital that is responsible—physician, nurse, carrier, source?" I cry out to Judy.

One of the residents takes me aside to tell me strict handwashing precautions are now in force since two babies simultaneously having so rare a disease makes everyone very suspicious of an infectious cause. Judy and I become even more despondent hearing this. We are furnishing good material for the residents to learn on. As we say on rounds, "Great teaching case!" Right on.

Standing next to Carrie's limp, unresponsive body amidst the noise and chaos, we decide to limit our visits to see Carrie to three times a day—morning, afternoon and evening. It seems pointless to just stand there all day agonizing. We can't hold her, we are always in the way, and Carrie isn't going to notice us while she is blindfolded.

The blindfold is to protect her eyes from the "bili lights," artificial light of a wavelength which, when it hits the skin of a newborn baby with an elevated bilirubin level, causes a chemical reaction which helps the body clear itself of the excess bilirubin. The bilirubin itself is a non-specific chemical product of red blood cell destruction frequently seen in premature infants, especially sick ones.

Many centers never use them at all any more, since it has been shown fairly conclusively that an hour of natural daylight every day is as beneficial as the "bili lights." Where bili lights are used, fifteen minutes every eight hours is considered optimal therapy. Carrie is under the lights almost continuously. I wonder if I should say something and decide not to. It isn't important enough, even though there is evidence that prolonged exposure of the genitals to the lights could cause chromosomal damage. It just doesn't seem very relevant to worry about mutations in the chromosomes of the eggs in Carrie's ovaries while she lies at death's door. So I file it away as one more worry to carry away from the hospital should she make it out alive.

On the way out of the hospital, we cannot stop ourselves from passing Carrie's alcove again. More notes are clipped to her chart.

FRIDAY, OCTOBER 14, 2:10 P.M.

Bone marrow biopsy report.

Cellular marrow aspirate with relative lymphocytosis. There is a "maturation arrest" at the metamyelocyte level with virtual absence of mature neutrophilic forms.

Impression: Non-diagnostic as described.

Carrie's bone marrow has indeed shut down, accounting for the low white blood cell count. No doubt this is the effect of her overwhelming NEC rather than the cause, since her white count had been normal at birth.

FRIDAY, OCTOBER 14, 2:30 P.M.

Radiology report.

Abdominal film shows multiple dilated loops with air-fluid levels. Again noted is pneumatosis within the wall of several bowel loops. A frothy appearance of the bowel is present throughout much of the abdomen. No free air or portal venous air is identified.

Judy and I look at each other in despair. Carrie's abdomen now shows pathologic findings diagnostic for NEC. Her bowel wall has "pneumatosis," that is, it contains gas within its layers. Her intestine is not functioning normally, as the infection rages within. No air is seen outside the bowel or in the liver's circulatory system yet. This means that the bowel has probably not perforated or broken open, an almost certain forerunner of overwhelming sepsis and death. However, perforation could occur without x-ray confirmation of "free air."

No antibiotics will help Carrie now, although she continues to receive them in the commonly held medical belief that "They can't hurt." Once an infection has seated itself and localized in the body, it is common medical knowledge that it will in most cases never resolve without active surgical excision of the infected area together with antibiotic therapy. In Carrie's case, surgery is not yet being considered.

Surgery in babies with NEC is fraught with uncertainties. Often the bowel appears dead in some parts, and viable in others, yet the apparently good portions go on to become gangrenous. Conversely, some babies whose clinical course and x-ray picture suggest imminent demise have a bowel appearing not nearly as bad as would be expected.

Reading all this terrorizes us. Judy and I decide, despite our earlier rationalization that we should limit our visits, that we have to stay.

Preparations for Carrie's white blood cell transfusions begin. Blood is sent for cross matching. At 6:05 the first unit of transfused white blood cells is given to her. A short while later, they begin giving her oxygen by nasal prongs because she is not absorbing enough oxygen from the air. That is due to a combination of her respirations being depressed by her overall weak condition and her gas-filled intestine pushing her diaphragm up into her chest.

We listen as her breathing becomes irregular. Spells of apnea (breath-holding) and bradycardia (slow heart rate) occur with increasing frequency, about twice an hour. A tube in her stomach continues to suck out what gas is accumulating there, but can't remove the gas from inside her bowel or the bowel wall itself, which could rupture at any time.

We watch as Carrie's abdomen continues to increase in size, as gas accumulates within the bowel. Once an hour a nurse measures her stomach with a tape measure.

I give an objective picture of Carrie's deterioration. At 8:00 P.M. her white blood count is repeated. It has fallen to 2,000 cells/cubic millimeter, less than what it had been earlier that day. There is no doubt Carrie is getting worse.

FRIDAY, OCTOBER 14, 8:30 P.M.

Judy and I stand next to her limp figure, holding her hand, talking softly to her. Is it really only twelve hours ago today that we'd gotten that phone call to let us know Carrie had taken a turn for the worse? It seems months. I am transformed by the day's events, now a victim, a patient as much as my daughter. I wonder sadly how did this loyalty to a baby I have barely held occur.

The nurses and doctors tell us not to worry, that she is "holding her own," but we don't even pretend to believe them. You don't have to be a neonatal intensive care expert to realize things look bad and are getting worse. We both feel Carrie will die soon.

We stare at Carrie's limp form. She has no reserves, no body fat to call on, little immunity. She is receiving no food or nutrition to help her sustain a fight. Every hour brings yet another procedure or piece of bad news. How long can an eighteen inch, four and a half pound baby go on? And to what gain? What kind of life would this child lead even if she survives?

Both Judy and I have always said that if one of us were to turn into a helpless, comatose shell, we'd expect the other to finish us off. Now we see our firstborn quickly fulfilling our worst nightmare about each other. Yet we are powerless to do anything about it.

Judy whispers, "Why don't we just take our baby home and put her in bed with us? If she dies, at least she'd have been with us."

"I don't know," I say. Trying to leave the hospital AMA with a mortally sick infant who almost certainly would die at home would probably be logistically impossible. I could see police, court orders, all the paraphernalia of modern medicine and the law being mustered to keep the baby in the hospital, us appearing as did parents of children with terminal cancer who'd had enough of chemotherapy, and took their children home under the glare of television lights.

I work at the hospital and everyone I work with would think Judy and I, health professionals, are crazy. I wouldn't be able to work there any more, that's for sure. The baby would die, and no doubt an ugly court fight would ensue over whether Judy and I were guilty of murder. It is preferable to let the baby die in the hospital. Yet, I just don't want her ongoing pain to continue. I've always had contempt for physicians who can't admit a lost cause and accept that death is preferable to a prolonged course of painful, aggressive therapy. Now the lost cause is mine.

Judy's mother has been scheduled to arrive at 10:00 P.M. She calls us at 9:00 P.M. Her plane has been diverted from Washington due to fog, and she'll be spending the night in Philadelphia and arriving tomorrow morning, Saturday, the 15th. "How is my darling granddaughter?" she asks.

I pass the phone to Judy who tells her. I think of Norma, sitting alone in a hotel room hearing the news that her first grandchild is now mortally ill. I feel all over again the sinking, empty feeling I'd experienced earlier that day (Was it really the same day? Unbelievable!). Judy hangs up the phone, crying.

"Mummy says she'll say prayers for her all night tonight, but she's sure the baby will be all right."

I shrug my shoulders. There is nothing to say. Finally, Judy presses my hand. "Let's go home, Joe."

I nod my agreement.

SATURDAY, OCTOBER 15, 8:00 A.M.

Somehow we sleep better than the previous night. Maybe it is because the overwhelming sense of events and shocks are over. Maybe it is the realization that the only peace we can find is sleeping. As soon as I wake up though, I feel the same tearing sensation in my gut as the day before.

"Call the hospital," Judy says, "and see how the baby is."

"I don't want to call the hospital or talk to anyone," I snap back.

She flashes me a dirty look.

But I can't help myself. I want to have as little to do with anyone else other than Judy as I can. I just want to get dressed and to see Carrie.

I call the hospital anyway.

"Neonatal ICU."

"Hi, this is Joe Stirt, Caroline Stirt's father," I say with a cheerfulness I don't feel. "Could I talk to her nurse please?" You quickly learn that the only way to get accurate information without having it travel through several people is to ask for a patient's nurse.

"Just a minute. I'll see if she can come to the phone."

I wait, resigned for the worst. "What else, I wonder, could have gone wrong?"

"Hi, this is Carrie's nurse."

"Hello, this is Joe Stirt, her father. How's she doing?"

"Well, really not much different from last night. She had an okay night, nothing bad happened, but she's still pretty sick."

"Okay, we'll be in soon to see her. Thanks a lot. Bye for now."

"Bye."

I tell Judy not much has happened, that Carrie is pretty much the same. We drive to the hospital. Once there, we go directly to ICU. As usual I read Carrie's chart to see what we've missed.

Nurse's note.

Lethargic when not disturbed. Fair grasp. Poor suck. 31% oxygen in hood. Tachypneic, mild substernal retractions. Occasional apnea and bradycardia. Abdomen distended and firm. No bowel sounds. Passed one very bloody stool. Slightly jaundiced. Central venous line operative site with dried blood underneath. On table with head of bed elevated. Bag and oxygen mask, laryngoscope, endotracheal tubes, succinylcholine at bedside.

"At this point her condition was essentially unchanged from when we went home," I tell Judy. "At least she's not worse." I don't tell her Carrie is requiring 31% oxygen now to provide enough for her body; last night 28% had been enough (room air is 21%). But Judy sees as I do more ominous equipment for emergency resuscitation is now at the baby's bedside. If she stops breathing for a prolonged period of time (in a premature infant her size, thirty seconds is life-threatening, so small are her reserves), a tube would be placed in her larynx to enable oxygen to be given easily via a bag. The news is, on the whole, not good. Carrie's condition appears to be worsening. A further discouraging note is attached.

Nurse's note.

Weak cry. Poor tone. Began nasal CPAP (continuous positive airway pressure) and 34% oxygen at 0600. Expiratory grunt present.

Seeing this confirms my suspicions; Carrie's prognosis is growing less hopeful.

At 6:00 A.M. they'd increased Carrie's oxygen concentration to 34 percent, and taken her out of the oxygen hood. Now as we stand over the bassinet, she looks even smaller. She is puffy-eyed when the blindfold is removed and the bili lights are turned off, her eyes slits within swollen, red lids. She is wearing a headband with nasal prongs on it, which distort her nose. These provide continuous pressure to her lungs against which she has to breathe. The theory is, the pressure keeps the weak airway walls from collapsing on themselves and helps get more oxygen in. The problem is that the constant pressure of gas in her upper airway also causes gas to

enter her stomach, which is just what her doctors are trying
to avoid by keeping a suction tube in her stomach.

The only alternative is placing a breathing tube into the
larynx. But, to me as an anesthesiologist, this technique also
means the end of the road is near. An intubated patient has
gone as far as she can go. There are no more maneuvers left.
Still it is either the tube in her larynx, which itself is fraught
with complications, both immediate and future, or gas in her
stomach. They have no choice, they have to choose one or the
other.

Since most patients in ICUs die with a tube in their larynx, I prefer just on those grounds alone the course they've
taken. I marvel, though, at how everything that happens continues to be in areas I know about so well, in which I can so
vividly appreciate the risks and about which ironically, I can
do nothing.

The old problems are continuing, and new, potentially
more serious ones arising. Carrie's white count is still low,
4,300, although better than yesterday, so another white cell
transfusion is administered.

Her platelets, the blood constituents responsible for clotting, are declining from a normal value of 250,000 per cubic
millimeter (small things, aren't they?) late Friday to 130,000
by 6:00 A.M. Saturday and 53,000 at 4:00 P.M. The infection
has suppressed her bone marrow to the extent it just can't
generate platelets fast enough, and she is using them up trying to stem the bleeding in her belly.

The dangers of a low platelet count are several: first, she
simply might not be able to respond adequately to bleeding by
clotting her blood at the site, which in her case is the entire
bowel, it seems; second, and just as ominous, premature infants have very fragile blood vessels in the brain, and bleeding into the brain is a real possibility now. The aftermath of
infants bleeding in the brain runs the gamut—mental retardation, seizures, blindness, deafness, paralysis, and inconti-
nence being some of the lifelong residuals of such an event.

The deck appears ever more strongly stacked against Carrie.

SATURDAY, OCTOBER 15, 11:00 *A.M.*

We watch and wait, growing more afraid as time passes. Carrie is getting x-rays every six hours now, her condition is becoming critical. If free air appears in the films, it will mean her intestinal wall has finally burst, rotted through by infection and the pressure of the gas formed by the bacterial growth inside. What then? Perhaps a rush to surgery to explore, or, mercifully, she might die soon afterward. Knowing how things are going, I am afraid an even worse possibility than either of these awaits her.

Carrie's course is complicated by the necessities of modern medical life. The hospital has one pediatric surgeon, who has been aware of her since her admission to the ICU yesterday (Friday) morning with NEC, but who plans to be out of town for the weekend, returning Monday. Thus, if Carrie requires surgery over the weekend, only the inexperienced resident and a general surgeon who cares for adults are available. A sudden need for surgery would probably result in a consult note stating that "Surgical exploration should be deferred until patient stabilizes," or some such polite refusal to get involved.

I sympathize with the plight of the surgical team. Many were the times I'd written similar notes, when I was in over my head and didn't want to let everyone else know it. Nor do I fault the pediatric surgeon for going out of town and enjoying himself all weekend as we agonized at Carrie's side. A doctor cannot feel his patients' pain all the time, because he won't be able to function. This is truth, this is reality. Ask the surgeon's wife if she'd stay married to him if he never left town when one of his patients was critically ill.

Perhaps once upon a time things were different, but remember, modern medicine with its endless array of interventions wasn't around then either. A physician did his best, and let nature take its course. Now nature never gets a chance.

In this charged atmosphere we keep our eyes focused upon Carrie, hoping for a sign, any sign of progress. We see none.

Carrie lies deadly still as if encapsulated in her own world. Her eyes are closed. She couldn't have opened them if she'd tried, and she isn't trying.

Blood continues to emerge from her bowel as the infection eats away her intestinal wall. She is limp, barely responsive, crying faintly. We continue to observe her, and feel part of ourselves dying. Finally it is time to leave the hospital and go to the airport to pick up Judy's mother. I clutch Judy's hand as we wait at the gate. It is all so sad, when it had all seemed so exciting and wonderful before.

When Judy's mother deplanes, she and Judy hug each other. I watch as Norma pats Judy on the back telling her, "Things will be okay, the baby will be fine." She looks at me gently. "I've said oh, very special prayers for the little one." I don't answer. We go back home and get Norma unpacked.

"How is she doing?" Norma asks me when we have a moment alone. "A bit better?"

"Not really, Norma," I say. "In fact, she seems worse." I hear the sharp intake of breath.

"Oh, my," Norma says turning away.

Norma is Jamaican by birth and upbringing. Premature babies with NEC don't live very long in Jamaica: the level of intensive care and ancillary support, all the machinery and equipment which is keeping Carrie alive right now, don't exist. On the other hand, parents don't agonize over a slow, progressive decline the way we are. It is over in a hurry. There's something to be said for that.

SATURDAY, OCTOBER 15, 2:00 *P.M.*

Hurrying back to the hospital, we enter the neonatal ICU, a place very familiar to Judy and me even before Carrie was born. To Norma, though, it is all new and very frightening. We watch her reactions; seeing things through her eyes. As most adults do when first exposed to high tech medicine, she becomes very childlike waiting to be told what to do next. "It is," she says slowly, "like stepping onto a strange planet." We nod sympathetically. Alarms, beeps, buzzers, and hissing noises fill the air, from all manner of machines. People dressed in blue scrub suits move purposefully in and out of little alcoves off the main hallway and crowd around bassinets laden with equipment. Phones ring incessantly, until the caller gives up.

We all scrub our hands dutifully, why I'm no longer sure. Carrie is already infected, she isn't likely to be catching anything else, and if she does maybe it would be all for the best.

Only two visitors at a time are allowed in the ICU, but Judy and I ask Carrie's nurse if it is all right for the three of us to go in. She gives us a stately nod. The nurse rules in the ICU. This is one of the things which counterbalance the extraordinary pressure and frustration of being an ICU nurse. Physicians may think they run things, but the nurse is the difference between survival and death quite often, more often than anyone but nurses (and doctors who are honest with themselves) know.

Cost-effective strategies are now being implemented in all hospitals nationwide, and "efficiency of care" is the new catch phrase. I have watched Judy sit on many a patient's bed, holding clenched hands and stroking sweaty, scared arms, reassuring, encouraging, crying herself. This will be a memory soon, and I for one do not look forward to that time in the hospitals of today, much less so to those of tomorrow. What nurses do cannot be quantified any more than love and kindness can be weighed. Without them we are all going to suffer.

Norma stands at the bassinet—actually, a flat plastic board with padding and a sheepskin on it, with a raised rim around it to prevent Carrie from falling out. Norma looks at her silently. She's come in with a brave smile on her face, but it has faded to a somber, wincing expression when she gets her first look at her first grandchild. Even with the blindfold and bili lights off, Carrie looks dreadful. Tubes and tape cover most of her body surface, her eyes are still swollen shut, her belly is hard and tight like a drum. She lies nearly unconscious on her back, naked, spread-eagle under the warming lights. There is no point in covering her up, since she needs to be constantly examined or have blood obtained.

She weighs four and a half pounds, and contains approximately two cups of blood. So much blood is being taken for tests that she will soon require a transfusion just to replace what has been removed. This is common in neonatal ICUs.

Norma is afraid to touch her or say anything. "Mummy hold her hand, and stroke her head and talk to her. She can hear us," Judy pleads.

Judy and I always touch her when we visit. We bend down and whisper in her ear. I tell her about all the good times we are going to have when she comes home. Do I really believe she'll come home? No. Can she tell, or somehow sense I am lying? I rationalize. Well, I believe it when I tell her; so much do I want her to be rid of this nightmare.

Norma takes one tiny, limp hand and puts her own finger in it. Carrie doesn't stir. Norma bends down, kisses her, and begins to cry. So much pain, and for what?

We all stand around watching Carrie for a while, Judy and I holding hands. "It is too much, too much to expect anyone to endure day after day," I say suddenly. "How does a baby survive a time when every touch leads to exquisite pain as one needle or scalpel after another pierces her skin, and fingers probe her tense, swollen belly?"

Norma is trembling, "Let's go," I say. She nods but doesn't move. She never would leave on her own, so loyal and fierce is her faith in her God who would look after little Carrie, if only we are strong for her. Finally I put my arm around her shoulder and lead her away. We leave the ICU, politely saying good-bye for now to the nurses and doctors. That the veneer of manners survives such a stress is, I suppose, the result of what we call civilized society. I don't feel polite, I feel bestial, but I can still say the right words.

We return a little after six. A new nurse's report is attached to the chart. It's not good.

SATURDAY, OCTOBER 15, 6:15 P.M.

Nurse's report.

Changes from previous report. Totally flaccid tone. Does not attempt to grasp. Muscle tone hypertonic at times, with extensor muscles in arms and legs extended, asymmetrical, not simultaneously. Right arm seen extended with wristdrop and fingers extended. Pupils reactive to light.

Carrie's neurological status appears to be deteriorating. The worst is occurring. Her body movements are indicative of the beginning of brain death, so called "decorticate" movements and posturing. When the higher brain centers are damaged, the lower centers take over, and produce just these sorts of movements. No one is doing anything for her. There is nothing to do.

I keep going back to the chart all day. Reading. Hoping. Only a one sentence note by Bill Young, the attending physi-

cian, appears in the record. No other physician writes a
word. There is very little to say, I suppose.

Judy and I talk with Bill again. He now seems a bit distant from Carrie and her problems, probably out of fear and
unfamiliarity added to the fact that she is a fellow attending
physician's daughter. "Go easy on Carrie," we tell him softly,
"Don't persist in ordering every test and therapy possible for
her right up to the bitter end."

He nods.

SATURDAY, OCTOBER 15, 8:00 P.M.

We come back in the evening, all three of us, and sit around
Carrie's bassinet, a vigil of depression and despair.

Carrie's overall condition continues to worsen. Tests to
determine the ability of her blood to clot show she requires an
abnormally long time to form a clot. She is at increasing risk
of catastrophic brain hemorrhage. All the clotting factors she
can muster from her depressed bone marrow are being used
up in a furious effort to stop the bleeding in her intestinal
wall.

We are pretty much left alone. All we can do is watch and
wait. Carrie lies still and unconscious.

An hour or so later we head home. We don't even try to
reassure each other.

SUNDAY, OCTOBER 16, 7:15 A.M.

Looking at her Sunday morning, nothing looks different. She
is still lethargic, although she occasionally cries weakly. Mercifully for her, I know she is too sick to stay as she is for long.
She is on borrowed time, entering her third day with NEC.

Talking to her we hold her hands, which is difficult since
both tiny scarecrow arms are taped to rigid boards from

shoulder to wrist to prevent her from disrupting the catheters that are in her arteries and veins, we notice redness at the base of her nose where the prongs rest. I am enraged, realizing the prongs have been left on too tightly and are cutting off circulation to the skin at the bottom of her nose.

The pediatric surgeon has returned from his weekend off and looks in on Carrie. He puts no note on her chart only a rubber stamped sentence saying, "The attending physician has seen this patient today and discussed current status and treatment with the house staff." I wonder if he feels as I do, there is nothing to say.

I have had experience with this before. During my residency I'd been called to consult on a patient who had been anesthetized two days earlier and had an NG tube placed for stomach drainage much as Carrie does. The tube had been placed against the patient's nose at an angle which cut off the circulation to the skin over the nostril, and the area became necrotic, or dead, tissue. Now I see this happening to my own daughter's nose. I feel absurd even noticing it, much less caring about it, since she is so sick. It is trivial. Yet just such details are what make up the whole. I call the nurse over, "Look at this," I say pointing to the prongs. The nurse sighs, she replaces the prongs with a smaller pair, which she carefully places so as to minimize the amount of pressure at the red, inflamed site.

Somehow, somewhere in my thoughts I must imagine Carrie somehow recovering from all this, I guess, or else I'd not have made a fuss. I picture her recovering from the NEC, and then going home with a facial deformity requiring plastic surgery to correct the scars. It seems like finally here is something I can help with, and get involved with, that finally I can do something for my child. I marvel that hope still exists anywhere within me despite all I know about Carrie's condition. I marvel and I despair.

At 3:00 the nurse scribbles a few more words. Quickly I read them over as soon as she leaves.

Nurse's note.

Small, fretful cries when disturbed. Otherwise quiet with some spontaneous movements. Fair tone, good suck, eyes open, trying to focus. Jaundiced.

What is Carrie seeing, I wonder? What emotions does she feel when the blindfold and bili lights are off, as she stares up at the ceiling? I long to pick her up, to hold her close to me and rock her as the day after she was born. Now she lies isolated, far from living touch, any warmth provided by heat lamps in what must be intolerable pain as her gut eats itself alive, distending her abdomen.

What has happened to her mind? Is she tuned out, so barely conscious that nothing registers? Is a life which has consisted so far of no feeling but intense, unremitting pain and discomfort worth continuing? And what kind of person would emerge, if one did emerge from this wreckage?

As Carrie lies in the ICU, hovering on the edge of death, the physicians' notes in her chart become increasingly sparse. In medicine, stability has little interest. "No change" means "Let's move on." When a patient is deteriorating, attention is intense, while an improving course invites us to bask in our success, writing enthusiastic notes of recovery on the chart. Carrie is going nowhere, so no one has much to say, except the nurses. Each day's nursing records contains pages of detailed physical examinations, tests ordered, results received, hourly notes on temperature, heart rate, blood pressure, respiration, fluids received and put out, all totaled and organized to afford the physician an accurate picture of just how Carrie is doing. Even as a physician, exposed to hospital record keeping and charting for over ten years, I gaze in awe at my daughter's records, a testament to what I can only call real love, that of Carrie's nurses for her. No mere job or sense of duty could yield such fanatical devotion.

SUNDAY, OCTOBER 16, 4:00 P.M.

Despite their diligent care though, Carrie is still very ill. Her body is producing so much acid as a by-product of her infection that she needs to have it neutralized with sodium bicarbonate. She is puffy overall (edema), which I notice when I press her shin bone and my finger has left a deep pitting impression. This means her blood vessels are leaking fluid into her tissues, an ominous sign, since if this happens in her lungs little oxygen can be absorbed.

No organism which could be considered the cause of her infection has been isolated from her blood cultures, which is not unusual. Even if an organism is isolated, it would be impossible to say it is the cause of Carrie's NEC instead of a result of it. Nevertheless, a lumbar puncture (spinal tap) is planned to try and identify an organism there, as well as determine if any bleeding into the central nervous system has occurred.

No one says a word to Judy or me about a spinal tap. Perhaps they think we'd do better not knowing. I perform spinal taps regularly, in the course of my job as an anesthesiologist. Spinal anesthesia remains a mainstay of modern anesthesia practice. Thus, once again, Carrie's treatment and my awareness of the complications of the procedure coincide and once again, my knowledge is useless.

Even if an organism is to be isolated from Carrie's spinal fluid, it will be days until it can be identified and sensitivities determined.

The problem with cultures is that often the organism cultured is a secondary infecting organism, and although it can be treated, in itself it is not the source of disease. It can even be an extraneous contaminant, and not at all the source of infection. As I meditate on this new complication, Judy walks up to me with a bit of a smile. "Carrie is more stable today than yesterday, Joe," she says, "at least in regard to her heart

and lung function." This is determined, in a clinical sense, by
the number of episodes of apnea and bradycardia ("A's and
B's") she suffers. Premature infants are prone to disturbances
of respiration and heartbeat, probably due to their immature
nervous systems which fail to generate and transmit impulses
as a mature baby's does. Sick premature infants are even
more vulnerable, as the controlling centers deep in the brain
stem progressively go awry. Saturday Carrie had four episodes of A's and B's. Sunday only one occurred. Thus, the
need for CPAP is decreasing, and slow discontinuance, or
"weaning," from CPAP is begun.

Later that afternoon Carrie is given a transfusion of
whole blood, her first. So much blood has been taken from
Carrie for diagnostic tests in the two days since she'd gotten
NEC, about 15 percent of her total body volume, that she
already required replacement since she's become anemic.
Again, I can only grimace. Each blood transfusion, no matter
what the amount, carries with it about a 1 percent risk of
hepatitis. Since Carrie has already received two white blood
cell transfusions to help her depleted bone marrow fight her
infection, this is her third exposure. Given enough blood, she
would be certain to get hepatitis at some point. Lurking in the
back of my mind is the specter of AIDS, which also can be
transmitted in blood, as well as other diseases whose carriage
in blood is as yet unknown. Our bit of brightness quickly dis-
sipates into more dismal worries by the time we leave to
catch some dinner.

When we get back later that night, I notice several red,
half-inch diameter circles on Carrie's thighs. Our nurse tells
me those are burns from the transcutaneous monitor. The
monitor works by heating an area of skin and then analyzing
the amount of oxygen in the blood vessels dilated by the
warmth. Unfortunately, after the device has been on for a
while, it burns the skin. Since the burn is superficial and goes
away, it is accepted as a necessary evil.

Again, I wonder what can I do?

I see Carrie's poor tiny nose still red and raw. There are

burns on her legs, all part of her therapy. What kind of mess are they planning to discharge, should she recover? How disfigured or deformed would she be? No one in the hospital really cares to the extent Judy and I do. To her nurses and doctors Carrie is a challenge, a disease to be overcome. To me she is my child, a person, with a life to lead should she survive. No one else seems to care much about the quality of her life. The bottom line here is survival. Success is measured in life or death. Any survival is a success, as looked at by her care team. I've often felt that way myself, as a physician. As a parent, it isn't that way at all.

In my heart I know selfishness plays a part, a big part in my thinking. Who would care for our blind, disabled, brain-damaged daughter? Who would wonder for years about what this crippled, forlorn thing might have been? Not her doctors and nurses. Carrie would be one more case, one more survivor in the impressive morbidity-mortality statistics generated by the ICU. I'd sent too many such survivors home, thanking God it wasn't my child, to fool myself.

Larry Cohn, a tall blond resident wearing glasses, comes over to talk with us. He pushes the glasses up on his forehead, "Carrie," he says slowly, "has developed a heart murmur earlier today." Judy and I clutch each other's hand as he continues. "It's a loud, continuous 'machinery' murmur that appears to indicate a patent ductus arteriosus, or PDA." In premature infants and those with heart malformations, one common finding is a patent ductus arteriosus (PDA), a channel which normally functions while the baby is in utero to divert blood away from the non-functioning lungs of the unborn child. The duct normally closes at birth, as lung function begins. In certain instances, however, it remains open or reopens, to take up extra flow if the lungs are unable to tolerate it. Carrie is accumulating fluid in her lungs and her body, sensing this, is reacting.

"We're going to get a Doppler ultrasound tonight," he adds. "Which should confirm or rule it out."

"What if she has a PDA—then what?" I ask.

"Well, she's not in the greatest shape for surgery, but we might try a prostaglandin inhibitor infusion."

"Doesn't that impair blood clotting?" I ask. He looks almost through me to a spot above my head.

"Well, yes, sometimes, which is why we're not rushing to do anything right now. We'll get the ultrasound and have cardiology see her tomorrow. She doesn't seem to be unstable right now, though, any more than she was."

Maybe not to him but for us and Carrie it is all going to hell. Amazing how many things can go wrong in that little body. Her lungs are filling with fluid, her heart is reverting to its fetal circulatory pattern to try to adapt to the water within them. The only trouble is, this means less oxygenated blood is flowing to her brain. This is my chief concern. I am not interested in growing a vegetable.

SUNDAY, OCTOBER 16, 10:00 P.M.

Radiology report.

Doppler ultrasound scan of peripheral arteries shows evidence of retrograde diastolic flow consistent with PDA.

Reading this note I realize that blood is flowing opposite from the normal direction as the heart fills, and that the shunt, or PDA, is thus directing blood against the normal flow. "Carrie, Carrie," I murmur as if reciting her name will somehow stop what is happening.

SUNDAY, OCTOBER 16, 11:30 P.M.

Radiology report.

Chest and abdomen remain unchanged from the previous study except that there is development of some increased haziness which would be consistent with third spacing of fluid.

Carrie's tissues are starting to leak. The blood vessels are becoming permeable to fluid, and water is being forced out of her bloodstream into her skin and other tissues. The "increased haziness" means fluid is beginning to accumulate in her lungs, which would make it even harder for her to exchange oxygen, and thus force her to work harder to breathe and make her heart work even more forcibly to circulate what oxygen is available. The picture is one of impending shock.

When overwhelming infection occurs, one of its hallmarks is a breakdown of the blood vessel's ability to constrict and prevent fluid from oozing out. Thus, water moves into surrounding tissues, producing the puffiness called edema, which Carrie has. The next step is often a drop in blood pressure, as the infection releases still-mysterious toxins which relaxes the blood vessel walls. The body, unable to circulate oxygen and remove waste with its now-impaired circulatory system, no longer functions, and death soon follows.

Intensive care medicine, however, fights back in the face of overwhelming infection, using up to five different antibiotics and a myriad of drugs to improve heart function and constrict the dilating blood vessels. Dopamine (a.k.a. no-hope-amine, since people receiving it seldom survive), digitalis, and phenylephrine are but a few of these last resort drugs, each capable of producing fatal toxic reactions themselves. Carrie is not on any of these, and I take some momentary comfort from this.

Yet our fear is that Carrie is neurologically abnormal. In a coma, unresponsive, her stiff, extended legs herald unknown disaster inside her head. Lying naked and blindfolded, covered with tubes, patches and wires emerging from every natural orifice and several artificially created ones, her tiny, thin, bony legs and arms rigid, her abdomen grotesquely swollen, laboring to breathe, and intensely red, she seems barely alive or human. We look at her, hold her hands, and say nothing. No words can describe it. If I could end it here and now without repercussions, I would. Judy, although believing Carrie will die soon, wouldn't. She says she has no hope of Carrie ever recovering to even a semblance of normalcy, but she still wouldn't just let her die. Which is not to say Judy hasn't dealt with this situation before, as a nurse, and felt differently. She has.

Carrie once again has created a dilemma. Her PDA is a response to her failing overall condition, an attempt by her body to adapt to her fluid-filled lungs by moving blood away from them to the rest of her body. This means that less blood will get oxygenated, however, and could result in lower oxygen transport to her brain. For this reason, therapy for her PDA is being considered.

Two types of treatment are available. Surgery to simply tie it off is the most common, and has been employed for many years. Most children with PDA, however, are not as overwhelmingly sick as Carrie, and in them the surgery was relatively simple. It is not "open heart" surgery as we commonly think of it, since the PDA is outside the heart, connecting the aorta, the main blood vessel of the body, to the pulmonary artery, the main blood vessel to the lungs.

In Carrie's case the excess fluid oozing into her tissues, especially her lungs, has caused the PDA to reopen to handle the overflow. She is not in any kind of condition for surgery.

Thus, medical therapy is the other option. In the past decade, it has been learned that infusion of indomethacin, a drug which opposes the tendency of the PDA to open, often can close a PDA permanently, without surgery. However, indomethacin has side effects and is contraindicated if jaundice or decreased blood clotting factors are present, since the drug causes jaundice and destruction of red blood cells, and inhibits blood clotting. Carrie has both severe jaundice and decreased platelets, so an attempt at closing her PDA with indomethacin would carry an exceptionally high risk.

It seems to me that all attention is now being focused on the PDA, and not on why it has opened or how it fits into her total picture. Carrie has responded to fluid overflow appropriately. By removing the ability to shunt extra blood out of her congested lungs, how would she respond? The fluid would simply continue to accumulate, drowning her. It seems to me that closing her PDA is a shortsighted attempt to do something, anything, in a case where for the most part, nothing is being done because nothing can be done.

As we stand around Carrie that evening, I place my hand lightly on her swollen belly, close my eyes, and wish that somehow I had some magical healing power and that as I touch her, her gut would heal and she'd recover. Nothing happens, but for these moments it is thrilling, imagining her coming back together, cured.

MONDAY, OCTOBER 17, 12:30 A.M.

Nurse's note.

No change from previous note, except now note red, raised rash over trunk and abdomen.

"Oh shit," I mumble when I read this the next morning, Carrie has developed yet another problem—a rash. What does it mean? It is impossible to imagine more going wrong, yet every visit seems to bring more bad news, some minor and some significant.

MONDAY, OCTOBER 17, 10:00 A.M.

Cardiology consult.

Color slightly dusky, probably secondary to peripheral vasoconstriction. Rhonchi, rales in both lung fields. Heart sounds normal. No significant murmur heard. Abdomen markedly distended secondary to NEC. EKG shows left ventricular hypertrophy by voltage criteria. X-ray shows slightly enlarged heart, lungs look wet. Echocardiogram shows decreased contractility. Both ventricles and both atria enlarged probably secondary to decreased ventricular function. No structural abnormalities noted. Impression: No evidence for PDA at present; decreased ventricular function, etiology unknown.

   Suggest: Inotropic agent of your choice would improve cardiac function. Dopamine or dobutamine probably best, to avoid arrhythmias which are more likely with digoxin.

A few hours later I read news that is more than significant. It is dire. Carrie's heart is failing. The cardiologist has written "etiology unknown" but one look at the baby and a glance through her chart is enough to see that overwhelming infection is now spreading through her body. My greatest fear now comes to pass: Carrie is placed on "no-hope-amine." They are going to flog her to the bitter end. "At least she doesn't seem to be feeling much pain," I murmur. This is how

I rationalize not simply taking her home right now to let her at least go quietly in my and Judy's arms.

It is difficult to oppose anything that is being done for her. It is all "correct," the proper therapy, by the book. True, I don't know enough, really, or have enough experience at actually treating sick babies, to say "Stop, enough, she's finished," but in my heart I think this is a convenient cop-out, an easy way to excuse passivity, watching the whole exercise. Perhaps for someone who isn't a physician, and doesn't have as vivid a picture as I do of the problems and ramifications involved in every aspect of Carrie's treatment, acceptance would be reasonable.

But I can't hide from what I've seen over the years, nor can Judy. No one tries to pretend with us, which probably makes the pediatrician's job much easier on the whole.

They all know I work here, and that Judy is an ICU nurse, but they also know we are now part of the great leveler, the ICU. No one can get more or less than medicine could offer here. Only one level of care exists—critical.

MONDAY, OCTOBER 17, 10:45 A.M.

Norma decides not to come to the hospital this morning.

"I just can't stand to see that poor little heart like that. Poor little heart," she protests.

I understand why she simply can't stand watching. I wish I could stay home too.

"I'm going to say prayers for her," Norma says. "I know the Lord is listening."

I hug her, then Judy and I leave.

When we arrive, we see to our bitter amusement that Carrie is still far and away the leader on the test board. "The 'Test Sign' is menacing. No one else is close," I say to Judy.

She nods. As we wash our hands and go in, we see an even larger crowd of people around Carrie than usual. "The 'Body Sign' is even worse," Judy interjects. We both know the

more bodies around a patient, the worse the patient is. It is
related to the "Service Sign," which simply reflects the fact
that as a patient's condition worsens, more and more consultations with other services are ordered, perhaps in an unconscious effort to spread the blame. Carrie definitely has a terrible Service Sign.

Judy and I smile at each other bitterly. Wearily I pick up
Carrie's chart.

MONDAY, OCTOBER 17, 11:00 A.M.

Resident note.

Fluids/Nutrition: Intake is strictly $D_{7.5}$ N.S. 160 cc/day. Maintain on glucose only until NEC begins to resolve.

Hematology: Platelets 88,000, up from 30,000 yesterday. Am
unsure of the cause of decreased platelets: coagulopathy vs. production deficiency. Bilirubin 7.1, continuing bili lights for now.
PT/PTT 14.9/11.9, 35.0. White blood cells 8,000, increased.

Infectious Disease: Blood cultures negative so far. Continuing
on ampicillin and amikacin.

Dermatology: Developed a blanching erythematous rash today, first on abdomen which has now spread to entire body except face. Most likely a drug reaction to ampicillin, but will check
with dermatology and consider change of antibiotic.

Cardiovascular: What was felt to be a PDA yesterday has resolved now, but echocardiography and cardiology exam find
biventricular hypocontractility of unknown cause. Suggestion for
an inotrope was adhered to and she was begun on dopamine.

Respiratory: On nasal CPAP 5 cm, oxygen 40%. She is requiring more oxygen to maintain oxygenation. Hope to increase pulmonary perfusion with dopamine. If this does not work, would
try to increase cardiac output with digitalis.

NEC: Abdominal girth increased 1 cm to 30.5 cm today. Abdominal x-ray shows decreased gas in bowel wall, but there is a
small persistent loop of bowel consistent with local necrosis. Abdomen has bluish tinge with palpable bowel loops today. A syrup-

colored rectal discharge still present. NG suction continues to be difficult to keep open.

Impression: Not a surgical belly at this time, but she is very worrisome. She looks worse, yet PT/PTT better, x-ray is improved, and pressures are stable. Problems will be to maintain adequate NG suction, closely monitor fluids, and jump on any change for the worse in the x-ray picture. Could perhaps be turning the corner with white blood cells, but if these are hers, they will be of poor phagocytic capability. Complications are: (drug?) rash, decreased heart contractility, peripheral vasoconstriction, all of unclear etiology. Her skin is a pale gray. Will watch her very closely.

There is no doubt Carrie is getting even worse. What has seemed rock bottom yesterday is just a resting place on her downhill slide. It is all coming apart. Today she looks dreadful, more dead than alive. Her overall color is a sickly gray. Her abdomen is shiny, tense and bluish, the gas-filled, dilated bowel loops pushing out against the skin as if about to explode. Overlying the blue and gray is a pink-red rash covering her entire body. Seeing her I want to run away.

"At least she is in no pain," Judy whispers. That seems evident. No pain medication is being administered in part because Carrie seems so out of it and in part because it would depress her respiratory and circulatory systems even more.

"She doesn't really need it," I say, "out where she is."

Walking over to a corner of the room, Judy and I begin to talk about Carrie dispassionately, as if we are not related to her, simply concerned friends. Protecting ourselves, I suppose. Yet two events shows me this is only a facade.

As we talk with Larry Cohn, one of the residents, he mentions in passing that a spinal tap had been performed on Carrie late last night. I register this information without reacting, but after he is gone, I begin thinking about it. Carrie's platelet count, a measure of the cells involved in blood clotting, as well as her PT/PTT, two blood tests used to determine

how long blood takes to clot, had been grossly abnormal yesterday. She is bleeding out of both ends of her gut, and her
infection has disabled her bone marrow to the point of shut
down, requiring transfusions of white blood cells to retain
any ability at all to fight off infection.

As I dwell on it, I grow more and more angry. One of the
rare complications of a spinal tap, or lumbar puncture, as it is
also termed, abbreviated as LP, is bleeding from blood vessels
around the spinal cord into the spinal canal or cord itself. The
result of such a bleed is a hematoma, a mass of clotted blood
at the site. Compression of the spinal cord by the hematoma
can cause partial or total paralysis of all body functions controlled by areas of the spinal cord from the affected area
down.

Unless the hematoma is removed surgically, soon after
recognition that it has occurred, paralysis is permanent.

Yet, it wasn't his decision, but that of another resident in
charge of Carrie's hour-to-hour (day-to-day was inadequate
to describe the speed with which events occur in the neonatal
ICU) care. I don't want to say anything to the resident, because although he's shown bad judgment in this instance, on
the whole he is doing a superb job. I've seen and continue to
see physicians whom I wouldn't let care for a pet turtle care
for patients, so I am grateful for our resident's fortuitous
presence on Carrie's case.

And fortuitous it is, because patient assignments in a
teaching hospital are usually strictly random. If two residents
are in a service, every other patient goes to each as they come
in. The only exceptions occur when one resident by chance
gets all the sickos, in which case an attempt to even the workload occurs, or when a case of special interest in one resident's area of expertise comes in. Few residents have enough
experience to have expertise, however, so this isn't often a
consideration.

What worries me as I stand next to Carrie's bed this
Monday morning, looking at my wreck of a child, is that she
might have bled into her spine after last night's LP and could

now be paralyzed from the waist down. It is impossible to tell. She is so far gone that she wasn't moving much anyway before the LP, so her limp legs could be simply her underlying condition. The lack of deep tendon reflexes (the little foot jerk that occurs when a doctor taps your knee with a rubber hammer) wouldn't tell me anything either, since she hasn't had them earlier. Suddenly an image crosses my mind. I imagine a miraculous recovery from NEC, only to find out days later that Carrie has been made a paraplegic by the unnecessary LP. You may mumble, "He's getting paranoid." I am here to tell you, things like this happen every day to people like you and me.

The rash is something else that bothers me. She's been given so many drugs and antibiotics already, it is now literally impossible to tell which has caused it, if indeed it is a drug-induced rash. Patients with severe infections often develop what appear to be rashes but what in fact are septic emboli, little agglomerations of infecting bacteria and blood cells which end up in the skin.

MONDAY, OCTOBER 17, 11:30 A.M.

Dermatology consult.

Patient is a 5-day old with NEC, who developed a blanching, macula-papular rash last night on the trunk which has now spread to entire body except face. On ampicillin, amikacin, and dopamine, previously on gentamicin. Condition critical. Blood cultures so far negative × 3 days. LP results pending.

Impression: Drug rash vs. fungal infection, most likely ampicillin reaction.

Plan: Would continue ampicillin and current drug regimes in view of overall condition, change now may not improve situation and may worsen it. Will follow.

A typical dermatology consult. Everyone in medicine makes fun of dermatologists, the country-club set whose worst emergency is an "Acute itch crisis." When I was in medical school I'd mentioned my thought of perhaps going into dermatology to a medicine resident who told me, "Wet on the dry, dry on the wet, and steroids if that doesn't work" is the essence of dermatology residency, and all I'd ever need to know about the subject to take care of almost any skin problem. I'd spent a month of my internship on a dermatology rotation as an elective, and later had treated a fair number of skin problems, for the most part succesfully, as a G.P. The resident was right.

Other worrisome thoughts cross my mind as I stand next to Carrie. These concern her drug regimen of ampicillin and amikacin. Amikacin is an aminoglycoside, a class of antibiotics which had been shown conclusively to result in permanent kidney damage and hearing loss unless blood levels of the drug are strictly controlled. Sometimes these problems occur even after optimum blood levels have been maintained. Carrie's exposure to those drugs means blood is being drawn several times daily to measure her drug levels to try and keep their doses within the ideal therapeutic range.

Even with an average dose for a patient's weight, some people metabolize the drug much slower than others, and are thus prone to high, toxic blood levels even with the "right" dose. Others are less vulnerable to seemingly "toxic" doses and do fine. Carrie's hearing, assuming she makes it out of the hospital, is at stake. Yet there would be no way of knowing if it had been damaged until much later. A favorite line from the movie *Young Doctors in Love*, supposedly a spoof of modern medical center "technomedicine" but in fact less of a satire than most of its viewers realized, comes to mind: "We won't know for sure until the autopsy."

Needing a break, we leave the hospital and go to the kennel to see our puppy, Gypsy. She'd been there since I'd returned from Atlanta. It seems so long ago, yet I have hardly given the dog a thought. Though I'd begun training and house breaking Gypsy a couple weeks earlier, I am certain I'll have to start again from scratch. Seeing us she turns somersaults and runs over. She licks us both with her pink wet tongue. Obviously she is happy to see us, so much so she then pees all over the kennel's anteroom. Laughing, we decide to take her home. "We need one survivor at least," I say to Judy. "I will continue my lessons with her, three times a day, using a book I've picked up called *Good Dog, Bad Dog*." It is something to do besides think about Carrie.

I am continuing to work, after a fashion. My job has several parts: one consists of teaching residents how to give anesthesia three days a week, and another is doing original research and writing papers. The research part is over for the duration of our ordeal. It requires real freedom and the ability to think about things optimistically, both of which Carrie's sickness has destroyed. Every hour I am awake I think about her, wonder and worry. I couldn't care less if I ever publish another paper.

My time in the operating room, though, is another story. Concentrating on a particular patient and a given problem, which I've dealt with umpteen times before, is both easy and a relief from the reality that my comatose daughter lies no more than fifty feet away, one floor above and down the corridor. I continue to work my scheduled days in the operating room, just to feel effective.

For now, at least, Judy has her mother so she isn't alone at home all day, in a new city, with no friends to talk with. She hasn't called her old friends to tell them the news about the baby's deterioration. As it is, having to write all our relatives to correct our initial telegrams heralding Carrie's birth seems an overwhelming task, which we decide not to do for the present.

We return to the hospital in mid-afternoon, and as we are washing our hands outside the unit, preparing to go in, a rotund, red faced man in a priest's collar comes hurrying up to us. "I'm Father McClune," he says. Shaking his head sadly he pats Judy's shoulder, "I just want you to know I'm always available if you wish to talk about the poor baby." Instinctively anger engulfs me. My hands clench. His words make me so furious I can't believe myself. I guess I am not as indifferent to Carrie's inevitable death as I'd thought.

Later I wonder how it happened that the priest was there. Did Carrie's doctors decide that she is now close to death, and put in a distress call? Did he just make rounds in the ICU every day, looking for children about to die? A ghoulish job. Who pointed us out to him as the parents? I hoped he hadn't gone from person to person, asking "Are you the Stirts?"

Here's another person, I think, who puts on a long face, sympathizes, empathizes, philosophizes, and then goes home to dinner, the paper, and a good night's sleep. Make no mistake about it: I had been one too. But not now. Not ever again.

MONDAY, OCTOBER 17, 2:00 P.M.

Radiotherapy consult.

Patient has neutropenia and NEC. Needs irradiation of WBC transfusion. Will irradiate blood products as needed.

Carrie's white blood cell count is being maintained by transfusion. In addition, she'd received more red cells and more platelets. So tenuous is her immunological status and ability to fight infection that her blood products are now being radiated, exposed to x-radiation, in an attempt to decrease the amount of immune response they produce in her body and lessen her rejection of the foreign cells. The principle is the same one behind the immuno-suppressive drugs given patients receiving heart transplants.

The risks of the additional transfusions register in my mind as I look at the bags of blood hanging at her bedside. "Three more potential sources of hepatitis," I mumble. Each bag increases her chances one percent or so. That makes a total of six so far, with who knows how many to come?

MONDAY, OCTOBER 17, 4:30 P.M.

Nurse's note.

Essentially unchanged from days, except increasing abdominal distention, increasing discoloration, increasing rash trunk and thighs. Dopamine continuing.

We go back and forth to the hospital, moving in a daze.

"She's so sick, Judy. The only thing I can say for sure is she can't stay where she is. I mean, she's getting essentially no nutritional support beyond sugar water, she's using up her own body's fat and protein at an incredible rate, and she's got no reserve at all: you saw her, a big potato belly with four toothpicks sticking out of it."

Judy sighs, "But somehow she's not giving in. You see her, lying there. She just won't die."

"But I can't imagine how she's going to get better. She needs to fight off an overwhelming infection, she's in a coma, her heart's failing, her lungs aren't working. I think she's almost gone. There's just no way for her to continue much longer."

I am trying to become resigned to her death. Any time the phone rings, I expect it to be the hospital telling us that

Carrie has died. The phone, by the way never stops ringing. Friends, relatives, the hospital insurance adjuster, co-workers all call and we've grown to hate it. I realize another sign has emerged to take its place among the others I've uncovered: The "Phone Sign" indicates how mortally sick the baby is. It is amazing. The frequency of the phone's ringing seems to ebb and flow with the baby's condition. Perhaps, though, the frequency isn't changing, and it is only our irritation and fear that changes as Carrie waxes and wanes.

The ringing carries with it a fatal insistence that it be answered. Many times I want to just turn the damn thing off and forget it, but Judy keeps saying, "What if it's the hospital and something's happening?"

Occasionally it is the hospital, Carrie's nurse calling to tell us she is doing fine and do we have any questions. It takes all the restraint I have not to say, "Yes, why do you have to call and tell me that bullshit when we were just there a couple of hours ago and saw the truth? Don't you think we've had enough for a while?"

It is impossible to say to the nurse, "Please don't call us unless there's a problem," for two reasons. First, it seems ungrateful, and we depend on the nurses for Carrie's well-being. Not just for standard care, if the near-insane level of meticulous attention given sick premature babies in the ICU can be termed standard care, but the extras—holding her hand, stroking her head, the contact with another person that for a change wouldn't hurt her. All this depends on the nurses' good will toward us. They've had plenty of babies to spend time with, and a lot of leeway as to who gets the intangibles. We want them to give them to Carrie as much as possible.

The second reason is that many, many nurses care for Carrie. Each works an eight-hour shift, so each day she has three different nurses in succession, and what with off days, vacations and the like, Carrie would be cared for by countless different nurses. It is impossible to tell all of them something —the lines of communication break down. The best that we

can hope for is shift-to-shift communication, as the nurse going off duty relays a summary of Carrie's course for the past
eight hours to the one coming on. Even then, it is a little like a
joke that gets told to one person after another in succession
and finally becomes unrecognizable, each person distorting it
just a bit more.

MONDAY, OCTOBER 17, 5:00 P.M.

Radiology Report.

Abdomen and chest: Abdomen continues to show the same persistent dilated loop of bowel in the right lower quadrant, but
again there is no evidence of pneumatosis or a perforation. The
previously noted haziness seems to have increased, suggesting
further third spacing in the abdomen. The chest x-ray remains
unchanged with the same bilateral patchy infiltrates.

On x-ray, Carrie's bowel seems to be improving, yet she
is continuing to pour fluid out of her bloodstream into her
abdominal cavity and lungs. So, although the primary disease
is apparently resolving, at least insofar as x-rays can show,
she is going downhill now as a result of the chain of events set
in motion by the disease. Or so it seems as no one really
knows.

TUESDAY, OCTOBER 18, 12:00 P.M.

Resident's note.

Fluids/Nutrition: Plan to begin hyperal today.

Hematology: Platelets decreased to 21,000. Will transfuse more platelets. PT/PTT 15.4/12.4, 42.9. Platelets may correct these values. White count down again to 3,200. Will transfuse white cells today.

NEC: Infections Disease has advised discontinuing ampicillin and beginning cefotaxime on chance that rash is drug-related. Other possibilities are Candida or viral, the former more likely.

Abdominal girth has increased by 1.0 cm, but abdominal x-ray shows no pneumatosis or perforation so far. Possible dilated loop seen indicating area of necrosis.

Cultures: Blood cultures from 10/12, CSF cultures 10/14, blood cultures from 10/14, breast milk, all negative so far.

Plan: Reculture everything. Continue antibiotics. White cell transfusion this afternoon.

Cardiovascular: Blood pressure now 63/42. Clinically improved peripheral perfusion.

The following are primary therapeutic questions about Caroline:

1. Volume status—needs very careful monitoring of intake and output, since seems to be sequestering fluid and third spacing.

2. Progression of NEC—continue x-rays every six hours; abdominal girths; surgery following.

3. Fungal/viral infection—rash? Reculture everything, consider amphotericin B.

4. White cell status—poor now (3,200), decreasing; plan WBC transfusion. This should improve numbers and function.

5. Coagulation—platelets decreasing. Platelet transfusion now.

Carrie is developing problems everywhere. A decision to begin hyperalimentation, or "hyperal," has been made. Hyperalimentation means infusing a solution of protein, fat, carbohydrates, and amino acids intravenously, usually into a major vein. Carrie had a large catheter surgically implanted in her jugular vein last Friday, when she'd become ill, so access is no problem. Evidently her physicians have now decided she might well hang on for a while, hence the decision to give her some nutritional support.

Since the advent of hyperalimentation several decades ago, its use has been refined and extended to enable many patients, adults and children, who otherwise would have wasted away from malnutrition superimposed on severe, long duration illnesses, to survive. Prior to hyperal, patients, unable to eat, simply died.

I wonder why they've waited so long to begin the hyperal. After all, she'd fallen ill Friday the 14th, four days ago, and over that time, sick as she was, had required enormous amounts of energy generated by utilizing her own body tissue energy stores. Maybe they'd thought she was a goner, and why bother complicating things? Perhaps they worried about other complications, because, like every other modern therapeutic advance, hyperal too carries a risk. One of its most common side effects is hepatitis.

For reasons still unclear, the solution causes inflammation of the liver in a significant number of patients. If there is no underlying liver malfunction, the hepatitis usually resolves on its own rather rapidly after the hyperal is discontinued.

Giving it to Carrie, however, is another story. Her liver is already damaged, and her liver enzymes and bilirubin are sharply elevated. If she reacts adversely to the hyperal, liver problems might cause irreversible liver failure and swift death. Thus, the doctors have been debating whether or not to risk it. Now it is decided. The hyperal would begin.

I agree with the decision. Kill her or cure her, I think, just don't let her end up in between.

Her platelets are down to 21,000/cubic millimeter, less

than ten percent of normal. This slow clotting time is dangerous in itself. But more importantly, she is a setup for bleeding
anywhere. Blood continues to emerge from both her stomach
tube and rectum. The transfusion might help, but Carrie's
dike is springing leaks faster than they can be filled.

Her falling white count heralds bone marrow failure, her
body is simply unable to keep up with the attack the NEC has
unleashed. She is vulnerable to almost any organism she
might contact, and in the ICU only the most virulent organisms survive.

The next day, Larry Cohn, one of Carrie's residents, talks
with us about her problems, telling us, "The white cells she
will get have to be type-specific, that is, from blood donors
who have blood type B negative as does Carrie." The previous
transfusions have been, but now there is a problem: there are
no B-negative white cells available.

B-negative is not a common blood type, and white cell
transfusions are not routinely performed, at least not in the
University of Virginia's neonatal ICU.

It is extreme therapy, a last resort procedure, of uncer-
tain value in any case, since it isn't clear whether even if she
gets a supposedly matched blood type her body won't attack
the cells as foreign. Blood types can differ in both major and
minor ways. There are a myriad of them which if mismatched
could cause dire consequences. There are a few which for the
most part are unimportant.

However, in Carrie, whose ability to withstand any stress
is severely compromised, a "minor" mismatch might be serious, and a major mismatch could kill her. Transfusion reactions cause the blood cells to clump and destroy themselves,
and the resulting outpouring of hemoglobin, a major part of
red blood cells, lodges in the kidneys and causes what is usually irreversible kidney failure and death.

Even if the transfused white cells survive, their ability to
fight infection and function effectively as scavengers really
has never been demonstrated conclusively. It is another of

those procedures that sounds good on paper, so it is performed.

Irradiating all of Carrie's blood products might diminish their ability to cause bad reactions in her body, but the irradiation also damages the functional ability of the cells as well—it doesn't perform selectively. That is why its use in cancer therapy is so difficult, because post-radiation damage to normal surrounding tissues occasionally is as bad as the cancer itself.

"I'm ready to try anything," I say slowly, desperately.

"Maybe you could ask around your department, and see if there are any B-negative people who'd be willing to donate blood for Carrie," says Dr. Cohn.

This is the problem of a small town. In Los Angeles there would have been plenty of the right white cells available for Carrie, but the population base here is so small, that just isn't the case.

Moreover, the cells she needs are a small fraction of the blood cells present in blood, and have to be obtained at the time the blood is donated.

Two nurses and a nurse anesthetist have B-negative blood and are willing to help. I am very moved, because to me it is like a gift of life, this generosity from people I barely know.

All three go down to the neonatal ICU and then the blood bank. One nurse is rejected because she has a cold. The other nurse and the nurse anesthetist, who'd just started working at the hospital recently, donate their white cells that afternoon. Carrie receives them later that same day.

TUESDAY, OCTOBER 18, 1:00 P.M.

Nurse's note.

Unsuccessful suprapubic tap.

A baby can't very well provide a clean, uncontaminated urine specimen on her own. So, to get around the problem, which also occurs in unconscious adults, a procedure called a "suprapubic tap" was invented. You take a syringe and needle, scrub off the lower abdomen right above the pubic bone, and stick the needle in, drawing back on the syringe until you get urine. This would be a clean uncontaminated specimen, ideal for culture. Simple, right?

Except, as always, it sounds simpler than it is. Here's where the procedure unravels. First, sometimes the bladder is empty. Thus you could be inside it, jam the needle through the back wall, and never know it. Second, other things live in the area; things like intestines, blood vessels, and nerves. A blind needle stick, especially in a baby with distended gut, runs the risk of hitting something like infected bowel, and then all bets are off. The spread of Carrie's bowel contents directly into her abdominal cavity means peritonitis, and that would be the *coup de grace*.

Nevertheless, in the same all-out spirit as the questionable lumbar puncture two days earlier a suprapubic tap is performed on Carrie and is termed "unsuccessful." That means, no urine is obtained. Who knows where the needle has ended up?

The reason for the dogged pursuit of fungal organisms in

Carrie's body is that the disease she has is devastating, but the treatment is almost as bad. One drug exists to successfully fight systemic fungal infection: amphotericin B, also known by those who administer it as "amphoterrible."

Carrie's abdomen is still enlarging; a one centimeter increase in girth is significant. The x-ray may indicate a gangrenous portion of bowel which has lost its ability to contract, but then again it may not.

All the cultures are negative so far, so her therapy is strictly guesswork. Perhaps she'd do as well or better without receiving every different antibiotic available in the pharmacy, but with today's medicine it takes a lot of nerve not to treat when a drug is available.

The advances of modern medicine make every physician, especially the younger breed, aggressive, believing that if only they get the right tests and give the right drugs, things will improve. Treatment failures are more often than not blamed on the patient ("He had bad protoplasm to begin with") or simply not recognized ("His electrolytes were normal, but he died anyway").

The toughest thing of all to teach is judgment, because there are no tangibles, only hoary chestnuts of examples which are sometimes as outdated and inapplicable. Thus, for the most part we press ahead as Carrie's physicians are doing, shunting considerations of the big picture aside in favor of increased attention to more immediate questions whose answers are black or white.

Until now I too have believed this the proper way to behave. Until now when it is my child being subjected to endless tests and agonizing procedures which seem to be going nowhere.

Today is an especially gloomy, wearing day. Carrie seems deathly pale, and watching her labored breathing Judy and I wonder why we are subjecting her to all this. Wouldn't it be more humane just to let her go?

TUESDAY, OCTOBER 18, 8:00 P.M.

Nurse's note.

Extremities cool, dry, fair perfusion. Receiving white cell transfusion 30 cc over three hours. Nasal CPAP continuing 5 cm pressure, 33% O_2. Respirations spontaneous, periodically slightly labored, occasional episodes of apnea and bradycardia requiring stimulation, moderate substernal and intercostal retractions masked by edematous, distended abdomen and torso. Both nares raw, red, and excoriated, occasional clot of blood on CPAP prongs.

NG tube producing large amounts of gas and moderate amounts thin rust-brown secretions, grossly bloody. Abdomen round, distended, shiny, tense to palpation, loop of bowel palpable at liver margin.

Skin pale grey to yellow, rash covering entire abdomen, spreading more sparsely down arms and legs. Labia and perineal area especially red and inflamed.

Other: bag, mask, succinylcholine, laryngoscope, endotracheal tube at bedside.

On and on it goes, some things worse, some things better. I wonder when the final whimper will come. Carrie simply can't stay as sick as she is for much longer.

"In two weeks we'll know one way or another," I tell Judy. "Either she'll be dead or she'll be a hell of a lot better. She won't be this sick, I guarantee it."

Judy's mother stays at home during our visits, probably wondering much less than we about the fate that has rendered us all actors in this tragedy. She sees it all as part of an intentional, greater plan, and so is more accepting of everything. As long as she doesn't have to go and see the baby "on the rack" as she is. I don't blame her for not wanting to see Carrie. Even faith can only take her so far.

TUESDAY, OCTOBER 18, 8:30 P.M.

Radiology report.

In comparison with the previous studies, there are again noted the persistent dilated loops of bowel in the right lower quadrant but there is no evidence of pneumoperitoneum.

Judy and I are in bed, reading. Trying to read, really. I'd look at the words, then start daydreaming and thinking about everything—about the baby's room we've had all ready for her, all her clothes and diapers and bedding in place, half-finished stencils on the walls that Judy had been working on the day she'd gone into labor. We'd thought there were still five or six weeks to go until term, but had gotten everything we'd needed months earlier, figuring we'd be in no shape right before the baby was due to round up a crib, changing table, and the million and one other things needed.

Now the room is dark, the door closed. Neither of us has gone in it since last week Thursday when Judy came home. We're both depressed, without our child.

"She's never going to come home," Judy says.

"Well, I don't know."

"She's going to die, and all her clothes and things are here. What will we do?"

I don't even try to answer. It seems nothing worse can happen. Then suddenly the telephone rings. It is Ralph Wells, Carrie's pediatric surgeon.

"Joe, I hate to have to tell you this but there are several

ominous changes including falling white cell count and platelets. Her abdominal films have improved somewhat, but there
are two persistent loops. I have performed an abdominal tap
which returned feculent, bloody material. For this reason I
plan an immediate exploratory laparotomy to excise necrotic
bowel and will perform a gastrostomy, ileostomy, and colonic
mucous fistula."

"Are you sure?" I say, too stunned to react.

"Yeah, there's no doubt about it. There's a lot of feces all
over her abdominal cavity."

"Can we talk with you personally at the hospital before
you go ahead?"

"Sure, we'll be here; just page us."

"When are you going to start?"

"We're getting the operating room ready now, and the
ICU is getting her ready for transport."

"We'll be right in."

I turn to Judy. "The news is awful. She perforated her
intestine."

"Oh my God."

"They tapped her belly because she was looking so
shitty, and now we know why. There's shit everywhere."

"Now what?"

"That's what I say. We need to agree on what we want to
do, and then talk to Dr. Wells before he starts. I don't want
Carrie to be a "bowel cripple."

"Can they do anything for her?"

"Well, I suppose if they only take out a small amount of
rotten bowel the best that can happen is that she'll have horrible peritonitis from all the contamination of everything they
leave in. She can die from that." I pause, the agony I feel
seeping into my voice. "Judy, I can't imagine her surviving
this."

For a few minutes there is only silence. Then I go on. "If
they can't leave her with enough intestine to digest her food
and live, I'd rather they just close her up again. I've taken
care of babies with all their intestines taken out. All they do is

pour fluid into their bowel bags constantly, and they're always in the hospital for one thing or another. They don't grow, they get infected, and they die. I just don't want to subject her or us to that."

Judy nods. Then her voice expressionless, she says, "If he can't leave enough to let her have a good shot at a normal life, I'd rather he just let her go."

We walk down the hall to Norma's room after we've dressed and tell her what is happening. "One way or another, Norma, at least she's going to be out of her misery."

"Poor little heart, poor little heart." Ever since Carrie's heart murmur and PDA has been noted, Norma has focused on her heart. To her, it is something that makes some sense, her sick heart being the reason Carrie is so ill. All the rest seems so remote and confusing. "I'll send up some special prayers for her. I know God is looking after His little one. She's very special to Him."

I don't answer. Neither does Judy. We are too stunned to make conversation. Frozen, we start on our way to the hospital to yet another debacle. You'd think we'd get used to it, but it hasn't happened yet.

We page the surgeon, and we go to a corner of the operating room lunchroom, littered with cigarette butts, empty coffee cups, and old newspapers. How many hundreds of times over the years have Judy and I sat in rooms like this, talking about life and death to families of patients who had to make decisions about their loved ones just as we are doing? No matter how experienced we are, this time is very different. Our past vanishes. Only the agony of the present remains.

Joan Lang, the chief resident in pediatric surgery, sits with us, listening. She wants to learn, perhaps, how to deal with people like us when she is the one making the decisions. For her, this meeting is interesting, and yet safe. No skin off her nose, whatever happens. That's one of the nice parts about medical training. You get to be a voyeur par excellence, with no penalties attached. Someone else takes the responsibility; you just do what you're told.

Next to her sits our pediatric surgeon Ralph Wells. He has operated on a number of babies with bowel disease while in practice, and had gone from one extreme to another in his approach.

He explains that, "At first, I was ultra-aggressive in my surgical approach, and operated and resected the entire intestine from baby after baby with extensive NEC. Then, as the years went by and many babies died after intense, exhausting, repeated medical and surgical procedures aimed at correcting all the problems occasioned by not having a gut, then I started to pull back, and finally, through trial and error, learned just how much intestine is needed to let a baby live and grow and have a chance at a somewhat normal life."

"What are you going to do now?" I ask wearily.

"Well, Carrie's obviously a very sick little girl," he says. "We'll go in and have a look, and see what's there. She obviously perforated . . ."

"How long do you think she's been perforated?" Judy asks staring at him.

"Well, the x-rays didn't show anything; so they're no help. She's been going downhill today, so I'd guess sometime in the last twenty-four hours. But she might have been perforated for days, just sort of walled it off and it's now breaking through. There's no doubt, though, that her whole belly has feculent contents in it."

I jumped in bluntly, no longer able to contain myself or choose my words carefully, "What's the prognosis?"

He stops to reflect a moment, "Well, if we can resect the necrotic portions of her bowel and clean her out as well as we can, she might do fine."

I clear my throat which feels hoarse and tear-filled; my eyes are wet, my voice shakes as I talk and Judy holds my knee. "If you find that so much of her bowel is involved that you can't leave enough for her to digest anything and lead some kind of life without hyperal, bowel bags and the rest, we'd both prefer you just closed her back up. We don't want her to live without any decent quality of life."

He nods and says quietly, "All right."

Here we are, possibly signing our daughter's death warrant, just as easy as that. I sigh heavily. In this situation, right or wrong doesn't seem to matter in any moral sense; we just don't want to be party to Carrie's drawn out suffering, or our own.

After we talk to the surgeon, we quickly leave the operating room area. I don't want to see the anesthesia resident or staff person who will be doing Carrie's anesthesia for fear of upsetting them even more than I know they already are. In fact, I feel sorry for them.

There's nothing more anxiety provoking than anesthetizing someone you know, or a member of their family. Both you and they know how easily things can go wrong. Now, not only do they have our daughter to anesthetize, but she is an emergency and critically ill to boot! A sick premature infant is probably the case I'd least like to do, ever. And the child of a fellow faculty member, in my own department, is even worse. So much can go sour. Babies like Carrie can die for many different reasons; you simply go ahead and hope for the best.

As I walk down the corridor I alternate between deep depression and an almost blithe sense of unreality, as if I am watching it all happen to someone else, can be objective, note my feelings and Judy's dispassionately. I marvel at my own ability to cope until I realize, looking around, I have left Judy far behind and, find that my eyes are so filled with tears I don't know where, in my own hospital, I am.

WEDNESDAY, OCTOBER 19, 12:30 A.M.

Judy finally catches up with me, takes my arm and we go to the waiting room to wait. The room is authentic hospital deco: couches with burst cushions, flickering fluorescent lights, lamp shades askew. It is overheated to the point of sweatincss. An elderly black woman lies slumped along one sofa, snoring, as the television flickers. Empty soda cans, mounds of old newspapers and magazines strewn about complete the picture. We sit there for a few minutes. Tense, wishing I could run away, I think of where I can hide. Somewhere, anywhere. Then it dawns on me, the call rooms!

Every hospital has call rooms, rooms where physicians who stay overnight can sleep if they get the chance. Call rooms range from the plush, i.e., color television, refrigerator, private bath, and clean sheets, to the scuzzy, like those at Los Angeles County-USC Medical Center, where I interned. There, four bunk beds circa 1940 were crammed into a space just allowing people to slide between them to get in. You woke up carefully, because the ceiling was about eighteen inches above the top mattress. One bathroom served all four bunks, such that it was almost always in use, and every time someone opened the door to the bathroom, the whole call room was flooded with light, since the bathroom light switch was broken and the lights were permanently on.

Just when you finally got to sleep, the door would open and a nurse would bellow "Admission for Dr. so-and-so." So you were awakened every twenty minutes or so, no matter what.

Fortunately, you were so punchy from working there, it didn't really seem that horrible. Moreover, the graffiti on the bathroom walls was outstanding. The best I've ever seen, before or since. Pungent jokes and harangues, poems mocking everything and everyone in the hospital, especially the physicians in charge of the residency program. I distinctly recall one aphorism directly above the toilet tank. It said, "You men are the scum of the earth—(Telly Savalas, *The Dirty Dozen*)." Every time I read it as I was peeing, I'd start laughing so hard I'd piss all over the walls and floor, which would make me giggle even more. It didn't matter, since the room stank so bad anyway. Then I'd flush the toilet, which was so loud it sounded like a missile was being launched, and laugh even harder.

"Hey, fuckhead, shut up," I'd hear, and I'd open the door to leave and then slam it as hard as I could dashing back to my bed. It was so dark no one knew who was who, and everyone would groan and wiggle around in the saggy creaky beds.

No wonder physicians get money-hungry. I've often thought that the bottom-of-the-barrel working conditions at big city and county hospitals do more to transform doctors into money-making machines than any other factor in their training.

I've never been in a call room at this hospital. Whenever I worked late at night, I'd rest on the couch in the anesthesia office. I ask one of the surgery residents where the rooms are. He points in the right direction and we head for them.

There are several, and one is marked "Anesthesia Staff." That is me, so we go in. Looking around we see a bed, a table, a lamp, and a wastebasket. The door locks from the inside, a key feature. Call rooms have functions beyond sleeping at night, at least in the eyes of house staff.

I remember one particularly ironic story that occurred during my anesthesia residency. It seemed a surgical intern at UCLA, which prides itself on being the "Johns Hopkins of the West," a reference to the pioneering (and brutally tough) surgical training program at Hopkins, had quite a way with women, and was systematically screwing his way through the hospital. One day, while he was on the Thoracic Surgery Service (which was headed by a particularly tough surgeon who happened to be Chairman of the Surgery Department as well as a Hopkins graduate) rounds began early, and when the team arrived at the bedside of Romeo's first patient, he was nowhere to be found to give his report on the patient's progress.

The Chief looked around and asked if anyone among the fellows, residents, interns, and medical students knew where he was. Now, the code of "Omerta," or "Silence," is almost as strong among house officers as among the Mafia, so no one said anything. The Chief thought for a moment, then turned on his heel and quickly led the group down fourteen flights of stairs to the house staff sleeping quarters, where he produced a key to let himself in. The pack followed silently in his path. Then he produced a second key. Successively he opened each door of the fifteen or so in the area.

Bingo! There on one of the beds in the OB-GYN call room was the resident, pumping away with a nurse. The Chief looked at them for a moment, then closed the door and rounds resumed. During that day word spread around the hospital, and I learned that the intern had been summarily fired that afternoon. Died in the saddle, in a way.

Flipping out the light, Judy and I sit down on the bed. "Let's go naked," I say feeling desperate. There is nothing to do now but wait, and who wants to sit and stare at the walls? I begin to peel off my clothes and then start trying to undress Judy.

"I don't feel like it," she says.

"You will, though. Just get undressed and we'll lie in bed together, and hug."

"I don't want to get undressed. I feel sick."

"I'll rub your back, or anything," I say. I am crazed, nervous, jumping out of my skin. This is the ultimate insanity, so why not be part of it? I want to feel something other than fear.

We lie down on the bed. I call the operating room to give them my number so they can reach me when the operation is over. We don't talk much, just lie there. Finally, I turn to Judy and grip her tightly, my mind is racing. Scrambled, jumbled thoughts fly by. "Yes, we had a baby, but if she died, it would be merely 'what-might-have-been.'"

"We don't know her at all," Judy says.

"Let's not talk about it."

"Remember how she looked when we first saw her."

I wince. We are already trying to forget Carrie as she is now, and remember her as she looked the first two days, a tiny little red thing, her face all mashed up and distorted from the birth. We have pictures of her a day old, but no more after that. It seemed morbid to document her as she became sicker and looked more and more like an advertisement for an intensive care monitoring equipment company.

At 2:30 P.M. the phone rings. "Joe?" Dr. Wells' deep voice penetrates our daze.

"Yes, hi," I say hoarsely.

"We're finished. You want to come on over?"

"Sure, we'll be right down."

"Well, Judy," I say. "Here we go again."

"How does he sound?"

"I don't know; like he always sounds, I guess." Quickly getting dressed we walk downstairs and over to the lunchroom to wait for the surgeon. He strides up, a warm smile on his face.

"Well, she's one tough kid, I'll say that for her. She did just fine."

"What did you find?" I ask quietly.

He hands me his report. Silently I curse his easy wordless rationality. And my new inability to match his facile emotionless manner. With trembling hands, I finger the page.

WEDNESDAY, OCTOBER 19, 3:00 A.M.

Surgery operative report.

Clinical Summary: This six-day old infant was born prematurely and developed NEC. She has not been improving clinically, and a paracentesis this evening demonstrated intestinal fluid within the peritoneal cavity.

Procedure: With the patient under suitable general anesthesia, the entire abdomen was prepped with Betadine solution and draped as a sterile field. A right upper quadrant transverse incision was made, dividing the right rectus muscle. On entering the peritoneal cavity, there was considerable intestinal content in the free peritoneal cavity. The proximal bowel was somewhat dilated. The small bowel was gently teased from within the abdo-

men. The proximal small bowel from the ligament of Treitz proxi-
mally to the mid-ileum appeared quite uninvolved. The distal 21
cm of ileum was heavily involved with NEC with several areas of
gangrene.

There was one area of perforation approximately six centimeters proximal to the ileocecal valve. The very last three centimeters of terminal ileum appeared relatively uninvolved. The
right colon appeared unremarkable as did the transverse colon.
The distal ileum was then resected. Interestingly, the grossly dilated loop of bowel which had been persistent on the last several
x-rays was not grossly involved with NEC and was proximal to
the area of perforation. This area was resected, however. The
proximal bowel was then fashioned as an ileostomy with interrupted sutures of 5-0 vicryl to approximate the serosa of the
bowel to the fascia of the abdominal wall in the right lower quadrant. The ileostomy was matured with interrupted sutures of 5-0
vicryl in a Turnbull fashion.

We were able to salvage approximately three centimeters of
the terminal ileum and this was brought out as a separate mucous fistula in the right lower quadrant. This was matured with a
single row of interrupted 5-0 vicryl sutures. The mesentery of the
bowel resected was ligated with interrupted 4-0 silk sutures. The
abdominal cavity was then irrigated copiously with sterile saline
to remove all of the fecal material. We had intentions of performing a gastrostomy, but on inspecting the stomach, there were
several areas of inflammation, suggesting involvement by NEC.
We felt it would be best not to violate the wall of the stomach in
view of this vascular compromise. The nasogastric tube was confirmed to be well positioned in the body of the stomach and was
secured in this region. The abdominal wall incision was then
closed with a single layer of interrupted 5-0 wire. The subcutaneous tissues were irrigated but left open. The wound was packed
with a Betadine-soaked gauze and a dry dressing was applied.
The patient tolerated this procedure quite well and was returned
to the neonatal ICU in stable condition.

Still silent, I pass the paper to Judy, thinking. In such flat
language is one's ultimate fate described. A critical, difficult,
pressured operation, a dying child, and you'd think spark
plugs had been changed. Yet, it is hard to imagine performing

surgery of this nature in any other manner. Thoughts of mortality and fate are out of place here, where human beings daily confront life and death and force the issues.

Years of experience, skill and judgment, are incorporated into every act, each thought: Do I take what now appears to be normal bowel but looked diseased on x-ray? Is it normal or diseased? Can this child live normally with what I'm leaving? Am I leaving too much, will we have to go back in and cut out more in two days?

Beyond decisions extends skill. What use is it doing the right thing poorly? A leak in the suture line, inadequate cleaning of the abdominal cavity, mistaken identity of a structure barely noticed and ligated when in fact it is a ureter, severance of which results in loss of a kidney just like that, all these myriad details conspire to finally make or break the surgeon. Why is it some physicians rarely have problems with patients postoperatively, yet others almost always do? It's a question of habits and details, the little things that go unaccounted for in the operative report. Reading one, nobody—layman, physician, or even surgeon—distinguishes healer from hack. It is all in the doing.

"As you can see Caroline had perforated her ileum," says Dr. Wells gesturing auspiciously, "and there were feces all over, as we suspected from the tap. We resected about sixteen inches of ileum, and made an ileostomy and a mucous fistula from her terminal ileum. She'll have to wear an ileostomy bag for the time being."

"Oh no," Judy says shaking her head.

I stare at her. My heart sinks. She'd known that would be the best result we could hope for, Caroline having enough functional bowel left to salvage, and that interrupting her intestine meant putting a bag on the end until she could be hooked up once again, down the road. The trouble is knowing something with your mind and feeling it is very different. Judy has taken care of a lot of cancer patients whose surgery resulted in colostomies and ileostomies. To her they mean death. These procedures are usually done on palliative operations to relieve bowel obstruction due to tumor. For Judy, the destruction of the surrounding skin when the bag adhesive fails, the leaks, all the frustrations of caring for dying patients, is associated with bowel bags. Now, our seven-day-old daughter has one.

"What else did you find?" I ask swallowing hard, trying to rid my mind of the same images Judy sees.

"Well, the rest of her bowel looked uninvolved, although it's hard to know if we got everything that was involved or not. Her stomach had some redness, so we decided not to put a gastrostomy tube in. She's a tough little kid, sailed right through like a champ."

"The right stuff," I say quietly, my voice emotionally charged.

Judy interrupts, "What happens next?"

Wells' eyebrows knit together, "Well, assuming we got all the involved areas, if she doesn't get peritonitis from the contamination, she may recover very nicely." He looks straight at me. I avert my eyes. "We would hope that after her bowel starts working again, we can reattach her and then, if she functions adequately and gains a little weight, she can go home."

I don't even consider asking "how long?" So many things, so many "ifs" are contained in that question, no one could hope to answer. Carrie would make her recovery, if recover she did, in an ICU, where anything could go wrong at any time. One mistake in drug administration, a switch left in the wrong position, and she was dead. At this point the only certainty is that she'd made it through a potential disaster in the operating room.

Of course, had her entire bowel been involved, not just the portion that had been removed, she'd be on her way out of her misery, with no doubts. Closing her back up would have meant a day or two more until death took her. I guess I am glad things have worked out as they have, but I know also that the weeks to come will, at best, be every bit as hard on Carrie and us as the last one has been.

Part of Carrie now lay in a jar of formaldehyde. What a macabre joke; her blood went to one lab, her bowel to another.

WEDNESDAY, OCTOBER 19, 7:00 A.M.

Surgical pathology report.

The specimen is submitted fresh in one part labeled "bowel" and consists of a fragment of what appears to be small bowel which is dark red in color. It measures forty centimeters in length and has a diameter of approximately one centimeter except for one area where there is fusiform dilation with a maximum diameter of two and a half centimeters. There appear to be areas of necrotic tissue and there are numerous areas of perforation with stool draining through the bowel wall. On opening the bowel longitudinally there is a brownish, somewhat hemorrhagic, exudative process seen throughout the mucosa. In areas where this is removed, the mucosa is seen to be smooth and denuded. Diagnosis: Excised small bowel; NEC.

Part of Carrie sits even now in a warehouse, pickled.

Back upstairs in the ICU, Carrie looks pretty much as she did late Tuesday evening when we last visited her, except now even less of her is visible. She has large dressings covering most of her abdomen, and a tube in her mouth which is connected to a respirator which does her breathing for her. Following abdominal surgery, this is commonplace. Nevertheless, I don't like seeing the tube still in.

Too many reports of disasters in patients with endotracheal tubes, too many near misses myself, make me nervous about Carrie. The tube can get plugged up with secretions quickly; oxygen flow can cut off without warning. Changing a tube is no problem, if you are an anesthesiologist. The trouble is, there aren't any in the ICU, just a pediatric resident and attendings learning how. So an intubation is a major thrash, the routine becomes an adventure. I don't want any more adventures for Carrie. The spinal tap affair still sticks in my craw.

The long-term consequences of the tube are nothing to anticipate, either. Quite often infants who have a tube in their larynx go on to develop areas of narrowing requiring surgical resection of the trachea, an enormously complicated and difficult operation with usually poor results. The problem with narrowing arises because of pressure by the tube on the tracheal wall, which is very delicate in an infant. The blood supply could be easily cut off, and the affected area of trachea simply die and collapse. The longer the tube stays in, the greater the chance for problems.

We stand next to Carrie who lies, as always, unmoving, her eyes still taped shut from the surgery. I reach up and peel off the tape. "Daddy's here, baby," I say, then redden when the anesthesiology resident who's done the case hears me and comes sauntering over. Knowing he overheard me, I quickly cover my remark, "Glad it's over, eh?" I ask him.

"Yeah, I'm glad," he chuckles. He's been in the program four months, and now this case has been thrown at him, with all its inherent difficulties as well as the burden of it being a staff doctor's baby.

He goes on, "She did really nicely. We gave her some morphine and some muscle relaxant, and she had no problems at all." He lowers his voice, "Blood pressure was very stable."

We are very fortunate that he happened to have been on call that night. Not only is he a very conscientious anesthesia resident, but he's just finished his training in pediatrics. Thus, he is comfortable with sick babies, far more so than I am.

He'd had enough confidence in himself to give Carrie some morphine and muscle relaxant prior to putting her endotracheal tube in. The procedure is often performed in babies like Carrie with the baby totally awake and unsedated. Doctor and nurses simply hold the infant down as the painful instrumentation is performed. That's the way I was taught to do it and told it's the safest way. Of course, what it means to a child's ultimate development no one knows. I can't see, though, how being brutalized this way can make you a better person.

We finally decide to go home at 4:00 A.M. Norma is up and asks us, "How's Carrie?" We tell her and she replies, "Poor little heart. I know she'll be fine now. She's a strong little thing, I think. I'm so glad she's got the worst over."

We hope so too but are too tired to really care by this point. We collapse into bed. The unreality of what is happening keeps accosting us. I don't see Carrie ever coming home nor does Judy. Too much has happened, too much still can.

WEDNESDAY, OCTOBER 19, 9:00 A.M.

We get up this morning just like all the others. Though our baby has had surgery, just hours ago, we don't feel any greater anxiety than any other time during the past week. The treadmill just keeps moving and we keep trudging upon it, keeping up as best we can, saving our energy, trying not to get excited by some seeming improvement and set ourselves up for the inevitable fall. Nothing is good; nothing is bad; everything just is.

The first thing Judy does is to use the breast pump, just as she's been doing this last week, three times a day. A few drops come out, we preciously harvest them in a little plastic cup; then I label it with the date, time and Carrie's name. Afterwards I take the cup downstairs to put it in the freezer. Peering inside I cannot help but notice the freezer is filled with little plastic cups, each with a teaspoon or two of milk which we are saving for the baby when and if she ever begins eating again. Seeing them all, I feel like crying but I don't, I just close the door.

The pediatricians have encouraged Judy to save her breast milk since it is better for the baby than formula, especially a baby whose gut has suffered so drastic an infection. Yet we can't help but wonder if she'll ever drink it and reflect on the fact that the pediatricians are the ones who'd started giving Carrie formula through a feeding tube the day after she was born when she was too weak to feed herself and Judy hadn't yet begun to produce milk.

Pumping her breast is painful for Judy and not getting much milk makes it even more so. Judy is so engorged she has to buy bigger bras, and yet she can't get the milk out. I try to help, squeezing and massaging her breasts, but nothing I do seems to help. The whole process is a tense one, which probably doesn't help the flow. Relax, the books say; just relax and let it flow. The books don't tell you how to relax, though, when your new baby is critically ill.

By the time we get to the hospital, both of us feel punchy, we are so exhausted emotionally. Lots of things seem funny. Just looking at each other we burst out laughing. Suddenly I say to Judy, "Maybe we are just going crazy." She nods.

But when we peer into Carrie's crib our laughter stops. Tears fill our eyes. It is not that she looks worse. Carrie is no picture of health, but she is no worse than last night before surgery. It is the question which pierces us as we look at her and that I hesitantly voice, "How much worse can she be and still be alive?"

As always, I pick up Carrie's chart to try to understand what is going on. The first thing I see is a doctor's notation.

Resident note.

Caroline went to the OR last night and had 30 centimeters of bowel removed. Currently has dopamine running at 6 micrograms/kg/min. Blood cultures negative so far. On cefotaxime and amikacin. Primary pathogens in the first week past perforation

are gram negative aerobes, adequate coverage should be assured
with amikacin. Second week will see increased incidence of
gram negative anaerobes, cefotaxime should provide good coverage. May consider adding mefoxin.

Receiving fresh frozen plasma today and platelets to support blood clotting, as platelets down to 59,000. Chest x-ray
shows improving aeration, decreasing heart size. Receiving morphine as needed for agitation.

"Interesting," I say bitterly to Judy, "how reality can
create itself. Already there is a disparity in what would seem
impossible to disagree on. The resident has written '30 centimeters of bowel removed,' yet if you remember the pathologist had stated in the report he handed me, 'It measures 40
cm in length . . .' "

"The pathologist is probably right," Judy retorts.

I nod, "After all he measured the damn thing."

We both become silent but I am thinking that either the
surgeon has estimated the resected bowel to be 30 centimeters long or he told the resident he'd taken 30 centimeters
when he meant to say forty (after all, it was 2:00 A.M. for him
too), or the resident has heard thirty when the surgeon said
forty (2:00 A.M. for him too). In any case, who cares, right?

Well someday Carrie might care a lot. Especially when
decisions are made about whether or not the bowel length
she still has is enough to let her absorb her food properly, or
whether she'll have to have dietary supplements and injections her whole life. On such initial misinterpretations as this,
major decisions not yet even imaginable hinge.

I try to make sense of the rest of the report. At one point
the note says there are totally negative blood cultures so far,
yet in the next breath gives a long, rational explanation of
why antibiotic coverage for Carrie's contaminated abdomen
is optimal. I sigh heavily. The present drug regimen has done
little for her up to now, that is for sure. It is a bitter joke that
no organism is known to be causing her NEC, yet she might

have died filled with antibiotics, in the infectious disease consultant's equivalent of a cowboy or a cocksman dying in the saddle.

Not so amusing is the fact that Carrie is getting fresh frozen plasma. This is the constituent of blood which remains after the red blood cells are removed. It contains most of the chemicals called "factors," which make blood clot. Unfortunately for its recipients, it is combined with plasma from many donors in bags for administration. Thus, the risk of contracting hepatitis, AIDS, or any one of a myriad of other blood-borne diseases, is not simply the risk of getting it from one donor, but from many. With all the other transfusions Carrie has gotten the odds are steadily mounting that she'll contract hepatitis at some time in the future, months, perhaps years, down the road—if she lives that long.

Dejectedly, filled with frustration, I put down the chart. Judy and I stare at Carrie lying spread-eagle as always on her back, her arms and legs secured by cloth bands which are safety-pinned to a sheep-skin mattress to keep her from wiggling around (not that she can move much at this point) and pulling out her IV lines. "I'd imagined all during your pregnancy how our newborn baby would greedily take in all the new sights, sounds, and textures of the world," I say sadly.

Judy nods, "Carrie is lying flat on her back, staring up at a steel plate above her bed."

"On the other hand, listen to the constant beeping of cardiac monitors, IV alarms, respirators, and humidifiers; they make her environment an insane asylum."

"Perhaps she is just shutting out the whole thing," Judy sighs.

"Either way," I say through clenched teeth, "overload or starvation, it isn't what I'd dreamed of, and it can't be good." I leave the hospital that day determined to do something about it.

At home I dig through my junk boxes, finding film containers, colored wood, anything with shape and brightness. I begin to construct a four-tier mobile. In several hours it is

done. I carefully pack it in a shoebox to take in that afternoon. It isn't much but I feel momentarily liberated from the
helplessness I feel. Until now I have had the sense that I have
no function, that I am a doctor who can't help his own child,
a father who can't be one. Then I look back at Judy who
stands behind me watching and realize that my frustration is
only a small fraction of what she must be feeling. After carrying Carrie for all those weeks, she is now being reduced to
pumping the liquid from her breasts into plastic bottles.

Wishing I could help her, I hand the mobile to her. She
flashes a warm smile. "Let's bring it to Carrie now," she says.

"Let's," I reply.

At the hospital, I put up Carrie's mobile—rubber egg,
film box, coaster, rubber spider and all, attaching it to the IV
pole next to her bed. The nurse tells me newborns are near-
sighted and can't focus more than two feet away from their
eyes. So I hang it to dangle about a foot over her head. Everyone oohs and aahs—I feel like a brain-damaged stroke victim
being congratulated after making an ashtray in physical therapy. It does look good enough, quite bizarre amongst all the
high-tech equipment. What did Dr. Johnson say? "Viva la bi-
belots!"

WEDNESDAY, OCTOBER 19, 7:00 P.M.

Nurse's note.

Awake, quietly alert, extremely responsive to verbal stimuli.
Tracked parents' faces and new mobile at approximately ten
inches. Hear murmur faintly audible. Peripheral pulses strong.
Extremities cool, pale, dry, without edema. Arterial line in left
wrist. Peripheral IV in right hand infusing dopamine. Scalp vein
IV for blood products and medication. Central line infusing saline with potassium chloride.

> On respirator; 35% oxygen, rate 22/minute. Few spontane-
> ous respirations. Moderate amounts thick blood-tinged secre-
> tions when suctioning endotracheal tube. Remains NPO [nothing
> by mouth], status post temporary ileostomy leaving 2 stomas at
> right of umbilicus. Nearest one expelling small amounts of air
> and fecal liquid. Further is dry. Abdominal incision dressed with
> betadine ointment, covered with sterile gauze, no drainage
> noted. Abdominal girth increased over last shift by 1.25 centime-
> ters.
>   Skin: On abdomen and extending down legs is light, flat rash
> of unknown origin, resolving since yesterday.

Judging by everything, Carrie is up fifteen hours after
surgery. Still, no one can be certain she won't abruptly go
right back down. Perhaps the surgeon has left some rotten
bowel, or more is becoming gangrenous. For this reason, the
surgeon has not sutured Carrie's major incision—a four inch
horizontal slash across the right side of her belly—shut, but
has simply closed the wound with stainless steel wire through
the subcutaneous tissue and muscle. If he has to go back in,
there's be no sutures to painstakingly cut apart or have gotten
infected, just a wire-cutter to snip the wire and he'd be there.

Staring at it, Judy and I wince. "Our poor baby," I say.
She nods, her eyes filled with tears.

WEDNESDAY, OCTOBER 19, 8:00 P.M.

In for our evening visit, we see on the back door of the
ICU rows of pictures of former ICU babies, all in various
stages of growth, smiling, playing. All around the snapshots
are cards and notes from parents of former patients. As we
stand around Carrie's bed, exhausted, depressed, seeing no
future beyond endless days and nights spent at her bedside,
under the fluorescent lights, I stare at these pictures and wonder.

What about all the babies who have died in this unit? It happens all the time. Already in the five days Carrie has been there—two babies have died, one during open-heart surgery to correct a congenitally deformed heart, the other of multiple central nervous system defects and brain damage.

What, too, of the far greater number of damaged survivors, the crippled, maimed and retarded babies who have been discharged as "cured?" What are their lives like, and their parents' lives, as these children drive a knife into the family's dream of a typical happy home-life? Children who can't walk, see, hear, or think adequately, in pain, coming back into the hospital for this or that complication, how do these parents feel? Do they rejoice in their good fortune, or do they secretly harbor guilt and anger at themselves for producing such a child?

It seems to me everyone should get their picture on the door, not just the successes. Let people see what really happens to babies who come through ICU, instead of pretending the disasters don't exist in numbers far greater than the successes.

Ask any ICU director anywhere. He or she will tell you, "Our cure rate is so much better now then it was ten years ago, we're saving a lot smaller babies now than we used to." Yes, but who's taking care of those babies after they leave? And is survival the bottom line? Would the ICU director want one of these blind, retarded "cures" as his own child, growing up totally dependent on the rest of his family, ripping apart his marriage?

THURSDAY, OCTOBER 20, 9:00 A.M.

Nurse's note.

Good suck and grasp. Responds appropriately to stimuli. Opens eyes, focuses, follows mobile above her when alert. Agitated and kicking spontaneously. Medicated with morphine, decrease in agitation. Right hand peripheral IV site infiltrated, discontinued, changed to right leg. CVP line—no wave form.

I look at the nurse's note as soon as we arrive at the hospital Thursday morning. Noting the short phrase "IV site infiltrated" I curse under my breath. A baby as small as Carrie has tiny, fragile veins, which can withstand catheters for only a day or two before simply bursting, or "infiltrating." Then another one has to be started. Starting IVs on a baby is a tough teeth-gritting job. Usually the child is moving and struggling, often screaming unrelentingly as she's held down and fine needles are tentatively, oh so gently, advanced into her. Often it takes five or ten attempts, each one bringing you closer and closer to blind rage as it slips in, then through, the paper-thin vessel wall, causing a bleeding lump or hematoma to form. The thoughts running through doctor's minds as they start pediatric, and especially neonatal, IVs would be revelation to those who think of pediatricians as the gentlest of all physicians.

Carrie's CVP, or central venous pressure line lost its wave form. This means that the catheter which had been surgically inserted into her central venous system, near her heart, the day she'd come down with NEC was no longer providing a clear impulse to the tubes that transmitted the blood flow and displayed it on a video screen. Either the catheter was no longer in the vein, or its end was clogged up with clotted blood such that you could infuse fluid through it but not get anything back—a one-way valve of sorts. So a new one had to be inserted, poor Carrie.

Still on the whole, Carrie appears to be coming back. Somehow, somewhere, she is getting the strength to hold together and begin to heal. Her brain seems intact, at least she isn't paralyzed or having seizures, and she seems to be able to look at things. This indicates progress, albeit small, but considering all she's been through so far, we rejoice.

The resident's note on her chart which we see at lunch time confirms my opinion. I give Judy a thumbs up sign.

THURSDAY, OCTOBER 20, 12:00 *P.M.*

Resident's note.

Caroline appears generally improved today. Suture site and ostomy site fine—stooled for first time, dark black stool. Abdominal girth unchanged all day. Belly soft, no bowel sounds as yet.

Rash markedly decreased; peripheral perfusion good. Abdominal x-ray unchanged, blood cultures remain negative, day 6. Amikacin level 8 (trough), ideal less than 10. Peak pending. Receiving hyperal, 38 calories per kilogram per day at present rate.

Hematological picture: platelets 39,000 this morning, down from 110,000 last evening. Given 1 unit platelets, count now 85,000. Bilirubin 4.2. White blood count 10,700.

Respiratory status: Oxygen 25%, spontaneous respirations increased to 25 min. Arterial oxygenation good.

Plan: Increase amikacin dose 20%; problems of restricting fluids yet providing adequate caloric intake continues. May require further platelet transfusions, but bone marrow and white cells appear to be responding. Bilirubin down, will discontinue bili lights. Will try to wean off respirator over next day or two.

The reasons she is getting better are as unclear as those explaining why she had gotten NEC. Removing her gangrenous bowel seems to have helped. But she cannot be allowed to rest on her laurels. More pricking, pulling and prodding now go on. For example, they begin regulating the antibiotic amikacin to optimal blood therapeutic levels by measuring Carrie's high and low blood concentrations ("peak and trough" values) comparing them to "ideal" values. Samples of Carrie's blood are obtained thirty minutes after ("peak") and thirty minutes before ("trough") one of her three daily intravenous doses of the drug. Afterward they are analyzed for drug concentration.

Too much drug doesn't do any better at fighting infection than too little, and leads to irreversible hearing loss and kidney damage. This had been discovered inadvertently years after the first few thousands of people had received the new class of aminoglycoside wonder drugs, of which amikacin was one. Once physicians understood that the drugs were hazardous, the pendulum swung the other way, and the aminoglycosides fell out of favor. Then, further research showed that the side effects seemed to occur at doses above those needed for optimal antibacterial activity, and so monitoring of blood drug levels, similar in principle to a diabetic's regulation of blood sugar, became standard when such drugs were given intravenously. Medicine is no different from fashion—hemlines go up and down in Paris; in medicine, drugs and therapies fall in and out of favor.

Judy and I know that Carrie's life partially depends on whether this year's fashion suits her.

What to believe is always a problem in the day-to-day practice of medicine. The sicker the patient, the more we trust in numbers, tests, and procedures that purport to be objective, thus "true," but often are simply objectively wrong. With a baby like Carrie, you can't ask the patient how she feels, you have to get answers some other way. Medicine, especially modern medicine, is a science, or pseudo-science, built on obtaining answers and acting on them.

Carrie's team of physicians are now evaluating some of these imperative "facts." At 10:00 P.M. last evening her platelet count was 110,000 (remember normal is about 250,000 per cubic millimeter). A platelet count is being obtained every eight hours, since she is so critical and her status so changeable. The 6:00 A.M. count came back 21,000, so low as to put her at great risk of spontaneously bleeding without stopping. The first thing her physician did was order a repeat platelet count.

In the same way the ancient Greeks killed the bearer of bad news, physicians ignore data or reorder tests whose results conflict with what they think is happening, or should happen, or want to have happen. This is often not a bad thing: in anesthesia especially, values generated by machines, if believed and acted on in preference to one's own clinical judgment, often lead to catastrophe. So, Larry Cohn, Carrie's resident, not wanting to believe this dangerously low number, "killed the messenger," in effect throwing away the lab report and choosing to try another one.

The next one was 39,000, still low but, after all, nearly twice the original. He liked this one better, so he wrote it down in his progress note, and ordered more platelets. The only evidence of the 21,000 result is the computer-printed laboratory slip buried amongst literally forty-five pages of printouts of blood count values for Carrie's entire hospitalization, and a nurse's faithful notation of the value, received on her shift and entered into the nursing record.

He, like I, knows that Carrie's blood clotting status and overall condition make her a high-risk candidate for an intracranial bleed, that is, bleeding into the brain itself. Often, in critically ill infants even without discernible blood clotting difficulties, hemorrhage into the brain occurs. This is a devastating complication. Once thought to be rare, intracranial bleeding is currently recognized as being quite common in ICU babies.

Later that afternoon, Cohn buttonholes Judy and I in the

hall. "Judy, Joe," he says, "I'm sure you can appreciate why I'm scheduling Carrie for a head ultrasound."

I freeze. I haven't thought about this particular problem as yet, so much else has gone wrong and is going on. Cohn rambles on about how "She hasn't had any seizures or anything to make us suspect she's had an intracranial bleed, and neurologically she looks intact, we still need to get a baseline in case anything changes."

I try to get my bearings.

The advent of sophisticated diagnostic tools such as CAT scanners, which generate exquisitely detailed computer constructed x-ray pictures of every structure in the brain, and head ultrasound, a similar technique which uses no x-rays, has revealed many previously undiagnosible CNS (central nervous system) bleeds. Thus any newborn baby in a modern ICU for any length of time commonly gets one of these tests, but the results can be fateful. The incidence of lifelong seizure disorders and learning disabilities in children who have had neonatal intracranial bleeds is frighteningly high, and the damage is permanent. There is nothing that can be done. So I am miserable about the prospect of Carrie having one. Yet I know to her doctors, its results can be important.

Cohn goes on: "We want to see if the cause of seizures or paralysis or palsies that might soon happen is already there or not." A reasonable thing to do, but now Judy and I will freeze every time the phone rings as long as Carrie is in the hospital, thinking it is a call telling us Carrie has had a seizure—that half her body is now permanently paralyzed. I'd seen those calls made, and thanked God it wasn't me making or getting one. The thought of Carrie surviving this brutal disease only to become a feeble half-wit is too much to bear, but we agonize about it from that moment on.

THURSDAY, OCTOBER 20, 4 P.M.

When we go into the hospital that evening, I walk around trying to find Larry Cohn. I am frightened to death. Finally, I find him in the doctor's lounge.

"How'd her ultrasound go?" I ask quietly.

"Normal. Completely normal. No bleeding at all."

"What a relief."

"Well, we had no reason to believe it would be abnormal; she's neurologically intact as far as we can tell." Carrie's father rises in me—I mumble to myself, turning away, "Why the fuck did you put me and Judy through this then, asshole? Goddammit, we have enough to worry about as it is."

But I turn back and answer the way he wants his fellow physician, Dr. Stirt, to do, "Well, let's hope she stays that way."

Reporting his words and my feelings to Judy my voice conveys my misery. She nods, "We're absolutely alone in this, Joe. No one else cares the way we do, because no one else is going to live with the consequences of what happens here."

When we return home that night we feel like people who have just barely avoided being mangled in an accident—survivors.

"How many more times do we have to sit and wait for some result which totally decides Carrie's fate?" I say, my voice breaking, filled with emotion I have spent the day hiding.

Judy shakes her head, "People just order a test, and if its a bad result, well, too bad for us."

"No skin off their noses," I finish her thought.

It is our vulnerability which angers us most. Our future and Carrie's is totally in the hands of her doctors and whatever they chose to do or not do. Our tie to them is both involuntary and undissolvable. Our lives no longer seem ours. We feel as victimized as Carrie, pawns in someone else's game, waiting to be moved to some destination of their choosing.

Dispiritedly Judy gets her breast pump out, and the ritual begins. She squeezes and kneads each breast holding the plastic funnel under her nipple to catch every precious drop. At first I'd lift when she did it, but lately it seemed to go better when I rubbed her back and neck. I'd tried sucking on one breast while she did the other, but it distracted Judy. Odd, I think that Carrie might never get to try it. At least someone in the family is.

After all Judy's efforts she only produces a few drops. We bring the frozen bottles into the hospital to be stored for Carrie, when and if she ever recovers enough to drink the stuff. We give the hard-earned milk to John Androdi, Carrie's doctor, a new resident. He holds up one tiny cup, "We'll get an antibody screen first, to make sure she's not allergic to anything in the milk, before we use it."

"Okay," says Judy her voice shaking, her head meekly bowed. We leave the room.

As soon as we're outside, Judy turns to me and says, "What the hell is he talking about? They gave her formula, she got NEC, almost died, and now they're going to test my milk for allergies? Why? It's my milk!"

Judy starts to cry. I hold her and wonder. What point is there in getting tests on the milk? How can it not be the best thing for Carrie, whatever is in it—antibodies, anything? It is her own mother's, for God's sake. Why didn't Androdi just take the milk and go get it tested, without telling us about it? It is obvious Carrie won't be able to drink it for days, if not weeks, until her bowel heals well enough for her to tolerate something in it, and chances are the tests on Judy's milk will be negative anyway. I know the answer. He just had no idea that getting the milk had been such an ordeal, an emotionally and physically exhausting task already made difficult by Judy's overall depression and fatigue—only possible because of her faint vision of Carrie drinking her gift, getting stronger and healthier somewhere in the future.

After all how can Androdi know what getting that milk means to Judy. Just as he can't know how we go through each day like zombies, simply going through the motions, alert for any new straw in the wind, deeply affected, yet not caring at the same time. Perhaps it is better he doesn't know, because the awareness might make him as well as the rest of Carrie's doctors and nurses so skittish around us as to make it unbearable for us all.

FRIDAY, OCTOBER 21, 2:00 P.M.

Resident's note.

Caroline had a very good day today with progress in many areas.

Now receiving 112 calories/kg/day including hyperalimentation and intralipid. Will increase protein and intralipid as tolerated.

Platelets 50,000 this morning, now down to 20,000. I am very uneasy about this consistent loss of platelets but etiology is still unclear. Will continue to evaluate and transfuse irradiated platelets as needed. White count 10,700, Bilirubin 4.1.

Blood cultures negative so far. Amikacin levels optimal both peak and trough. Continue on present regimen.

Respiratory status improving; will attempt to wean from ventilator to oxygen hood later today.

Family status: Dad *very* helpful and supportive of wife. Today grandmother in to visit; was able to hold Caroline.

I read these words grimacing. So, two days after they have cut out her guts and ours, she is better overall.

FRIDAY, OCTOBER 21, 2:30 *P.M.*

Nurse's note.

Good tone, suck; grasp untestable due to IV boards bilaterally.
Awake, alert and active. Good peripheral perfusion, extremities
warm. Bowel sounds active, moderate amount ostomy drainage.
Incision site gaping open at one end—dressed with ointment and
gauze. Triggering respirator 20 times/minute.

Reading this hope flickers within me. Carrie is more
awake. She seems to be recovering. Her bowel, what is left of
it, which has been incised and manipulated, has once again
begun to function. Her blood clotting status remains a problem, though. She is losing platelets somewhere, faster than
she can replace them, so she continues to receive them by
transfusion. Every time I see a bag hanging up at her bedside,
dripping in, I also see more chance of her getting hepatitis
and yet another series of complications. X-rays continue too,
twice a day, to evaluate her belly. She is too small to have her
ovaries shielded, and I wonder how, if she survives this affair,
all the x-radiation she is receiving will affect her both, in
terms of the sharply increased risk of cancer or leukemia, and
any children she might have. Her ovaries, tiny as they are,
already contain the fully developed eggs that will someday
form half of her children. She has had multiple exposures to
x-rays, medications, anesthetics. Who knows the long-term
outcome? And, at this point, who cares.

Studies of such effects are far and few between, mostly
because there are so few survivors of illnesses requiring such
intense care. Only recently, for example, has it become appar-

ent that children with childhood leukemia, apparently successfully treated and "cured," have a much higher than normal incidence of a second cancer years afterwards. Is it the therapy, the combination of toxic chemicals and radiation, that causes this, or are such individuals more susceptible? No matter what the reason, the attitude in medicine is, arrest the disease no matter what the price in the future. It's easy to take this attitude when you know the future doesn't affect you.

I wonder if we'll tell Carrie, if she survives and grows up, that having children might be risky, or would we then be as out of line as the resident telling us about the antibody screen on Judy's milk? Maybe we'll just see what happens. Chances are, nothing out of the ordinary, but what if Carrie has a child with some bizarre deformity? Then what? What would she feel? Would we have betrayed her by our silence? We'd be no different from our medical colleagues, I guess, mortgaging the future for the present.

FRIDAY, OCTOBER 21, 2:00 P.M.

Nurse's note.

Caroline was on pediatric respirator with #3.0 endotracheal tube, end-tidal CPAP 5 cm. Extubated at 3:00 P.M., placed on 40% oxygen hood. When extubated it was noted that inner circumference of endotracheal tube was decreased due to build up of thick, solidified secretions. Blood gases prior to extubation, on ventilator, were: O_2 [oxygen] 70, CO_2 [carbon dioxide] 39. After tube removed $O_2 = 95$, $CO_2 = 39$. Tolerating extubation well in oxygen hood. Plan blood gas analysis every 2 hours, and as needed, continue suctioning.

Two and a half days after her operation, Carrie is breathing on her own. Everything is fine, right. Pretty much so. She is doing better breathing on her own than when the respirator was breathing for her. But wait—had she ever needed the respirator that long? When her breathing tube had been removed, its inner surface had been noted to be covered with hardened mucous, markedly decreasing the area available for gas to flow. Three millimeters, the inside diameter of the tube, is not much, about one-eighth of an inch. Narrow this even a little, and you make it very hard to exchange gas—a lot more pressure needs to be exerted, either by a respirator pushing air in, or a person inhaling. This pressure increase can cause fluid to be pulled out of the thin-walled blood vessels in the lungs, and water thus accumulates in the lungs, a condition called pulmonary edema, simply meaning "water in the lung."

Carrie had been noted on physical examination to have "wet, course rales," which is a term for water moving in the small lung airways, and to have "mild substernal retractions," that is, her chest wall pulled in visibly when she tried to take a breath. Was this because she'd been trying to breathe, but was unable to do it, through even a narrower area than the breathing tube allowed? The x-ray picture seems to confirm this:

FRIDAY, OCTOBER 21, 3:00 P.M.

Radiology report.

Chest, portable, 1400 hours. In comparison from the previous study, the chest continues to show improvement in streaky haziness in the right upper lobe, although hazy infiltrates consistent with increased fluid persist in both lung bases. The heart remains prominent.

Several times in my career as an anesthesiologist, in the midst of otherwise smooth anesthetics in children Carrie's size, their breathing has suddenly changed, becoming more difficult. A small baby can only tolerate fifteen to thirty seconds without respiration before its heart rhythm begins to become irregular. Then oxygen supply to the brain begins to diminish. This is an immediate emergency. In the past when it happened on my cases I'd note the sudden increase in pressure required to force gas into the baby's lungs, and the lack of chest movement. I'd turn the head from side to side, thinking it was only a kink in the breathing tube that had developed as the tube warmed to body temperature and softened (the soft plastic the tube is made of does this).

The tube used for infants is too small to attempt to pass a catheter through and check if it is indeed blocked, a maneuver often used in adults when sudden tube obstruction occurs. So only one solution remains: pull out the tube and put in a new one. Unfortunately, these obstructions usually occur during cases like cleft palate repair. The tube unfortunately is right in the midst of the area operated on which by then is filled with instruments, packing, blood, and saliva, all hastily extracted as I replace one tube with another.

Each time, the result is the same: the new tube works well, easy respiration resumes, and all is well. The problem with the old tube, however, isn't always so clear cut: The last one I changed, a couple months ago, was indeed completely clogged with dried, caked blood and mucus, an obvious cause for the problems I'd encountered. Others, though, seem fine, with no appreciable obstruction. Perhaps I'd knocked a chunk of material off the tip in pulling it out.

In any case, mechanical problems with endotracheal tubes, or any kind of technical difficulties in medicine, can be devastating. Because the pediatricians taking care of Carrie lacked expertise, they pulled the tube. In fact, she did well in spite of, not because of, the timing of their decision. A near miss is the same as a distant one, if nothing happens. So much of "getting well" in medicine today consists of tests and procedures intended to be performed, but inadvertently forgotten, with the realization later, when all is well, that they obviously weren't necessary anyway.

Carrie continues to do better all day Friday. She requires less and less supplemental oxygen. When she no longer needs extra oxygen, but can breathe air alone, she'll be taken out of her open pallet, unfastened from her restraints, and placed in a plastic isolette, a closed incubator which has two portholes similar to those in nuclear power plants, to prevent entry of germs and outside contamination.

Isolette is an apt name for the box, because inside it you really are isolated. To test it out, I find one and put my head against its porthole. Then I press my ear against the plastic to seal it flat and plug my other ear with my finger. All I can hear are muffled sounds. The plastic blurs things as I look through the opposite wall and out.

The exercise plunges me into depression again. How much Judy and I had wanted our baby to touch, feel, hear, and see her new world; instead her nightmare would continue. The horror of it is we no longer care. Our only goal right now is to see Carrie finally able to live in an isolette. To think of her at home is impossible. We will keep the door to her room shut.

While I'm evaluating Carrie's future box home, yet another platelet transfusion is given to her. All her blood products are now being irradiated (placed under x-rays), prior to being given to Carrie. The radiation decreases the potential for Carrie's body to react to the foreign cells, but it also damages, to a degree, the cells themselves. It is another therapeutic trade-off. Still, what else can the doctors do? Carrie's body seems so reactive to the blood products that they have been destroyed as fast as they are administered, or so it seems. No source for the continued low platelet count has yet been uncovered.

A further concern is Carrie's elevated bilirubin, now down to 4.5 from a high of 11.1. When blood cells are destroyed, the free hemoglobin, a protein which makes up the bulk of the red blood cells, is converted by the liver to bilirubin, an excess of which produces jaundice. Carrie seems to be recovering from her jaundice, and irradiating her blood products seems a prudent thing to do to minimize the amount of red blood cell destruction in her body.

X-radiation of blood cells works by simply destroying the antigens, making the recipient's body less likely to produce an antibody response to the cells and thus attack them. More and more diseases whose causes were once shrouded in mystery now appear to be caused by the body's abnormal antibody response rather than any infecting agent, and are thus termed "autoimmune diseases."

Arthritis, for example, seems to be a disease of excess production of antibodies to the body's own antigens, or identifying proteins: The body appears to attack itself, in effect committing cellular suicide. Myasthenia gravis likewise seems a disease of self-identity gone amok: when the blood of myasthenic patients is cleaned of antibodies, symptoms promptly resolve. Multiple sclerosis likewise is now considered a disorder of the immune system.

Cancer seems a disorder in the opposite direction. Current theories of the origin of cancer differ from those of even a decade ago, which held that a single cell in the body, for some unknown reason, went amok, reproducing itself rapidly and eventually producing a tumor. Today's state-of-the-art envisions multiple cancers constantly occurring in every individual. These tumors, however are destroyed by the body's own antibodies which recognize the aberrant cells as "foreign" and eliminate them. The occurrence of clinical cancer is thus seen as a failure to eliminate the microscopic tumor array, a lack of normal "immunologic surveillance."

Thus, the conceptual basis for radiating Carrie's blood

transfusions is established. What is less clear is the potential for cancer induced by x-ray induced changes in the transfused cells. She is now receiving X-radiation; felt to cause mutation in the cells radiated, it is a well-known cancer inducer. Are the treated cells Carrie is getting a short-term panacea, propping up her falling platelet count, yet perhaps planting a seed which foretells her doom from yet another direction? Perhaps. Again, no one knows. I care, but it doesn't matter much. If she survives her acute illness and a year later leukemia occurs, no one would argue that she shouldn't have received the irradiated blood products, or that this is the cause of her cancer. So much else has occurred, no one could possibly pinpoint an inciting factor.

Judy and I put these morbid thoughts of *maybe* and *might* away. It is Friday night. The weekend, I sigh, "Let's go home and try to get some sleep." We both know, weekend or not, we'll be back first thing in the morning. To watch, to wait. Our lives now circumscribed within these walls, where once we'd been casual observers of others' misfortunes.

SATURDAY, OCTOBER 22, 10:00 A.M.

A stamp appears in the chart. "I have ___x___ (have not) ____ seen this patient today and discussed current status and treatment plans with the house staff." An illegible signature follows.

It's Saturday. I guess the attending pediatrician has taken the day off. One of his associates is making rounds for him. That's all right as long as everything is going well and you've got good house staff. To try and deal well with a new problem, requiring understanding and a "feel" for the case, on such short notice is impossible.

A certain intuitive understanding of a patient's status and course develops over a period of time, at least for some physicians. That's why continuity is so critical. Something unsaid but understood gets left out in transitions, and disaster often ensues from what in retrospect was obvious.

The feeling I suddenly have in the pit of my stomach is fear. It is true Carrie is getting better, but no one knows better than Judy and I how suddenly she can go sour. We try not to dwell on this though. And the doctor's note at noon makes me a little less anxious.

SATURDAY, OCTOBER 22, 12:00 P.M.

Resident's note.

Last blood gas value improved on 23% oxygen. Platelets 42,000. Chest x-ray looks clear with good expansion. Continuing on antibiotics, day 3 of 17. Weight unchanged. Belly soft; abdominal x-ray looks good. Is stooling from ostomy. Mildly present bowel sounds.

    Plan: Wean to room air;
             Continue hyperal;
             Discontinue intralipid;
             Platelet transfusion.

I sigh. This is a relatively short note, 25 percent of the length of several days' previous. It is short for two reasons. One, Carrie is improving. Modern medicine has little to say when things are going well. Second, it is Saturday. Even though illness doesn't recognize time or day of the week, those who minister to it do. Thus, Saturday and Sunday rounds are always shorter, and tests are ordered for Monday since few of the special technicians required to run the machines work on weekends. I never use to agonize about this reality. But now that my tiny daughter lies here, I do. "What ifs" crowd my mind. I brush them away and try not to think about them.

SATURDAY, OCTOBER 22, 1:00 P.M.

Radiology report.

Portable chest/abdomen at 1300 hours. In comparison with the previous study, there is increasing aeration of the right upper lobe, and the rest of the lung remains clear. The cardiac silhouette is slightly prominent on this expiratory film. An N-G tube is noted in the stomach. There continues to be a paucity of bowel gas through the abdomen, but no evidence of free intrabdominal air is seen in this patient who has had abdominal surgery and whose metal clips lie transversely across the abdomen. The abdomen shows no evidence of pathology.

The radiologists are following Carrie from afar. To be more precise, from two floors below, in the subbasement, the catacombs of the hospital, where radiology and x-ray departments are traditionally housed. Granted they need no outside light, and can just as well be located in the basement, there's no real reason why they should, simply habit on the part of hospital designers. Perhaps their days spent in the dark, shadowy film reading rooms and fluorescent lit hallways make radiologists seek the opposite: they are invariably the most tanned physicians in any hospital.

Their contact with patients is two-dimensional, displayed on their viewing boxes. They'd watch from a distance as Carrie's bowel distended and exploded, then was repaired, and now is healing. None of them had ever seen her; their films are taken and developed by technicians, then brought to them. It makes for a much more carefree existence than that of the pediatricians, who have to deal directly with miserable infants and depressed parents. Radiology is sometimes the refuge of fine, extra sensitive, caring physicians who simply cannot handle the misery and pain of treating people person to person.

SATURDAY, OCTOBER 22, 4:30 P.M.

Nurse's note.

Awake, alert, good suck, muscle tone. Has had long active/alert episodes. Respirations unlabored, relatively even. Suture line is split. Central line leaking, no blood return, flushes fair. Small amount of red drainage around central line insertion site, surgeons aware.

On rounds Friday, two days after Carrie's surgery, the surgeon, elated with how well Carrie was doing, ripped off with a grandiose flourish the sterile bandage which had been all that was keeping the skin over Carrie's wound together. He didn't notice one end of the incision was not yet quite knitted. Now it is crusting over, the wound likely to heal more slowly and with a much more noticeable scar. This irritates me, because there is no reason for it to have happened, and yet I understand the surgeon's triumphant feeling and expression of it.

He'd probably said, "This child doesn't need this bandage any more—she's cured!" And ripped off the dressing. Now the wound is gaping and Carrie would pay for his moment of hubris with a prominent scar, if she ever got out of the hospital.

The pediatricians and surgeons had told us it would be a minimum of two weeks following surgery, if all went well, before Carrie could have anything to eat, and that she'd then have to demonstrate she could absorb her food and gain weight before her intestine could be reconnected. After the reconnection of her bowel she'd have to recover for another two weeks before she could begin eating again. Then once again she'd have to gain weight and show she could absorb her food. "The way I see it," I said to Judy, "we are looking at the rest of the year in the hospital. If she gets home by the end of December, it's the best we can hope for."

What bothers me about all this is that Carrie will be spending so much time in the hospital, much of it in the ICU, where problems and complications always occur if you wait long enough. It is like routine medical testing. Take any healthy person, bring them into a hospital, draw blood, take x-rays, examine them, really give them a work-up, and I'll guarantee you this: there will always be an abnormal value or result somewhere if you look hard enough—something which can then be pursued with even more specialized tests and procedures. The odds favor something somewhere being a little off or askew in everyone once in a while. Good clinical judgment lies in knowing when not to pursue the ultimately trivial and meaningless.

Being an infant in a modern ICU is worse than being an adult. For a baby being exposed to so many hazards, tests, and procedures almost inevitably leads to something disastrous. The odd thing is, you can't anticipate what it will be. You never know what you miss when things go well. So much just whistles by our ears unnoticed. Even so, every tube or line in Carrie's body carries a risk. Problems can occur anywhere, anytime, for no apparent reason. Just as there appears to be no reason or a million why she'd gotten NEC in the first place.

Being so critically ill so young has been devastating for her. Already premature and small for her age, Carrie is now in a holding pattern, unable to get the material she needs for what should have been a period of extraordinarily rapid development.

The infant brain and body double in size during the last month of pregnancy. Carrie had been a month and a half early. Not only did she miss that critical six weeks growth, now she is faced instead with total absence of food and nutrition, growth and development halted in their tracks. She has only been receiving intralipid (an emulsion of fat and dextrose) and hyperal (which supplies some of the amino acids and protein she needs) instead of breast milk which would have supplied everything she needs for nutrition. Even more disturbing, she has received no handling or warmth, no stimulation but the painful thrusts of needles and the irritation of tape being removed from her reddened, tender skin. What is this doing to her? Could she ever recover to what she would have been? I have my doubts.

It is now well established that critical periods in the body's development once missed, can never be regained. This has been most dramatically illustrated in the case of vision and blindness. During a certain limited period in the first two years of life a temporal "window" of sorts appears, such that the retina establishes permanent connections with the visual centers in the brain. If, for any reason, the retina does not get its proper input of focused images during this one to two month period, it can never again establish the connections, and vision is lost forever. Subsequent correction of the eye's ability to focus on the retina produces nothing but a jumble.

It seems to me that much of the body and its ultimate development will prove to be similarly dependent on proper stimulation at the correct time for proper function. Thus, the known tendency of sick infants to have developmental and growth deficits appears to me to be simply a case of "not enough when it is needed." Carrie might have all the promise in the world, but the centers buried deep in her tiny brain simply might never get the critical messages they carry across to the rest of her body in time. She might seem to catch up, but we'd never know what she would have been. Of course, if she hadn't been sick but was run over by a car at age four, we could say the same thing. Thus do I rationalize her illness and her fate.

Even though she seems to be recovering her platelets have stayed down. Some new research suggests an association of intralipid with a drop in platelets, so on Saturday Carrie's intralipid is discontinued. Scratch the fats, crucial components of a diet for growth, from Carrie's intake. Quantifiable short-term gain (platelet count perhaps improved) traded for unknown long-term effect (decreased constituent of brain and nervous system growth). It all boils down to, "I don't want this patient to die on my service."

For physicians, dying is a personal affront, as well as a paperwork nightmare. Every effort is made to make certain a patient doesn't die when you are responsible for her. Thus, a pulseless, unconscious trauma victim is rushed from the emergency room to surgery ("He didn't die in the ER," say the ER doctors). The anesthesiologist urges the surgeon on, trying to get the patient to the ICU alive ("He didn't die in the OR," says the anesthesiologist). Finally, the patient dies in the ICU.

Carrie isn't in any imminent danger right now, but every decision that has possible long-term complications is weighed against short-term gains. Then a decision is made in favor of the present. It is simply a mind-set that is passed on and on to medical students year after year; you are on a service four weeks, take care of your patients as best you can, then you're gone, and they're someone else's problem. I can't argue—I am a product of the same system. Just like the surgeon who'd pulled off Carrie's bandage. He wouldn't be around to deal with the scar when it became bothersome, assuming Carrie made it that far.

I laugh at myself. In the midst of life or death decisions about Carrie I am still wrapped up in whether or not the scar on her stomach will be bad. Things must be getting better, I think. Then I reconsider. No, it is just the way I am. I have a tendency to focus very intently on the trivial. Perhaps it absorbs my worries while I repress what I can't deal with. Whatever it is I can't stop myself.

I keep on imagining scenarios. Carrie could wear a one-piece bathing suit, and no one would see the scar. Or perhaps by the time she is old enough to care, punk and S&M will have reached such a popularity level in this country that scars will be in and she'll end up a model because of hers. On the other hand, if we want them off, we'll have to wait until she is older and able to lie quietly while the new wounds made by a plastic surgeon heal. Still I wouldn't want to make a big deal of it and make her self-conscious, so perhaps we'll wait until she wants them off. That would probably be the best way to handle it. Wouldn't it? Just as I am about to finally definitively answer yes, I think of another contingency. But by then, she won't heal nearly as well. On and on it goes.

SUNDAY, OCTOBER 23, 12:00 P.M.

Resident off-service note.

Parental course and birth unremarkable, tube feeding begun with breast milk every three hours; baby seemed to do well until approximately 4:00 A.M. October 14 at which time an increase in abdominal girth was noted, as well as bright red blood per rectum. Abdominal x-ray showed gas in bowel wall consistent with NEC, and patient came to ICU. There she deteriorated over the next five days, developing a heart murmur consistent with patent ductus arteriosus, heart failure requiring dopamine, a total body skin rash of unknown etiology (perhaps drug-induced), decreased white cell and platelet levels requiring repeated transfusions, jaundice, and decreased neurological status progressing to coma.

An abdominal tap on October 18 returned feculent material and surgery early on the 19th showed gangrene and perforated bowel. Resection of 32 centimeters of the ileum was performed.

Postoperatively she was greatly improved; she is now 4 days post-op.

Respiratory function and NEC itself appears to be markedly improved; however, platelets have been a real problem. Etiology of thrombocytopenia [platelets are also known as thrombocyte] is unclear, but differential includes intralipid-induced, non-specific effect of sepsis/NEC, autoimmune or familial problem (doubt seriously). Have held intralipid today and yesterday. Platelets now 164,000 twelve hours after last transfusion, when normally they are beginning to decrease again by now. The problem here is that she really does need the intralipid.

The blood bank has been *outstanding* in their help, devising special ways to make sure Caroline has her reds, whites, platelets and plasma when needed. We are irradiating all of her blood products for now.

Central nervous system: never asphyxiated, but neither was her bowel, we thought, yet she got NEC. To rule out intraventricular hemorrhage [bleeding into the spaces or ventricles, within the brain] we got an ultrasound which was normal.

Feeding: She is currently getting 52 calories/kilogram/day, about half of what she needs. We will have to reintroduce intralipid somehow. We plan to begin oral feeding in 2–3 weeks.

Family: Very supportive of each other and good parents. Dad seemed fatalistic at first but has a better outlook now.

Central venous line: Hyperal, intralipid and blood products all run through this line. Some have suggested we discontinue this, but as long as it is working I'd keep it. I would even get a new one put in if it fails, but there may be other opinions. I feel more comfortable with a central venous line, despite its potential complications, since:

1. central line complications in this ICU are down in number lately;

2. it affords good large-bore access;

3. her veins are poor and she has at least three weeks left here;

4. repeated blood samples and IV sticks only cause her more pain;

5. amount of dextrose in water is quite limited through a peripheral IV versus a central line, and she'll need the calories. It would be nice to be able to give her what she needs;

6. the central venous line is less grief for her and us, and she is not out of the woods yet.

Arterial line: again, this is less bothersome to her if lots of labs are drawn, but as we decrease them the risk of complications will override this.

Current labs:

Vital signs every 4 hours;

Arterial blood gas every 8 hours;

Chemistries and electrolytes every 12 hours;

Calcium every 12 hours;

Complete blood count with differential every AM;

Platelet count every 8 hours.

So, 3–4 blood draws/day if all is well. Good Luck!

Arriving Sunday, I read through this detailed note from Larry Cohn and turn pale. I am jolted. He is going off Carrie's case. I know a new resident joining the team will need a toehold from which to grasp the situation which he'd suddenly encounter.

To house staff or attending physicians, a change of rotations is routine; every four weeks, usually, you leave your service, and someone else replaces you. Usually the change is structured so that interns, residents, and attending physicians all shift at different times, to ensure some continuity of care; this way, at least someone remains on the service who is familiar with the patients.

Depending on which service you've been on, and where you're going, a change of service can be great or depressing. To go from admitting on ward medicine to, say, dermatology clinic, is exhilarating; you spend every day dreaming of derm, and counting down. To go the opposite way is depressing: from nice hours and no stress into a pit of sweaty, sleepless, eye-burning, body-aching painful nights.

Being on the patient and parent end of a change of service is a whole different ball game. When we learn that Carrie's resident Larry Cohn is going off the service and someone else will take over we are frightened.

Larry knows Carrie so well and has gone through hell with us. Now, someone else is stepping in. He or she will be trying to get the "feel" of our child instantly, as well as five or six other critically ill babies. From my own experience coming on-service, I know that this is impossible. You bumble around a lot for days, basically trying to avoid any major decisions, until you have some grasp of what you are dealing with. We had great confidence in Cohn, who apart from the nurses, spent more time involved with her than anyone else in the world. What if his successor is a shmuck, incompetent, ignorant, and a pain in the ass to deal with? There are plenty of these types around. To us, Judy's experience as a nurse dealing with house staff has been as sobering to her as my own feelings about being one were to me; this change is a crisis.

To me, Carrie's departing resident was outstanding. Not only did I feel his love and concern for our child to be intensely real, but he knew what he was doing, and he was not intimidated by the fact that I'd know instantly if he didn't. It proves to me again that in the murky medicine game no one knows everything.

Nevertheless, in his off-service note he stated that Carrie had gotten NEC while being fed breast milk, when, in fact, there'd been no breast milk, and she'd gotten formula by feeding tube. Not really important now, I suppose. The fact of the matter is she'd gotten sick. But this mistake is the sort that gets perpetuated over and over again, to the point where, if I tell a future physician that no, Carrie had gotten NEC with formula and he read in the chart "breast milk," he'd assume I was mistaken.

Future research studies on the cause of NEC would put Carrie in the "fed breast milk" group, for the sake of compiling statistics in which type of feeding was more likely to precipitate NEC. This is why I am so skeptical of all the studies I read. They are usually based, ultimately on some pieces of misinformation just like this. Then the error is perpetuated forever.

Later that afternoon going into the ICU, I see my friend and fellow anesthesiologist Dick Pettit. He'd come on the staff of the anesthesia and pediatric departments just when I'd arrived from Los Angeles, a couple of months ago.

I could let my hair down with him, and had, throughout the last nightmarish week and a half. He is one of those rare people and physicians who make you feel better just by talking with them even when you feel terrible. Now he takes one look at my gray-tinged face and knows something is wrong.

"Joe, come on," he says, "let's get a cup of coffee, I'll buy, I'm feeling rich."

In spite of myself, I smile. If there is one thing we both know, it's that material success and medical residents don't mix. On the way I tell him about my concern over losing Larry Cohn as a resident.

In the cafeteria he points me to an empty table. "I'll be right back." He comes back with two steaming cups and we both sip our coffee, then he asks, "Who is the new guy?"

"Someone named Greenbach," a wide grin spreads across his face.

"You've got no problem. Your kid may be all fucked up, but you're getting the best resident in the whole department!"

"Really? Is he that good?"

"Outstanding. You're in good shape."

I am giddy with relief.

"If Carrie keeps looking good, maybe we're out of the woods," I say.

"Maybe," he says dubiously, "but, Joe, that's just not realistic. I predict more problems before she goes home."

I wave him and his remark off and go back to ICU. I don't want to believe him. How could anything else go awry? Especially now when Carrie is looking better every shift.

The rest of the afternoon seems to fly rather than inch by as most of our hospital visits. The only discordant note is the nurse's report attached to Carrie's chart at 4:00 P.M. but not read by us until we come back for our evening visit.

SUNDAY, OCTOBER 23, 4:00 P.M.

Nurse's note.

Central line leaking. Surgeons in. Central line pulled back, good
blood return, flushes easily. Moved to isolette 3:00 P.M. Breathing
room air without difficulty.

The central line can be a prime source for infection which
can track directly into the heart and bloodstream, since it
terminates inside the right atrium of the heart. Larry Cohn
had devoted a good part of his off-service note to it. You
wouldn't think such a seemingly trivial thing as an IV catheter could be so important, but this one is, both as a route for
the many fluids Carrie requires and for a possible life-threatening infection. Unfortunately the fluids themselves are excellent culture mediums, encouraging bacterial growth. Added
to this, the constant leak of fluid around the insertion site in
her upper chest was worrisome because the best culture me-
dium of all was blood, and the area is constantly bloody as
well.

Pulling the line back a bit, as the surgeons had just done,
seems to free the tip of the catheter from being obstructed;
this might lessen the amount of leak around the catheter.
Catheters become more obstructed the longer they remain in
place. They have a tendency to accumulate small blood clots
and debris on their tips when they remain in the bloodstream.

Anesthesiologists are experts at resolving this problem,
unlike other specialties, which ponder and wonder whether
or not to gently flush an obstructed line, replace it or just
leave it alone. In anesthesiology we take no prisoners. A pa-

tient comes down for an operation, and excellent IV access is crucial, as all our drugs and medications are administered IV, directly into the bloodstream. Not for us the intramuscular injection of the surgery or medical services. We need results now.

So, confronted with a balky IV, we don't shilly-shally; a syringe of 5 milliliters of sterile water or saline solution is drawn up and injected, blasted, right into the IV line. One of two things happens. Usually, the patient says "Oww," as the force of the fluid clearing off the catheter tip is felt in the arm where the catheter lies, and the balky IV suddenly runs like a champ. Or, it doesn't. If the latter occurs, the IV was no good anyway, and we've just confirmed it, so we start a new one.

When I started in anesthesia I was reluctant to use the "big flush" technique, and some still are. What I worried about then, and still ponder, is what happens to that ball of cellular garbage I flush off the end of the catheter? Where does it go? Apprehensive, I used to wait a few seconds and see if a patient got chest pain after I flushed, figuring that the clot had gone back to the heart, then out to the lungs and might act as a sort of man-made pulmonary embolus. It's never happened. So I now figure, it just sort of dissolves, disappears somewhere. I still wonder where.

Anyway knowing all this, Carrie's IV problem is not just a vague concern to me, as it would be to anyone who didn't play with IVs for a living, but a potential hazard. Judy, too, is aware of the possible complications, having dealt with the consequences far too many times herself in the ICU.

Still, we try hard not to dwell on the possible and instead to take comfort from progress. Carrie has been moved. She is now breathing room air and having no difficulties. She goes into an isolette, where she is less exposed to the potentially infectious ICU environment. Of course, the fundamental insanity of having the sickest and most vulnerable babies the most exposed and out in the open, as she'd been for the past nine days, is just sort of taken for granted. One of the many oddities and inconsistencies of modern medicine.

Excited, Judy and I rush in to see her. In the isolette, amidst the tangle of tubes, wires and electrodes, Carrie is looking around, seemingly awake and alert. I remember seeing her this way for the first time and feeling like a piece of shit having created so much misery for such a tiny undeserving person. Now looking at her, Judy and I rejoice. "Hurrah for Carrie," Judy says, her eyes shining. Indeed what a difference a few days and much trauma can make, I think biting my lip, in one's judgment.

MONDAY, OCTOBER 24, 10:00 A.M.

Nurse's note.

Parent-Infant Separation:

Subjective: "Look at her. She really is looking good. I didn't ever think she would look like this again" (Mom).

Objective: Parents visit Caroline several times a day. When they are here they hold her and talk to her. Seem more optimistic about her outcome. See her acting and responding to their voices and touch.

Assessment: Good bonding between parents and baby; very loving and concerned; seeing her more as a baby now that she has less equipment and is doing better.

Plan: Allow them to express frustrations, provide support as needed, encourage them to help in care.

We leave the hospital for a few hours and when we return our Monday afternoon visit starts uneventfully. We slowly help untangle the nest of tubing and wires so we can lift Carrie out of her isolette. What must the average parents think, I wonder, as they wait helplessly for this to be done for them each time? It must be frightening, so remote and mysterious, all the hardware. So foreign, so distant, from what life was like for the great majority of people who never would see the inside of a neonatal ICU, much less see their child there.

Suddenly I notice that half of Carrie's mattress is soaking wet. From where? I wonder. Urine? I stick my fingers in the wetness and smell it; it isn't urine. Then I see the problem. A needle connecting the hyperal solution to Carrie's central line has poked through its rubber housing and is dripping her hyperal onto the mattress. I point this out to the nurse, who seemed a little irritated with me, probably because I noticed it and she didn't, and it is her job to notice things like that.

As we wait for the doctors to come I reach out for Judy's hand. There is still another complication to agonize over. Two surgeons saunter in the room. They study Carrie's hyperal line. As we wait, they suture it into her chest a little more tightly, hoping to decrease the leak around it. Judy and I grip each other's hand more tightly now. I know, Judy knows, and they know that this is a cosmetic procedure only, and that the line is leaking from inside her chest back out. All they have done is hide the leak, but not fix it, like a plumber who tightens a faucet joint so no water drips into the sink, pretending the excess pressure won't destroy a joint buried in the wall, where the new leak will gradually destroy the wall and floor.

"Is Carrie going to be 'in trouble again?' " Judy says, her voice breaking.

I shrug my shoulders defeatedly, "There's nothing to do but wait and see."

MONDAY, OCTOBER 24, 1:00 P.M.

Resident note.

Slowly increasing fluids, weight down 9 grams to 2200 [5 pounds]. Follow urine output and weight, use Lasix if necessary.

Day 7 of cefotaxime, day 10 of amikacin. Plan 4 more days antibiotics. Plan to discontinue cefotaxime, change to ampicillin because of decreased platelets.

Respirations stable on room air. Hematological status: platelets down to 38,000, 1 unit being transfused, follow-up count pending. Will try discontinuing cefotaxime, since cephalosporins are known to cause low platelet counts.

Cardiovascular system: continues with systolic and faint diastolic murmurs, cardiology feels to be decreased—plan to follow, and slowly increase fluids as tolerated. Arterial line discontinued.

We feel somewhat relieved. Carrie's heart is functioning better as the infection resolves. The catheter has been removed from her artery, which in one sense is good, since the risk of it clotting, and causing gangrene of her fingers or hand is now eliminated. She no longer needs to have arterial blood analyzed for oxygen, carbon dioxide, and acid content, since she is breathing without special support.

One worrisome note though is that Carrie's platelets still seem to be disappearing even as she gets better. To stop this condition a straw is grasped at—change antibiotics. The doctors decide to try ampicillin again. No matter that Carrie developed a total body rash when she'd been on ampicillin before, now that rash is being attributed to her overwhelming infection at that time.

The antibiotics are being given to forestall postoperative infection, which is common in patients after bowel surgery when antibiotics are not employed. Of course, surgical time and skill are even more important, but not nearly as easy to quantify, so everyone gets antibiotics. Antibiotics have side effects, though, besides allergies. They depress the growth of normal bacteria native to the body, thus predisposing to yeast or fungal infections. This happens to Carrie. So, in addition, Carrie is put on oral mycostatin, an anti-fungal drug, for what appears to be thrush, a yeast overgrowth in her mouth.

We try not to be overanxious at these seemingly minor problems. After all Carrie is now in an isolette, and so not attached to a respirator, and to as many monitoring lines (all she has attached now are two IV lines, four wires to her heart monitor, and her ileostomy bag on her abdomen). We can take her out and hold her when we visit. It takes some help from the nurses, but it is progress. She is still tiny, about five pounds, and still very squash-faced and funny looking, I hope from the birth process and not forever. Although at this point it still seems impossible to imagine her out of the hospital. She almost seems to fit into the hospital atmosphere so naturally now.

I've anticipated holding her in my arms, reading and rocking her to sleep every day since she was born. Now that I can hold her, I do just that. It is an incredible feeling. For the first time I allow myself to love and touch Carrie. To get to know the soft, sweetness of her. I do not remind myself that Carrie will probably die. I steel myself against feeling too much.

Our puppy is now back at home, three months old, and I am trying to train her. So I combine my need to read to Carrie and learn how to train Gypsy to sit, lie down and heel: I buy a book called *Good Dog, Bad Dog,* and begin reading it to Carrie, showing her the pictures as we go through each lesson.

Judy isn't thrilled with my choice of reading material. But I feel damned proud sitting in a corner of the neonatal

ICU, rocking my fragile daughter enrobed in pink blankets and a tiny pink stocking cap to keep her head warm, reading *Good Dog, Bad Dog*. She doesn't seem to mind and my concern for appearances is fading. I don't really give a shit what anyone else thinks.

We are all beginning to relax—at least just a little. So it is even more debilitating when on Tuesday morning we arrive to visit and the radiologist throws us a curve.

TUESDAY, OCTOBER 25, 9:00 A.M.

Radiology report.

Portable chest and abdomen. Comparison 10-24-83. In the interim, the heart appears sightly larger than on the previous exam, and a right pleural effusion is identified. The pulmonary vascular pattern is somewhat indistinct. These changes are suggestive of cardiac decompensation, possibly from fluid overload.

Slightly more bowel gas is seen within the intestinal loops. No dilated loops of bowel or pneumatosis is identified.

Wearily I read the words and my pulse quickens. Despite the fact that Carrie appears better, on x-ray, she seems to be going backwards a bit. Can it be that her heart is beginning to fail in its ability to move blood ("cardiac decompensation")?

Judy and I feel like we have been hit in the stomach with a handball.

"Look let's not over react," I say putting an arm around her shoulder.

"Is that what we're doing?" Judy says dejectedly.

"Sure," I say with a lot more conviction than I feel. "Just look at our little girl."

"That's true, Joe," Judy smiles. "She does look a lot better."

The nurse's note later that afternoon bolsters our shaky confidence.

TUESDAY, OCTOBER 25, 4:30 P.M.

Nursing note.

Awake and alert, good suck, grasp, and tone. Heart murmur audible, peripheral pulses palpable 4 extremities. Making spontaneous unlabored respirations on room air. Breath sounds clear and equal bilaterally, chest moves symmetrically. Bowel sounds active, jejunostomy draining small amounts green stool. Skin warm, dry and pink. Central line site has small amount old blood under dressing, no leakage noted, dressing dry and intact. Abdominal incision site partially split but has granulation tissue. Parents in, held and bathed baby.

"Not only the content of the note but the fact that it is sketchy is a good sign," I tell Judy.

"That's true," Judy replies heavily sighing with relief.

In fact despite the radiologist's sour note, things do look good.

Carrie's vital signs are now being taken every four hours instead of every hour or less. Blood is drawn once every eight-hour shift to check her platelet count, which for the first time is remaining stable without transfusions.

Carrie is two weeks old. It is a week after her operation and she's miraculously coming back. Seeing all these signs our bad mood turns good, even though we still keep the door to her room at home shut. We aren't that optimistic, not yet.

Still Carrie has begun to respond to us. She sometimes cries now when we leave, making the guilt of leaving her overwhelming. We hate to end our visits, feeling we are consigning her to her little prison box each time we go.

So, now we begin to worry about Carrie's surroundings. Although nursing coverage in a neonatal ICU is as intense as exists anywhere in medicine, there is never ever enough time for a nurse to pay attention to Carrie's every cry and need; there are other patients with needs as great or greater. The odd thing is, or perhaps it isn't so odd, on second thought, as Carrie improves, she gets less and less attention from the nurses. She needs no blood drawn, no new drugs given, and requires no feeds or "hands-on" attention as she'd once desperately needed. So more and more she is left alone. Such is the fate of a recovering baby in a neonatal ICU.

We are as careful and patient as we can be with the nurses, knowing at firsthand where their priorities lie. Enormous volumes of paperwork, as well as expert observation and bedside care, take up every moment of their time. Our visits, occurring every shift, require them to stop doing something vital, come over and help us disentangle Carrie's wires, leads and IV tubes in order for us to take her out of her isolette and hold her.

On the one hand the nurses are glad to see us, knowing our presence is good for the baby and us, but on the other it is irritating, a constant distraction from their other tasks. Thus, we are very passive, waiting quietly for a nurse to finish whatever she is doing, trying never to ask for help with Carrie once our presence is known. When your baby is critically ill, there is a trick to playing the role of good parents, and we are going to play it to the hilt, if it is to Carrie's benefit.

Still inside we simmer. Really, why should we act as supplicants at some religious ritual? She is our daughter, wrenched from us before we'd even had a chance to start, and now we are supposed to play hospital child's parents. If we'd had her at home, holding her, with free and easy access to her whenever we wanted, we would have been unable to even conceive of having to go through some third party to get to her, suppressing every urge and desire that nature has created in us, squelching our feelings in favor of reason. This reasonableness we carry around with us, this smiling facade that makes us so likable to the nurses and pediatricians, is only that; we don't believe it for a moment. Moreover, maintaining it through gritted teeth takes a hell of a lot of energy.

That afternoon, I have a brainstorm and say to Judy, "Why don't we buy a little tape recorder and some nice tapes, Mozart and Beethoven, and leave them in Carrie's isolette, ready to play, so that when she's alone she'll hear something besides monitors beeping?"

Judy smiles, "Finally she'll hear something besides these damn machines."

I go to the drugstore and buy a recorder, then to the tape store for some music.

That evening when there are fewer people around, I bring tapes in with us, hidden in my duffel bag and ask Dorothy, Carrie's night nurse, in an "Oh, by the way" fashion as we are leaving if it will be okay to leave the recorder in her isolette and the tapes as well. We don't want to make waves, at least not big ones; attitudes towards the family are important in terms of the overall care a patient gets. No one will ever admit it, but it is true. The human factor exists, perhaps better and more easily masked in a "high-tech" environment, but it is critical nonetheless.

Dorothy looks at me kind of funny and says, "Sure." I put the recorder inside, with Mozart's 21st piano concerto in it, and turn the music on. I bend my ear down to the armhole in the isolette to hear how loud it is, as sound doesn't carry very well through the thick plastic.

"Look, Carrie seems to like it; her eyes crinkle up reacting to the sound as she looks around at me." Dorothy nods, her attention occupied elsewhere but I show her how to operate the machine, how to turn the tape over, and the like. She promises to tell her fellow nurses how. When we leave the hospital that day the music is playing and the machine is in the "on" position. When we next arrive the battery is dead.

Instead of beating on the nurses to turn the tape over, or at least turn the machine off once the tape is finished, I run out to the drug store, buy a couple dozen batteries and leave them under Carrie's isolette. No way am I going to say, "Keep track of the music, okay?" The nurses have enough to do besides worrying about my follies.

I cannot stop thinking about how delicate an effort it has been just to let Carrie hear some music. If she'd been home, we'd have been sitting in a rocking chair every evening, listening to whatever we wanted to, without asking anyone in a special way. We are reminded again that in the hospital she is no longer ours, but the hospital's; their child, whom we see at their discretion. For someone like Judy or me, not accustomed to listening to others in a hospital environment, this is hard to stomach. Yet, having worked for many years in this same environment, we know we have no choice. It's their game.

WEDNESDAY, OCTOBER 26, 11:00 P.M.

Nurse's note.

Overall condition unchanged except skin now becoming increasingly mottled and red, appears to have flat red rash on face and arms.

THURSDAY, OCTOBER 27, 8:30 A.M.

Returning to visit Carrie, I read the nurse's note and can't help frowning.

Carrie had developed a rash previously, when she'd first gotten NEC. At the time, the dermatology service had attributed it possibly to an ampicillin sensitivity and allergy, so she'd been taken off ampicillin. The resident now on the service, hadn't noticed the reason in his review of Carrie's tumultuous course up to then, and Larry Cohn the resident going off-service had not mentioned it in his off-service note. The attending pediatrician, much less involved in the day-to-day minutiae of the case, had forgotten about it.

Sometime yesterday morning, they'd started Carrie on ampicillin again. Learning this, I hurry downstairs to question Jerry Greenbach, her new resident. He's surprised when I explain why she's been taken off it before, and, much to his credit, unlike the reaction of the typical physician at being caught, in a sense, with his pants down, reviews the chart and tells me he'll consult with the senior members of his team. I go back to my vigil at Carrie's bedside. A little while later he comes to tell me. They've decided that the rash had probably not been due to ampicillin, but was simply a non-specific accompaniment to Carrie's NEC, and that she is not allergic to ampicillin and can safely receive it. I swallow hard. It's a reasonable decision. But maybe a fatally wrong one.

When I inspect Carrie I notice there is a new rash other than the one seen by the night nurse. We mention it to Doris, her morning nurse. Doris, a wiry blond has been toughened by twenty years of ICU neonatal care. "The doctors are aware of it," she says abruptly leaving it at that. So do we. Carrie seems okay, her usual self, if a baby can be usual in an ICU unit. We just don't want to seem to be nosing in too far, the overly involved parent syndrome. Sure, the pediatricians would still be polite to us, but resentment builds easily, especially if you are already unsure of yourself and your decision. We don't need that and neither does Carrie.

One wag who'd written an account of his internship had said of his patients, "They can always hurt you more." So can doctors, if you are a patient or family who doesn't play the game.

Moreover, obsessing on one problem seems useless, when others crop up so quickly we can't keep track of them all. For instance, Carrie had first developed thrush, a noticeable yeast or fungal overgrowth in her mouth, on the 24th, three days earlier, and it is being treated with mycostatin, a potent anti-fungal agent. The rash has also appeared around her arms and perineum, so mycostatin cream is being applied there three times a day as well.

Yeast infections caused by the organism Candida albicans are not infections at first, simply excess numbers of an organism normally present on all humans. When the bacterial flora or immunological status of the body changes, Candida flourishes. Thus patients like Carrie, on prolonged courses of potent antibiotics which suppress the bacteria normally present in the body, have an overgrowth of yeast, usually in moist, dark areas which favor their multiplication, areas such as the mouth, where it is called "thrush," or the pubic region. The overgrowth can quickly become an infection capable of entering the bloodstream and seeding any part of the body, presenting a life-threatening situation in an already debilitated patient. Carrie's team of physicians thus had a second possible cause for her rash: Candida.

Despite these problems Carrie is doing much better. Therefore, no one really wants to disturb the status quo—if it ain't broke, don't fix it. Thus, she is getting x-rays only every three days now and the nurses' and doctors' daily notes get ever shorter. Still, knowing how quickly the picture can change, Judy and I don't know whether to feel relieved or anxious waiting for the other shoe to drop.

THURSDAY, OCTOBER 27, 4:00 P.M.

Resident note.

Feeding and nutrition status: Weight gain + 20 grams; electrolytes normal, urine output good—increase fluids.

Infectious disease: Day #12 amikacin, on ampicillin as well; 13 days since NEC. 9 days since surgery. Plan at least 14 days amikacin. Consider starting feeding on Monday, October 31.

Hematology: Hematocrit 45.7, platelets 146,000 and stable.

Cardiovascular: Continues with PDA murmur, breathing well without problems.

Jerry Greenbach, Carrie's new resident, sees us and walks over. He is smiling. "The surgeon has decided Carrie is doing so well, he'll consider starting to feed her orally on Monday if she continues as good as she is."

Judy and I hug each other. "There's light at the end of the tunnel," I say.

"Thank God," Judy adds.

"Of course," he continues with a slight wave of his hand as if making an aside, "Carrie has to have her bowel reconnected as well."

I nod, "But even that doesn't seem so remote now that feeding is imminent," I add stroking my chin thoughtfully.

"The surgeon said six to eight weeks after the first operation he'd reconnect her intestine if all went well."

Judy interjects, "That means four and a half weeks from now at the soonest."

"Judy, it doesn't seem so long now, somehow," I smile. Faint hope has returned.

We go home that afternoon floating on air. Carrie is finally going to eat. That is, sort of, because first it will be clear
electrolyte solutions, so as not to stress her bowel, and test
her surgical site, but if she tolerates that well, she'll be allowed to nurse. Judy has rented an electric breast pump a
couple days earlier, but hasn't yet used it. She is somewhat
scared of it especially its appearance. Now that it appears
Carrie will soon finally be able to drink from her breasts, she
runs to the closet and pulls it out and plugs it in, a big smile
on her face. I look at her and smile back. I know how miserable and frustrating it has all been. How different from the
idealized picture of her breast feeding our baby we had both
imagined.

The manual breast pump had required tremendous physical effort to repetitiously squeeze the little suction bulb. The
electric version looks like an ancient engine of war, gears and
a motor encased in a bell jar-like housing, a flexible vacuum
tube extending to a cup which fit over the nipple and sucks
the milk out. I sit down now to watch the machine in action.
It works. Milk doesn't exactly gush out, but it is a hell of a lot
easier than doing it manually. We look at each other in
amazement. What would have seemed horrible only a few
weeks ago now seems wonderful as we harvest the precious
drops.

FRIDAY, OCTOBER 28, 1:00 P.M.

A historic day! At 1:00 P.M. we give Carrie her first oral fluid
since she'd gotten so ill. Ten milliliters, about two-thirds of a
tablespoon, of clear electrolyte solution. What excitement.
The nurse measures it into a bottle, and gives it to me. Although I want so much to be the first to feed Carrie, I give the
bottle to Judy, instead—hell, no one has suffered as she had.
Not even I. No one could appreciate this moment more than
Judy.

We congratulate each other. "Thank goodness I kept up

that awful pumping for two plus weeks," Judy said unable to keep the pride from her voice.

Rose, a nurse standing nearby quickly injects, "Oh, that's not the record. One woman kept pumping her breasts for three months while her baby was in here, until he could feed. She used to sit right in front of the isolette looking at her baby and use the pump."

That shut us up. We feel both admiration for this devoted, determined woman, whoever she is, and guilt at feeling so proud of ourselves when we are obviously nothing special. Though Rose has meant no harm in relating the story, we both feel a little humiliated by our braggadocio. I know Judy finds the pump, this mechanical substitute for a child, basically offensive, and to use it in public, in full view of other people in the ICU, would be impossible for her. Awkwardly I put my arm around her now, trying to tell her I understand. She says nothing but I see the tears glistening in her eyes.

As we sit there in the ICU, rocking Carrie and murmuring little nonsense words to her, a sleekly coiffured woman in a black gabardine suit strides in.

"Are you the Stirts?" she asks in a deep throaty voice.

"Yes," I reply confused.

"Oh, good," she smiles showing a mouth filled with large completely even white teeth. "I'm Eugena Elsworth from the billing office, and I'd like to talk with you about Carrie's insurance."

Now I realize the joke's on me. Embarrassed, my face a little flushed. I say, "Sure." Getting up I walk her to the little anteroom.

As soon as we are seated, she gives me another horse grin. "Do you have medical insurance, Mr. Stirts?"

"It's Doctor Stirt and yes, I have two policies. One through the university, where I work, and my own personal policy."

My mentioning the "Doctor" title obviously doesn't impress her.

She continues to zero in, "Can I have the policy numbers?"

"Uh huh, here."

I smile to myself as she quickly writes them down.

When Carrie had been in the hospital for a week or so, I'd thought about what all this might cost. It seemed horrible to have to consider the cost of keeping my child alive, but there was no way out. I had to make plans. How else could we handle the bills? It struck me then that even if she did very well, she'd still probably be in the hospital a couple of months, the bulk of it in the ICU, and my best guess was she wouldn't be home until the end of the year, three months or so in the hospital.

Considering the cost of being in a neonatal ICU when you counted the tests, medicines, physicians fees and all, a six figure price tag seemed to me to be likely for Carrie's hospitalization cost if all went well. Of course, ironically, if she died, as seemed most likely at the time of her operation, it would be much cheaper. A hooker was the possibility that she'd recover but then need frequent rehospitalizations and operations, which would blow the lid off any possible estimate I could make.

Miserable, I scrutinized even the fine print on my university-supplied Blue Cross plan, and found to my dismay, that Blue Cross benefits were limited to a total of $250,000 for life for any person covered. Well, once upon a time, ten years or so ago, that was well in excess of anything one would likely (or unlikely) approach. Now, though, with medical costs skyrocketing, $250,000 didn't seem like such a great cushion. Luckily I'd converted my old group policy to an individual one to pay for Judy's pregnancy and delivery costs since my new policy didn't cover pre-existing conditions.

Realizing that Carrie's hospitalization might use up most, if not all, of her lifetime Blue Cross coverage with the possibility she might need many more hospitalizations if she survived, I decided to keep my private policy as well. Looking at Ms. Elsworth panting for proof that I wasn't indigent I realized I made a fortunate decision.

Then with a sinking feeling, I also realized how even a family which thought it was well covered with medical insurance could be devastated by a major illness, and I shuddered to think of the destruction of poorer families' lives that occurred daily in this country due to the cost of medical care.

SATURDAY, OCTOBER 29, 10:00 A.M.

Nurse's note.

Caroline had a heelstick K [potassium] at 2:00 A.M. today of 8.1. She was receiving pedialyte 15 ml every three hours P.O., and she was then made NPO (due to K). An EKG strip was done, and the house officer was called in to check it. At 2:30 A.M. she was given 2 mEq $NaHCO_3$ slow I.V. push and 2 ml $D_{10}W$ IV. Numerous arterial stick attempts for K were made at two different times. A repeat central line K came back 6.7, then later another repeat K was 5.4.

Assessment: Hyperkalemia from unknown reason.

Plan: Feedings resumed with D_5W at 15 cc P.O. every three hours per house officer. Hang hyperal this evening with decreased K. Electrolytes every shift for next three shifts.

We sleep a little late the next morning. After all Carrie is finally getting some nourishment. Judy and I are breathing a little easier, feeling a bit more confident. So when we got to the hospital and see the nurse's note we are doubly agonized, first because Carrie's slow upward progress can quickly slide backwards at any moment and then because we, who ought to know better, keep grasping at signs of hope only to have them snatched back.

Things are so changeable now. We don't know how to react. "I'll go find Jerry Greenbach," I say not looking at Judy at all.

He explains what has happened. "Carrie had blood drawn by heelstick for routine electrolyte analysis, which will continue until she is off hyperal and feeding normally. As you know, the heelsticks are the easiest way to get blood, although very painful for her." I nodded. Her heels looked like masses of scar tissue after two weeks of this, but what can anyone do? Her veins are so delicate and tiny, those that are left have to be reserved for IVs as the ones in place infiltrated and "blew."

His voice drones on. "Heelstick lab values are okay when the results are normal, but immediately suspect when abnormal numbers come back."

I want to say, look get on with it; come to the point; I'm a doctor too. But, of course, I don't. Instead I say politely, "Yes, go on."

He gestures widely, "The reason is, extreme pressure must be exerted on the foot to sort of "milk" the blood out, drop by drop, and the pressure may force an excess concentration of elements in the surrounding tissues into the blood samples, giving misleading or erroneous values." Why we believe the results when they fall in the normal range, and discard them when they're abnormal, tells a lot about how selective medical thinking can be in order to suit its own purposes.

"When K or potassium level gets too high or too low, trouble can occur, major, big-time trouble. Carrie's potassium was 8.1. Definitely high. High enough to trigger all the alarm bells and buzzers in the lab and a call to the ICU."

"It could cause cardiac arrest and death," I murmur. It is his turn to nod.

"So we did an electrocardiogram. There doesn't appear to be any changes in Carrie's EKG."

I take a deep breath. Two facts temper his assessment. First, there are no recent previous EKGs to compare the current one with, rendering the resident's assessment "EKG appears normal" essentially meaningless. Second, and equally important, the pediatric house officer's ability to diagnose hyperkalemia on the EKG is not much better than my dog's. He is not a cardiologist, and rarely has anything to do with EKGs. On his own, late at night, tired and scared, his interpretation is probably worthless.

I pay strict attention anyway. I have to. It is all we have to go on. "Carrie then received some sugar water," he says scratching his chin. "The idea being that the sugar would be absorbed into the cells, and by a complicated transport mechanism, potassium would also be carried into the cells, out of the bloodstream. The sodium bicarbonate will, of course, neutralize the blood acidity."

I glare at him, I can't stop myself. This is all well and good, except for one thing: the resident has forgotten a crucial part of the treatment of hyperkalemia, even assuming that Carrie needs such a vigorous response, which is doubtful.

In order to carry K inside cells, sugar needs to be utilized. Insulin is the hormone which effectively moves the sugar. Sugar without insulin is useless. The resident either doesn't know this or is aware of it but doesn't know how much insulin to use, so chooses not to use any. Too much insulin could drop the blood sugar precipitously and produce more trouble, such as seizures and cardiac arrest. No one else was around; he didn't have anyone to ask, and he didn't want to call and wake up a senior resident or attending physician and admit his ignorance, so he plowed on alone. Such is the course of many crucial early morning decisions in hospitals every day.

Following the attempt at therapy, they tried to obtain blood for analysis from Carrie's arteries, which would yield a more reliable number than the heel stick values. These attempts failed, so the central line was used. This was generally forbidden, since infection could spread easily into the bloodstream through the heart the more the catheter leading to it was handled and contaminated. In this situation, considered an emergency by the resident, anything was permitted. In medicine many decisions are made just like this, deciding an immediate problem has absolute precedence and letting the long-term consequences be what they may. After all, you'll be off the service by then. I want to throttle him but I can't allow myself the pleasure. I count to ten slowly and try to assess the situation.

Looking at the whole episode, several things become apparent. First, Carrie is not in any danger now—she appears fine. This is always the first and most important determination in any clinical situation: is the patient stable? If yes, you have plenty of time to decide, first, if anything is really wrong (it usually isn't), and second, if anything needs to be done (usually not, just awareness of a problem's existence and appropriate decisions made in its light).

Carrie's resident had little experience with babies with high heelstick Ks; maybe none. He had no more experienced doctor to tell him that, one, the value was probably erroneously high and two, even if it wasn't, the baby was in no imminent danger based on clinical signs. When you're young and a resident, though, you hesitate to trust your clinical judgment and experience, because circular argument that it is, you essentially have none; that's why you're doing a residency, to learn good judgment.

In a story that may or may not be true, a young resident once asked his attending, a world-renowned clinician, famous for his diagnostic acumen, "Professor, what is wisdom?"

The Professor replied, "Wisdom, young man, is good judgment."

"How do you get good judgment, then?" asked the resident.

The professor replied, "Years of bad judgment."

Residency and medical training are, essentially, the years of bad judgment which, hopefully, cause a minimal amount of damage as they help form wisdom.

I look at Carrie's chart for the several days previous to

the "sudden" hyperkalemia. As far back as the 26th, two days earlier, Carrie's K values had been in the abnormal range, about 6.0 consistently. Thus, the current value is not a sudden change from a run of normal values, but a shift up from an already elevated baseline. Putting things in perspective yields much, almost as much as looking at the patient instead of the numbers.

The nurse on duty, in her written note in the chart, recorded values of 8.1, 6.7, and 5.4 as various blood samples were drawn and analyzed. The resident, in his notes, recorded values of 6.5 and 6.1. The nurse who summarized the events ten hours later, in the early afternoon, lists values of 7.2 and 6.8. The computerized laboratory printout lists values of 6.9 and 6.7. So where is the truth, the "real" value? The value of a good physician lies principally in his or her ability to temper the plethora of facts and objective data with reality based on experience and judgment. Over and over I use the word judgment, but there is still no substitute, or anything even close.

Finally, this whole episode with Carrie demonstrates one more thing about medical decision-making, namely, that the decision made is in large part a function of the physician making it, not of the patient or the disease. The illusion that treatment is simply an extension of diagnosis is a holdover from simpler days when patients were supplicants and doctors were gods. Today patients are people, and doctors are finally perceived as people also, not curators of some mysterious knowledge insulated from the common man by "medspeak."

SATURDAY, OCTOBER 29, 7:00 P.M.

It is amazing how quickly these frightening episodes occur. What is also amazing is that Judy and I have become so used to them they also quickly fade from our minds. When we return to the hospital that night Carrie is feeding orally, sucking down a whole tablespoon of clear electrolyte solution, every three hours, and again things are looking up. We take the change at face value and begin talking of taking her home.

As we chat with each other about Carrie, the subject drifts around to the other babies in the unit. We are quite aware of who else is there, the comings and goings, since we come in so often. Each day we look at the board (the "Board Sign") and see instantly who's gone sour during the last shift, and who's been admitted in critical condition.

Now I check to see whether any nurses are nearby. For parents protocol and etiquette in the neonatal ICU means never inquiring about other babies. Perhaps it is more than that, and superstition plays a role. In any event, it quickly becomes clear that you are never to ask how another baby is doing, or pay obvious attention to any other child. Occasionally the nurse will bring another baby up as a topic of conversation, and then it is okay to join in, but otherwise, no.

Now thinking I'm being careful to be discreet I turn to Judy, "I wonder how Carrie would have done if she'd been a boy?" I am surprised to hear someone pipe up.

"Not very well." It is Sadie, a gray-haired nurse two isolettes away. Two others quickly echo her.

"What do you mean?" I ask, "A boy would be just as tough as a girl, if not tougher, and thus better able to deal with the ordeal of being critically ill from birth."

"Girls do a lot better than boys in the unit—they seem to bounce back better and recover quicker. And they seem to not have as many disabilities when they leave. It's like they're tougher," Sadie frowns.

Her words fascinate me. I've never heard of a sex difference being present in terms of response to illness, either in children or adults, and now I am being told there is indeed a noticeable difference. I tend to believe nurses' observations. They are the foot soldiers of medicine—they march beside their patients—they *know*.

I wonder what inborn survival advantage girls have over boys—is it hormonal, some increased resistance to the stress of being ill? It has been well established in recent years that female and male brains and nervous systems are wired differently from conception, a result of hormonal differences in utero—does such differentiation affect survival? Certainly more males died in utero than females. The difference the nurses in ICU perceive is consistent—but what does it mean or imply? Can survival be improved by looking more deeply into this observation, I wonder?

SUNDAY, OCTOBER 30, 7:30 P.M.

Resident's note.

Fluid and nutrition: weight 2000 grams (down 220 grams from yesterday). Unable to explain this. Patient with stable I & O's and doing well clinically. Potassium, 6.5; will continue to recheck K regularly. Continue to feed D_5W 15 ml every 3 hours, hyperal and oral intake to total 140 ml/kg/day.

GI tract/Infectious Disease: Today is day 14 of amikacin, discontinue both amikacin and ampicillin after today's dose. Abdomen soft, bowel sounds active. White count 15,800—will follow.

Hematology: hematocrit 42.9, platelets pending.

Cardiovascular: PDA murmur not heard today.

Feedings: Begin 1/4–1/2 strength breast milk feeds in A.M.

I read over Jerry Greenbach's note and feel confused. Carrie continues to look better each day, yet somehow she has lost a half a pound, fully 10 percent of her body weight, in the past day—how can this be? Every drop of fluid she took in or put out (I & O, "intake and output") is quantitated, her diapers are weighed to the nearest milligram to determine her urine output, yet she's mysteriously lost a half a pound, equivalent to fifteen pounds in an adult, yesterday. This is

where clinical judgment comes into play, and where understanding the ultimately futile nature of attempting to quanti-
tate a human being is crucial. In effect, the resident had decided to ignore this information. He seemed to be saying, "I
don't know and I don't care about her 'weight loss,' because
she's looking fine."

It seems reasonable to suppose someone has made an
error somewhere in the two weights, perhaps not subtracted
the weight of a dry diaper (one half a pound?) or perhaps the
scale had been fixed or reset or changed, but really no one
would ever know what had happened.

Carrie's K is still elevated, for no clear reason—again,
his response is practical: just let her have sugar water.

He also decides it is time to stop her antibiotics—for us
an exciting happening as it is every time another medication
or procedure or monitoring device was removed. It means
she is getting that much closer to making it on her own and
recovering.

Of course, there is a dark side to discontinuing drugs on
which she is doing well: perhaps the antibiotics are keeping
her free from infection, and now without them she will be
vulnerable. The next few days will be critical. She's been on
heavy antibiotic coverage since birth, eighteen days ago.
Eighteen days. It seems several lifetimes, so much has happened. So much crying, depression, gloom, self-flagellation
and guilt, and now it seems to be ending.

Uncertainty persists: Carrie's white count is still abnormally high, 15,800 instead of the 5,000–10,000 it should be.
This indicates infection, but clinically she appears well, so
again, no major effort is indicated or made to find evidence of
infection.

Her blood picture looks (another one of those ambiguous
words) stable, no evidence of anemia or bleeding. Her heart
murmur has disappeared.

On the whole, she looks so good that she is to start her
first breast milk feedings tomorrow morning. We are ready,
and plan to be there to give it to her. One-quarter to one-half

strength breast milk, thawed and warmed, from the stock Judy has built up in the ICU refrigerator, will be used.

The thought of Carrie actually resuming her feedings is exhilarating and frightening. It means she is closer to recovery, but in the back of our minds is the specter of the events two weeks ago, when she'd had several feedings (of formula, not breast milk) and suddenly gotten NEC. What if she just can't tolerate her feedings, and NEC returns? It is horrifying to think about, but it is on our minds all day Sunday.

We make our afternoon visit to the hospital about 5:00 P.M. We spend the afternoon holding Carrie and reading to her, making small talk. At 6:30 P.M. or so, we put her back in her isolette and say good-bye to the evening shift nurses. We have planned a special dinner out that night. A short time to be alone. To talk. To try to hold on to the vestiges of a normal relationship.

"Will you be back to feed her later?" asks Jessie, a tall well-built brunette and one of the very best nurses in the ICU.

Judy and I sort of stammer, looking at each other and say, stumbling over our words, "No, I don't think so, we're going to get to bed early and come in early for her breast milk feeding tomorrow," and "maybe, we might, I don't know."

"We'll call you," I hesitantly say, "and let you know whether or not we'll be back so we can feed her if we do come back in."

"Okay," Jessie answers, smiling. "See you later."

We leave the ICU feeling depressed. Jessie's innocent question has opened the floodgates of our guilt and self-doubt about ourselves as parents. We never get over, nor do I suspect we ever completely will, the feeling that somehow Carrie's suffering is our fault, the result of something we did wrong somewhere along the line.

The nurse's question has jolted us, making us both feel we are neglectful, selfish parents to be thinking of enjoying ourselves instead of being in the ICU our every waking moment holding, talking to, and caring for our daughter.

Yet the environment is so foreign, so hostile even for us,

experienced medical and hospital employees, that we dread every visit, the inability to have the kind of easy intimacy and privacy with our daughter and each other, moments everyone who doesn't have a child in an ICU takes for granted. We know how it would feel, our imaginations let us know how warm it would be—and when we look around at the cold starkness of ICU it makes everything all the harder to take.

Parents of sick babies are vulnerable, exquisitely vulnerable, to every seemingly innocent comment, question and infection. We harbor enormous doubts about ourselves and our adequacy as parents and human beings. Asking us if we'd be back later, the nurse has unmasked our doubts, and in our scramble to seem responsible, we destroy our anticipated evening.

Now we can't escape the pull of the hospital. Having to call in, in a couple hours when Carrie's next feeding is due, to let the nurse know we won't be there, is an irritation we can't forget or brush away. "Joe," Judy says plaintively, "I know we ought to go but . . ."

My anger at myself for letting all this get to me mounts.

"But," I repeat, "but what? Is one dinner alone, away from this place too damn much to ask?"

"Maybe it is," tears run down Judy's cheeks. "How the hell am I supposed to know? I don't know anything anymore."

I turn away. The tension and anxiety that has been building between Judy and me is composed of such things.

MONDAY, OCTOBER 31, 10:00 A.M.

By the next morning when we return to the hospital to give Carrie her first milk our heated interchange has turned to ice. We barely talk or look at each other. I feel my pocket to be sure I've remembered the book I read to Carrie. It is there. Reassuring, almost normal. A father who reads to his child. Then I look around me and realize nothing can be normal, not here where death is only a moment away and anything can happen and does.

Inside, Judy and I go to our usual scrub sinks where for five minutes we wash our hands of the outside world and all its potential contaminants that could devastate a population of sick, premature, immunocompromised and infected babies. There is always a feeling of distancing to me in this act, necessary as I suppose it is. One more barrier to the free and easy contact parents take for granted with their infants. Everything in the hospital routine is ritualized, stylized, such that spontaneity is eliminated. It simply can't exist. It is easy to become accepting of this mindset, and simply do what you are told, unless you are an anarchist at heart, a troublemaker from way back.

As we turn from the scrub sink to enter Carrie's room, we both stop stock-still. Carrie isn't there. Frightened, our first thought is that she's died, and second, we think perhaps she's been rushed to x-ray or surgery for some emergency procedure, and no one has had a chance to call us. Through our minds pass the memory of when Carrie had first gotten NEC. She'd started spitting up at 3:00 A.M. and we hadn't learned anything was wrong for more than five hours, until they called us at 8:30 A.M. So it isn't unreasonable for us to think the same thing has happened again. To us anything is possible now.

We walk into Carrie's room, another baby is in her spot near the window. By now we feel totally disconnected, disoriented. Ringing starts in my ears. In the corner we see a group of house-staff, interns, residents, and attendings crowded around another baby. I am bewildered. Judy looks anguished. Neither of us says a word to each other, we are too afraid to. It is like we've walked into a strange hospital in a foreign country. Finally, I see Sadie, a nurse I recognize. In a voice I don't recognize as my own I ask where Carrie is.

"Oh, didn't they tell you?" she smiles brightly. "They transferred her to the NIN earlier this morning."

"Oh, thanks," I reply, overwhelmed by relief. Judy and I

shake our heads at each other communicating without words. It never stops, and it never will until we get her out of here.

Slowly we walk toward the NIN. I sit down next to Carrie's isolette and continue to read, *Good Dog, Bad Dog,* the book which I carry with me. Judy glares at me. "Great material for a baby."

"It seems to me," I say, "she doesn't care what we read as long as she hears our voices. You know I don't have much time off and the puppy has started to chew the furniture plus peeing all over the house. I have to learn how to train her and this way, I can read to Carrie and learn at the same time."

"How practical," Judy says, "the nurses must think we're going to be great parents."

I sigh. I no longer care so much what people think. I do care about what's happening to Judy and me. I care but can't seem to do much about it.

Perhaps a fundamental cause of our increasing difficulty with each other is Carrie's turn for the better. After steadily growing more depressed and falling together into a vortex of despair and aching loneliness, isolated from everyone but each other, believing yet not really believing it was all happening, we'd touched bottom intact, closer and more strongly linked than before. As Carrie improved, visibly stronger and more lively each day, we seemed to withdraw from each other, each of us pulling back from the bonds and connections we'd relied on to hold us together for a rough ride down.

Little things that seemed insignificant a week ago now become irritating; my newsprint-laden fingerprints on every doorjamb in the house becomes an issue. Judy's speedball driving style provokes me. It seems we just can't deal with good fortune. The unknown is too frightening. We have become too used to despair.

MONDAY, OCTOBER 31, 1:00 P.M.

Nurse's ICU transfer note.

Caroline was transferred today to the NIN [Neonatal Intermediate Nursery, another handy acronym] at 1:00 A.M. She is stable and in no distress, heart rate 145, respiratory rate 42, temperature, 37.2°C. Patient is on PO feeds of D_5W 15 ml q 3° [every three hours]. She is tolerating the feeds well with no emesis. Her ostomy site looks good with no signs of infection, draining greenish fluid. Mucous fistula left open to air. Incision site patent [open] with no redness or swelling. Only med is mycostatin 2 cc PO q 6°.

   Plan: Care according to NIN routine, change ostomy dressing q shift, increase feeds as tolerated, give support to parents.

MONDAY, OCTOBER 31, 3:00 P.M.

Resident's progress note.

Feeds changed to 15 ml one half strength breast milk q 3 h today. Tolerating well. Will advance to 20 cc q 3 h as tolerated. Abdomen soft, nontender, good bowel sounds. Platelets stable 172,000. Cardiovascular: PDA murmur *not* heard.

MONDAY, OCTOBER 31, 4:00 P.M.

Nurse's note.

Social: Parents at bedside. Mom doing ileostomy bag change, dressing change, bath and diapering. Parents do very well with her.

I read the first two notes quickly lingering only on the third which stabs a weak spot. If only she could see how we are really doing, within ourselves. Still, it is the best day yet for Carrie. For that we are both thankful. The worst seems over, the best yet to come, and it is about time.

TUESDAY, NOVEMBER 1, 9:00 A.M.

Arriving to feed Carrie we are still buoyed by yesterday's happy time with her; we even suspend our state of undeclared war with each other. But walking into the NIN our hearts begin to pound. Carrie's isolette is there, with her name on it and the mobile I'd made taped to the inside of the lid, but no Carrie. I stand still rooted to the spot. Looking around I feel myself trembling all over. I don't even begin to know how to react. I feel as if the hospital is playing games with us, daring us to get excited or upset, yet there can't be any conscious pattern to this sort of thing. No one would be that diabolical (would they?). But nevertheless, for the second morning in a row, our daughter is not where she'd been when we'd kissed her good-bye the previous night. I am dumbfounded.

Finally I spy Jessie, one of Carrie's nurses. Trying to find my voice I clear my throat and ask hoarsely, "Where's Carrie?" She looks at me surprised.

"Oh, didn't they tell you? She's been transferred back to the ICU."

Judy and I bolt out of the NIN into the hallway and towards the ICU which is just around the corner. I stop short of the massive steel door and its automatic button opener. Judy and I go into the stairwell immediately adjacent, there we've had many talks over the past several weeks, this being the only privacy we can find in the hospital. We don't say anything, just stand in the stairwell and hold each other, tears flowing, knowing that somehow once again we've gotten involved in something very terrible and out of our control.

Neither of us want to go into the ICU and find out what new catastrophe has befallen Carrie: The news can only be bad. We cling together in the shadowy, dank stairwell, cold from the wind whistling up from the outside door below. We feel numb inside. After a while I notice I have a hard-on, and begin grinding it into Judy's crotch. She pushes back, and we twist against each other, locked together.

"Now I understand how come all that fucking went on in the London subways during the Blitz," Judy whispers. "I used never to be able to figure out how people who were frightened could care about sex, but now I see it. It's not that you want it or anything, it's just a sort of desperation, the only thing that's yours. . . ."

I begin unzipping her jeans.

"Shall we?" I ask.

"Why not? What does it matter anymore?" says Judy. After we finish we are more miserable than ever. We walk to the door of the ICU, push the button, and stand back as the thick steel door swings open.

Slowly, like mummies enshrouded, we stiffly walk through it and stop in front of the big board. There it is again, our name STIRT, just as before, with hordes of colored buttons denoting all the blood tests and needle sticks and lab work Carrie is undergoing and will continue to suffer through for who knew how long.

The nurse's note explains the details. I scan it my eyes widening in horror.

NIN nurse's note.

At 3:00 A.M. perfusion appeared poor, patient appeared dusky and jaundiced, less active, lethargic. Began having bradycardia and apnea. Blood gases attempted, difficult due to difficulty in sticking vessels. Respiratory: periodic long pauses without breathing. At 2:00 A.M. heart rate fell from 140 to 70, then resumed at 140. By 6:00 A.M. heart rate occasionally dropping to 40, requiring bag and mask. Feedings held. By 6:00 A.M. tone poor, cry faint. Transferred to ICU at 6:30 A.M.

"Where is she?" I ask the clerk in a hoarse voice. I see her smile through my misting eyes.

"Second alcove on the left." Judy and I walk down the sterile white hall groping our way as if we have never been here before. Finally we arrive at our destination. Looking in, we see Carrie lying very still. A crowd of doctors and nurses hover over her, probing and jabbing at her with needles, reestablishing the monitoring routes and lines that she's so slowly and gradually discarded as she improved in the past week. Anguished I stare at Judy. Her face mirrors my feelings. Back to square one.

It would be interesting and instructive for those individuals who make laws instructing hospitals and physicians on mandatory treatment of sick infants to have a child of their own who is in a position to get such aggressive treatment. It is very easy as a doctor or lawmaker or concerned citizen to

decide if freedom of choice, the right of the parents to determine the level of care, is right or wrong. It feels a lot different
when the child is yours.

I have been an active and, I suppose, a consenting par-
ticipant in the past, during my internship, in the very aggressive treatment of terminally ill infants, such that death on
several occasions occurred on the operating room table during an operation ostensibly intended to prolong the child's
life. Now I am a pawn in the same game, without any voice in
the matter of whether or not Carrie should once again be put
through the wringer. No one asks Judy or I how we feel about
what is happening; it is taken for granted that we are "all for
everything," and if we aren't, tough shit. It would be done
anyway.

Yet we are expected to love and care for Carrie for all the
years to come, after all is said and done, and after whatever
damage illness and treatment has inflicted on her has occurred.

The recent "Baby Doe" bill states that treatment should
be withheld only when the infant is chronically and irreversibly comatose, when treatment would not correct all of the
infant's life-threatening conditions, when treatment would
merely prolong dying, or when treatment would be futile or
inhumane.

A member of the House Committee who drafted the bill
stated, "No one has the right to play God with the lives of
these babies, except God himself." But who will raise these
children, and try to keep together a family and marriage
which can shatter so easily under the strain? For every family
we read about in *People* or *US Magazine*, united around a
chronically ill, deformed, or retarded child, there are ten
more marriages catastrophically damaged or destroyed, di-
vorces, and bitterness, financial disasters, and ultimately personal tragedies: suicides, murders, and illness to rival in misery any fictional tale one might imagine.

Yet who will speak for these suffering, silent, victims,
under siege, one that is neither requested nor invited. They

become quiet and bitter as they watch their lives diminishing into shadows of what might have been, wrought by what could never have been imagined.

On this day we are one with them. Without a word we wash our hands and go in. Carrie lies once again on a flat, padded, pallet. She is lethargic, her complexion yellowish-gray. When I squeeze her hand she doesn't respond, she just lies there with her eyes closed, working to breathe. How the fuck has all this happened to her since we'd gone home last night?

I try to compose myself to think rationally as I stand at her side, seeing but not seeing all the technicians, nurses, and doctors moving in and out of the room, commuting to and from her to wherever the data and specimens are being taken. Once again, the crisis mode has struck, and all are mobilized to support it. The other patients in the unit might have not been there, so great is the contrast between the activity required to "gear up" a patient for ICU care and that required to maintain it. Establishing a new level of routine is the essence of ICU medicine—the routine itself is like any other pattern, easily followed once established.

The frightening past floods my mind as I watch scene after scene almost recreated. Carrie had originally gotten NEC one day after beginning to receive formula in the NIN. Now, one day after beginning to receive feedings in the NIN, nearly three weeks later, after a brutal hospital roller coaster course, she's collapsed once again. Is it merely a coincidence? Even the initial observations of the nurses in the NIN are nearly identical: on October 14, she'd been "Apneic and dusky, sepsis work-up begun:" today, she's become "Dusky, with apneic episodes consistent with sepsis."

I can't shake the feeling that this is somehow a glitch in reality, a sort of time warp in which the film has been reversed. Perhaps some diabolic fate has decided to put us all through it again. Perhaps to help me get it right. I am certainly getting it, no doubt about that.

I force myself to stop feeling self-pity and to concentrate

on what has happened. Is it the feeding that has destroyed Carrie? Does she have NEC again, a relapse? Is her bowel simply unable to deal with food, rendering her a nutritional cripple, dependent on IV feedings forever? Maybe something about the NIN causes problems for her, some virus or bug in the air, some bizarre hyperactivity or some nurse. Anything is now possible, at least in my mind. My view of what is illogical and therefore, impossible has blurred over the past several weeks. To me the impossible no longer exists. It is Judy's and my daily reality.

TUESDAY, NOVEMBER 1, 11:00 A.M.

Resident's note.

Feeding/nutrition: Feeds stopped, on HAL. Weight up 25 g.
Infectious Disease & Sepsis: Patient with acute decompensation today as noted, with possible sepsis. Abdomen and chest x-ray look okay—searching for cause. Begun on triple IV antibiotics: ampicillin, gentamicin, and nafcillen.
Addendum 12 noon. D/C ampicillin, begin clindamycin.

The above note looks like it was written with a pen held between the writer's toes, so disjointed, illegible and illogical is it. A disquieting note. I've written many notes like it myself in similar circumstances. What has to be done isn't paperwork, it is coordinating a million and one tests and procedures, orders to be written, consultations obtained, parents dealt with, all on not nearly enough sleep, with your gut grinding and cramping after a non-stop diet of greasy hospital cafeteria food.

The progress note in a situation like this is just a scribble, an acknowledgement for the records that someone knows things are happening. When things deteriorate, those who continue to write nice notes are suspect as either ignorant, or borderline personalities. Maybe both.

TUESDAY, NOVEMBER 1, 6:30 P.M.

Radiology report.

Portable chest at 0630 hours: the central line is in the superior vena cava. The lung fields are clear of infiltrate. The cardiac silhouette is unremarkable.

Impression: Unremarkable chest with central line in place.

Flat Plate of abdomen at 0900 hours: The bowel gas pattern is abnormal in that there are elongated air filled loops in bowel. There is no mass effect noted. There has been no significant internal change since 10/29/83.

I run my hand across my aching forehead. The damned x-rays don't indicate a thing: no pneumonia, no sudden perforation of her bowel, no heart failure—she is the same "on x-ray" as she'd been for days. Once again I dwell on the past few days. "When something goes wrong after making a change, consider the change as the source of the problem." I learned this years ago in medical school from some clinical type who hadn't opened a book or journal in years, just relied on his experience and observations.

What has changed recently? Breast milk feedings were begun yesterday and all antibiotics were stopped yesterday as well. Now, twenty-four hours later, Carrie is critically ill. Coincidence? Not to me. Either she'd reacted violently to the feedings, her NEC once again exploding into her gut, or else whatever infection the antibiotics have been suppressing has emerged in their absence.

The stable x-ray picture, and the fact that her abdomen is still soft and not distended, with active bowel sounds and stool passing into her ostomy bag, seems to argue strongly against a recurrence of NEC. That leaves infection. This is the path being actively pursued by Carrie's doctors: blood is once again carefully drawn for cultures, and a spinal tap once again performed to try and isolate an organism that might have spread to the central nervous system. This I dread more than anything, meningitis or encephalitis on top of her already precarious status—the ever present possibility of permanent brain damage is horrifying.

To test all possibilities urine is also needed—since it is impossible to really get a "clean catch," that is, a sterile specimen, from an infant, another suprapubic tap is performed. Fortunately for Carrie, she is so lethargic by this time, she doesn't even need to be restrained.

I ask to talk to Carrie's attending physician and am told he's gone off-service. This stops me cold for a minute. "Attendings change on the first of the month every three months," says the ward clerk in a monotonous tone. "Do you want to talk to the new attending?"

"Sure, please page him for me, will you?" I ask. I feel bile rising to my throat.

Great. Two and a half weeks through thick and thin with one attending who finally got to know Carrie inside and out, and now, hours after she's suddenly "decompensated" and "turned to stool," as we put it, someone completely new is coming onto the service, in charge of the entire ICU and all its sick babies, and he'd be in charge of Carrie's care.

I am profoundly depressed. This just goes on and on I think. One thing after another. Forget about the fact that my marriage is slowly falling apart, our new house lies empty, I am not doing a thing at work besides showing up more or less as a functioning zombie-robot and going through the necessary motions, ignore the general pall of grey that descends on each day as I awake, wondering when both the day and the depressing repetitive nature of these days would end.

Every aspect of Carrie's life in the hospital seems more and more difficult. Problem after problem arises, each one draws me deeper into my brooding about the imbalance of it, the absence of contrasting good news. I suppose, if I think about it, the fact Carrie hasn't had a seizure or a central nervous system problem yet is good news. When you are there in the midst of a calamity the absence of bad news is, in itself, I guess, good news.

Hal Davis, the tall, gangling new attending physician, approaches us in the coffee room, introducing himself. "Let's sit down," he says motioning toward some plastic chairs littered with debris and clothing. We toss the stuff onto a nearby desk and bookcase, having both been in the business long enough to know you never put things away where they belong, nor do you move them out of the room they are in—you just change their location for whatever purpose suits you.

"Hi," I begin. "Pleased to meet you, but I've had enough," I try to smile.

"I can understand that," he says. "That little girl has been through the wringer, and she just won't stop, will she?"

"I think it's just a test to see how tough Judy and I are," I bitterly say. "We know how tough she is."

"No doubt about that," he says.

I am already tired from trying to make small talk when I can think of nothing but Carrie. I begin questioning him in earnest.

"What's wrong with her, do you think? Does she just have a congenital aversion to the NIN?"

"I wish it were that—we'd keep her in the ICU and send her home from here," he chuckles.

"Don't laugh—that's not such a bad idea," I reply. "If she comes out of this one, I'll be plenty worried the day she goes back to the NIN."

"I hope we get to that point," he says gloomily. I notice his tone and my heart quickens. "She looks to me like she's septic, from where or what organism I have no idea. We've cultured everything, and started her on three antibiotics that should kill everything growing in, on, or near her body."

"What about the central line?" I prod. "It's been in for two and a half weeks, she's got Candida in the mouth and perineum, she's had total bacterial suppression by her antibiotics since she's been alive—maybe you should pull the central line?"

"That's a consideration," he nods rubbing red sleepy eyes.

I look at him more closely. A good decent man, hardworking, from the look of him. But he's young, probably under thirty. How much experience can he possibly have, I wonder agonizingly? Not enough for this, not enough for Carrie. Still he's all we have. I force myself to concentrate on what he's saying.

"The trouble is, she's not eating anymore since she's so lethargic, and she's got to have nutrition—the hyperal is the only thing she's got."

"Maybe you could take out the old central line and put a new one in," I say more insistently.

"We'll talk to surgery and see—the trouble is, if we take this one out and use the other side, that's it—we don't have any other options should we have to put in another line. I don't like to be backed into that kind of corner."

I don't say it, but it seems to me this is as much of a corner as he'll ever be in—there doesn't seem to me to be any other option, and this situation seems exactly one which demands a site change. Many ICUs changed insertion sites routinely on a weekly or every ten days basis to prevent possible infections and colonization of the central line site, which, after all, is a direct, unbroken route from the outside into the bloodstream and heart.

I leave my meeting with him feeling a little better—he seems open, easy to talk with. He is humble yet appears secure about his decisions (I am to learn much later that despite his youth, he had done considerable research in this area and in fact had published papers on NEC, the disease Carrie had, a fact he never mentioned, dealing with me on a professionally equal basis, never alluding to his special expertise even when I questioned his judgment or decisions). Yet a half hour earlier I'd been apprehensive and depressed at the change. So do points of view and reality itself change.

TUESDAY, NOVEMBER 1, 8:00 P.M.

Nurse's note.

Resp: In room air on table. Spontaneous respirations 42/min, deep with slight substernal and intercostal retractions. Color of extremities blue. Occasionally becomes apneic, color very dusky, vigorous stimulation does not stimulate breathing. Heart rate decreases down to 45 [normal is about 150]. Requires oxygen by bag and mask. Periods of apnea and bradycardia last 2 minutes. Nasal prongs for nasal CPAP [continuous positive airway pressure] inserted. Color becomes less dusky but remains pale. Breathing is now periodic.

Neuro: Fair muscle tone. Responds to painful stimulation with movement. Fair suck, weak grasp reflex. Very, very lethargic.

Cardiovascular: Central line site and skin around site is red. Ped. surg. is aware of site.

Skin: labia red, swollen, edematous. Has raised red rash on perineum, right side more than left.

Assessment: Severe respiratory difficulties not responding to stimulation.

Plan: Continue to monitor breathing. Discuss problems with parents.

When we come in that evening (we'd learned one thing in the past several weeks at least, namely that no matter how bad Carrie was, we should stick to our three visits a day, not simply sit in the corridor staring at the walls all day and night. There is even less future in that than in Carrie getting out of this damned prison), we go directly to her bedside, and there ironically, she is. A bitter sweet surprise of sorts, compared to the last two days of Carrie's unexpected frightening transfers in the middle of the night and our terror at not finding her where we'd last seen her.

We stand around Carrie's isolette, Judy and I. She lies there, silent, eyes closed, not moving, breathing irregularly, lines, wires, and tubes once again emerging from everywhere. I squeeze her hand: nothing. I flick the soles of her feet: nothing. I pinch her shoulder hard, harder: nothing.

"Judy," I say softly now just holding Carrie's cold, blue, tiny limp hand, "Carrie's in a coma." Judy is a neurosurgical ICU nurse by training with years of experience, who knows a hell of a lot more about coma and its evaluation than I do.

"Oh no," she says plaintively.

We both know Carrie's brain is shutting down. All the higher centers, consciousness, movement, response, are in limbo, non-functioning. The primitive, simple centers of the brain, those that regulate heart rate and respiration, the most basic functions needed to sustain life, these centers are beginning to ebb as well. I stare at our tiny baby, my heart breaking. What is going on in that little head, and why? Is this part of an illness, a profound, fatal sickness or infection, or is it a protective response to shield the delicate controlling centers from overwork and damage as her body hunkers down for its final battle?

I cannot stop the tears which roll down my cheeks. I do not bother to brush them away.

WEDNESDAY, NOVEMBER 2, 7:00 A.M.

Nurse's note.

Neuro: occasionally very lethargic, more so at some times, with floppy, flaccid extremities. Now and then makes spontaneous, weak cry.

Resp: weaned to room air by 5:00 P.M., then began having episodes of apnea and bradycardia requiring bag and mask oxygen and controlled ventilation. Color and heart rate improved immediately but once again bagging stopped, condition again worsened. Bagging continued for approximately 20 minutes. Infant then placed on 25% oxygen with CPAP with no subsequent spells this shift.

Carrie is on the brink, teetering. Comatose, cyanotic, apneic, she is nearly dead, being brought back each time her condition deteriorates. Many ICUs, good ones, would not continue with the extraordinarily intensive level of observation and care now required to manage Carrie. Instead, an endotracheal tube would be inserted into her larynx, and the tube attached to an artificial respirator, a ventilator, which would automatically control her breathing.

No nurse would then have to sit next to Carrie, watching every breath and reacting instantly should she stop breathing and turn blue, as she'd been; the machine would do it all. But the machine also did other things, like occasionally blowing holes in the lungs or working even if the tube slipped out of the windpipe. The tube itself, riding up and down on the lacy, delicate lining of the tiny larynx and vocal cords, did damage, often causing permanent scarring requiring multiple dangerous and difficult surgeries to correct.

Thus, the respiratory expertise of the physicians and nurses of this ICU is welcome and fortuitous, especially to someone like myself who knows what could happen. The University of Virginia Hospital Neonatal ICU director had worked and done extensive research in the field of CPAP, so he and his staff were comfortable with it; at other hospitals, unfamiliarity and uncertainty would have led to inserting a tube in Carrie long ago.

WEDNESDAY, NOVEMBER 2, 9:30 A.M.

Radiology report.

Chest/abdomen portable at 0930 hours: both lungs are clear. The heart is normal in size. The abdomen is normal.

Nothing new here. I take a deep breath and try to relax going on to the next notation.

WEDNESDAY, NOVEMBER 2, 11:00 A.M.

Resident's progress note.

Infectious Disease: Positive blood cultures aerobic bottles, both central line and peripheral line growing yeast. Spinal and urine cultures negative. Will begin amphotericin 0.2 mg/kg/day IV over six hours. Plan to increase to 0.4, then 0.5 mg/kg/day, over one week. Repeat cultures in 2–5 days.

Continue other antibiotics (gentamicin, nafcillin,

clindamycin) until few days of non-bacterial growth. Infectious disease will consult and follow.

Possible trouble here. I begin to breath less easily.

WEDNESDAY, NOVEMBER 2, 1:00 P.M.

Pediatric Infectious Disease consult note.

Request: Three week old white female infant S/P NEC, on broad spectrum antibiotic therapy since birth, on hyperal via central line for two weeks, now with blood cultures positive for yeast. Please evaluate and advise therapy.

Patient well-known to Infectious Disease service. Now with blood cultures positive for yeast (presumably Candida). Clinically septic. Cerebrospinal fluid, urine suprapubic tap negative thus far.

Recommend: 1. continue present antibiotic regimen, 2. add amphotericin, begin at 0.2 mg/kg/day, advance to 0.5 mg/kg/day. Repeat cultures in a couple of days. In light of poor venous access and need for long-term parenteral nutrition and antimicrobial would try to clear infection without removing central line. If not cleared with 0.5 mg/kg/day amphotericin, would push to 1.0 mg/kg/day. If this fails would need to discontinue central line. Duration of therapy should be 7–10 days after negative culture. 3. Follow urine culture as you are doing. Consider renal ultrasound if possible although this will likely be of low yield. 4. Ophthalmological exam to look for retinal fungal lesions. Thank you for this interesting consult.

The worst of all possible events has occurred: Candida sepsis. Not only is the disease often fatal, but its nonfatal complications include problems such as blindness, or slow, indolent kidney failure. Not only that but the cure, amphotericin, a.k.a. "amphoterrible," is often worse than the disease.

I watch the frenzy of activity and excitement among Carrie's doctors surrounding the discovery of the positive yeast growth in the blood culture bottles (when a culture result comes back positive, the reaction among the patient's physicians is similar to that felt by shareholders in an oil well drilling operation when a strike is made, or stockholders when a split is announced—pure ecstasy!). Now there is a diagnosis, a reason, a cause for Carrie's sudden deterioration. It presupposes that the cause is treatable; she can be cured. There is no doubt on the part of Carrie's doctors or the infectious disease experts that indeed Carrie is suffering from systemic Candidiasis, and needed amphotericin. I have some doubts though.

Somehow, it seems to me I, her father, am being more objective in evaluating what I see than her own doctors, who want so badly to find a cause, a reason. How can I, an anesthesiologist, totally without experience in this area, even question the diagnosis? Yet when I look at the facts, how can I not?

First, consider how the blood cultures have been obtained. Normally, a valid blood culture is drawn from a carefully scrubbed, prepared area of the body, a fresh vein or artery—never through an existing catheter or line. The reason: The line in place may well have yeast on its tip, and any blood drawn through it thus will pick up the yeast and grow out positive. The incidence of positive yeast cultures of removed central line tips approaches one hundred percent.

In Carrie, finding a fresh vein, especially when she is as dusky as she's been when the cultures have been drawn, is essentially impossible. All her veins have been used up, she is a mass of needlestick holes, and there is no way to get the volume of blood needed for a blood culture except through her IV.

Thus, blood has been drawn back from both her central

line, which has been in place for nearly three weeks and is almost certainly colonized with yeast, and her peripheral IV, which has been in place for several days and is probably also infected. Such blood would almost certainly grow yeast, but does that mean the bloodstream itself is rife with Candida, or just the catheters through which the blood has been drawn? It is a very important consideration, it seems to me, especially considering the nature of the drug which will be used if Candida sepsis is the diagnosis.

Carrie's physicians are no fools—they recognize this possibility too. Thus, they have also obtained urine through a suprapubic tap and cerebrospinal fluid through a spinal tap at the same time—growth in cultures from either of these two locations will cinch the diagnosis. But the urine and cerebrospinal fluid cultures show no growth. This information is disturbing to all. Carrie's doctors want these sites to be positive, because they want to be certain they are treating her in the right way.

Me, I am not at all eager to see positive cultures in her urine and especially in her cerebrospinal fluid—fungal meningitis, invasion of the brain and central nervous system by Candida, is very bad news—a brutal retardation-inducing disease. Judy and I don't want Carrie to be a vegetable. So I guess our interests and desires differ sharply here from Carrie's doctors who just want her to survive.

The second thing about the diagnosis that gnaws at me as the day goes on is everyone's sudden unawareness or lack of concern at the degree of yeast infection Carrie has had for days, both in her mouth, tongue and gums, covered with white exudate, and around her perineum, her vaginal and anal areas are swollen and reddened. In addition, her nurses for days have been noting the reddened, raised area around her central line site. Carrie has yeast everywhere, especially around the central line site, where almost certainly it has infiltrated along the catheter into the central venous system. The question remains, is it just on the catheter, or is it indeed wildly spreading through her whole body?

Yes, Carrie collapsed suddenly yesterday morning, a classic picture of sudden, overwhelming sepsis, but is it Candida? Or is it a bacterial infection, due to ceasing her antibiotic? Or is it something else, something not so easily pointed at, which has brought her so ominously close to death again? Arthur C. Clarke once wrote, "If confronted with the technology of a far-advanced civilization, we would call it magic." Confronted with physical occurrences we don't understand, we as physicians do everything in our power to make them conform to one diagnosis or another. Medicine is a closed universe, in a sense; it allows nothing to lie outside its purview, but yet has no explanations for so many, many things.

The reason I'm worried about giving Carrie amphotericin is that it is so highly toxic, not only to the various organ systems of the body but also to whatever blood vessels it flows through. It cannot be given through one of Carrie's small peripheral veins for long: It will quickly destroy the vein. This could lead to more serious consequences such as gangrene.

Adding the drug onto her already pathetic physical status seems to me to be the last straw, the *coup de grace* of high-tech medicine, a real big-time send off to a little girl.

Maybe she'll have a cardiac arrest, I bitterly think, which everyone will blame on her already shocky septic condition instead of the amphotericin, since no one will ever really know. Then, finally, they'll leave my miserable little person alone.

They know and I know using a central line of larger caliber is preferable. In babies without pre-existing central lines, surgery to insert such a line is performed in order to give the drug. Carrie's problem in this regard is that she now critically needs her central line for hyperal—it is her only nourishment; she is no longer eating, being comatose, and feeding her through a tube is probably unsafe, since she is already having respiratory difficulties which, if she regurgitates or vomits, will be compounded.

I don't reveal any of my fears outwardly, even to Judy. I

don't want her to know how concerned I am at this new turn
of events, because I don't think she'll feel any better knowing
how worried I am. Instead, when we finish our visit that afternoon, I excuse myself and go off to the medical library to
become an authority on systemic childhood Candida infections.

Inside the library I quickly begin my invasion of the cu-
mulative indexes, finding a stack of current texts and articles
which I read and xerox, annotating furiously. This is no research paper, this is my daughter's life!

Several hours later, I emerge for air. Medicine is curi-
ous. You wouldn't think a random subject like Candida infections in infants to be of great interest to many people, yet on
my first look through the *Index Medicus*, the encyclopedic
compendium of the medical literature, twenty-five articles on
the subject show up.

I learn a lot, most of which is depressing. First, Carrie is
a set-up for Candidiasis, whether or not she has it. A review of
the incidence of the disease shows that antibiotic therapy is a
predisposing factor for it. The second most common predisposing factor is prematurity. Central catheterization is the
third factor commonly cited and hyperalimentation is the
fourth. Carrie has every one of these risk factors.

The outlook for infants with such infections is grim. The
treatment often causes problems as grave as the disease, and
treatment is often unsuccessful, with relapse common. I become more and more gloomy as I read on.

Nevertheless, I dutifully trudge over to the Xerox machine and begin copying the most informative articles, making two copies of each, one for myself and one for Carrie's
doctors. Much as they want to, I know they'd have no time to
spend hours in the library stacks as I have, doing the kind of
research necessary to become up to date in the disease; thus,
like most of us, they'd rely on personal experience, what little
they had, and what they'd read in some textbook or other,
already out of date. I want them to have every possible edge.

As I read that afternoon, one name comes up several

times, Dr. Sybil Connelley. She is the author of the chapter on
systemic infant Candida infections in a very authoritative,
yearly updated pediatric therapy text. I note she is on the staff
at Harbor General Hospital, an affiliate of UCLA where I'd
done some of my medical school clinical rotations. An idea
germinates: what if I call her pretending to be one of the
doctors on Carrie's team, and ask her for advice on Carrie?
Who could possibly give better advice? I'd hear the objective
stuff too, not filtered down to soften the blow. I let the idea
percolate as I continue to copy article after article.

Just then George Helpern, one of the other anesthesia
faculty members, walks up to the Xerox machine and sees me.
There is no way I can hide what I am doing. The titles of the
journals and articles scattered about belie any comments I
can make about their anesthesia-related nature, nor can I do
much about the tears in my eyes as I copy as fast as I can.

"Joe," he says looking around obviously taking it all in.
"How's it going?"

"Not that well, George, I'm copying all the articles I can
find for our baby's doctors. It's her latest crisis." I continue
working furiously knowing he probably thinks me a bit mad,
but I don't really care. Nothing else seems to matter. He
doesn't say much, just nods.

The following week, I learn from another member of the
anesthesia department that at church that Sunday, he had
gotten up and asked everyone in his congregation to say a
prayer "for the little Stirt girl." When I hear it tears well up
in my eyes. He doesn't really know me or Judy very well, and
certainly not our daughter, but my pain must have been very
evident that day in the library.

The ironic thing is, Judy and I are essentially faithless
people in a formal sense, not having had much to do with
churches or religion for many years. Now each of us pray for
the baby and ourselves, but we don't know quite how to do it.
A stanza from Auden's "Lullaby" runs through my head when
I try:

> "Lay your sleeping head, my love,
> Human on my faithless arm."

I do not know why, but somehow it seems to comfort me.

I go home, and tell Judy I am thinking of calling Dr. Connelley the specialist at Harbor.

She sighs, "Don't you think that's going a bit far? I'm sure the people here know everything she does."

"Maybe, but probably not. This lady has written a lot about Candida, and I have a feeling she sees more of it at Harbor than they do at Virginia." Even though it's a major teaching hospital, the University of Virginia is small compared to mammoth county-type hospitals in big cities, which have enormous patient populations and censuses, and see relatively large numbers of everything.

Of course, as I prepare for my call, with pen, paper, articles I'd read all arrayed around me, my heart pounds; I fear I won't be able to reach the woman. Her chapter and articles state she is at Harbor, sure, but those are years old. In academic medicine, movement is a given, and she'd almost certainly moved to another hospital, promoted to division chief or something.

If she hadn't moved, I felt sure she'd be on vacation, traveling (almost certainly out of the country), at a meeting, or otherwise unavailable.

Pessimistically I call Harbor, ask for the Division of Infectious Disease, and ask for Dr. Connelley's office. I am transferred to her secretary (surprise!) "Is Dr. Connelley in?" I ask. My heart skips a beat.

"She's out of the office now, on rounds, but I can have her call you back in an hour or so, when she gets back."

"She'll be back this afternoon?"

"Oh, yes, she always comes back after rounds."

"Okay, would you have her call me? My name is Dr. Joe Stirt from the University of Virginia Medical School." I gave her my number and hung up.

It has always struck me how easy it is for a doctor, if he's really serious, to get though to anyone, either by phone or by letter. Very few secretaries will not inform their boss that "Dr. So and So returned your call." Even if they've never heard of Dr. So and So, who knows for what reason he's calling? Syphilis? Gonorrhea? Cancer? That call always gets returned. The same with correspondence. Marked "Personal and Confidential," with a physician's return address, that piece of mail always goes through.

An hour and a half later the phone rings. I can hear the long distance hiss as I pick it up.

"Dr. Stirt?" a woman asks. "This is Sybil Connelley."

"Hi, yes, hi, Dr. Connelley," I reply. "Thanks for calling back so promptly."

"What can I do for you?" she asks in a lilting, sympathetic voice. Opening the floodgates, I begin. I pretend I am an anesthesiology resident doing a rotation in the neonatal ICU, and that Carrie is one of our patients. I give the whole detailed history from day one (she probably thinks "Hey, this guy is really on top of his patients) and she listens quietly, occasionally asking for more details. Finally, I finish and ask her what she thinks and what she'd do. I mentioned in passing that I have called her because her work seems the clearest and most based on experience of all that I've read.

"I think you're doing all the right things," she thoughtfully replies, "But one thing especially bothers me. It's almost unheard of, in fact. I can't remember a case of systemic neonatal Candidiasis with positive blood cultures that didn't also have positive urine cultures. The Candida concentrates itself in the urine and bladder and almost always produces positive urine cultures. Are you sure they're negative?"

"Certain," I say. "I rechecked the results this afternoon. The blood cultures have Candida, the urine bottles have no growth."

"That's unusual," she says sounding puzzled. "Were the blood cultures drawn from fresh sites or through existing lines?" she asks.

"Through existing lines," I reply. "We just couldn't find any other vessels."

"I understand," she says. "That's always a problem. We occasionally do cut-downs to get our cultures if we're really suspicious, just to avoid the situation you're in, but that's no picnic either, as you know. Have you taken out the central line?" she asks.

"No," I say. "The baby has such poor veins and is on hyperal; the surgeons are reluctant to do it." I hear her sigh.

"Well, I would give serious consideration to pulling it out. It's almost certainly colonized with Candida, and God knows what else. You can always start another one on the other side.

"I'd repeat all the cultures, blood, urine, and CFS [cerebrospinal fluid via spinal tap]. Although, if a child has meningitis, it's very unusual to have systemic symptoms prior to meningitis becoming apparent, with seizures or spasticity. Has she had any CNS [central nervous system] signs?"

"None," I reply.

"The other important thing is, have you checked her eyes?"

"No," I say.

"Well, Candida endophthalmitis occasionally occurs in babies with sepsis, and if she has it, you want to know it from the beginning. I'd get an ophthalmologist to dilate her and look at her eyes. Kids with ophthalmitis have fluffy white retinal and vitreous infiltrates, and if they have eye involvement, amphotericin isn't enough. Eye penetration of amphotericin is poor, so you'll want to add flucytosine to her therapy if she does have eye involvement.

"The trouble with that is, flucytosine and amphotericin are a very, very toxic combination. They can cause real severe kidney, liver, and bone damage, so you really have to be on the lookout."

"All in all," I ask, "Do you think this kid has Candida?"

"Well, with negative urine cultures, I'm not convinced. Positive urine cultures almost always accompany

Candidiasis. I'd try more urine cultures. Also, that central line bothers me. Young up at UCLA, who's really an expert, has said that a positive blood culture for Candida doesn't establish the diagnosis of sepsis, especially if the patient has an in-dwelling central venous catheter. He said that if Candidemia is found in a patient on hyperal, it's often sufficient to remove the catheter and observe the patient, especially if there's no other organ involvement. Personally, I'd pull the central line and see what happens."

"If she has Candida, what's the time course for improvement on amphotericin?"

"Well, if you pull the central line and start the amphotericin, you'll never know which was the thing that helped her. On amphotericin, documented Candida sepsis takes about a week to get under control. If she gets appreciably better any sooner, especially if you can't isolate any Candida from her urine, I'd have to say she was never really septic with Candida."

She pauses as if meditating on what she is about to say then she goes on, "You can always stop the amphotericin. The trouble is, it's hard to know if those kids are sick because of the amphotericin or because they're septic and need more amphotericin, or both."

"What about feeding her?" I asked. "She's NPO [nothing by mouth] now. Should she stay that way?"

"If she's got positive bowel sounds, I'd feed her. If she's too weak to eat, put in a feeding tube and feed her that way. These kids need everything they can get in."

"Okay. I'll mention what you've said to the other people on my service," I said. "I really appreciate it. I think it'll help us do a better job on the kid. Can you send me any materials you have that might be useful to us; any references or papers you find worthwhile?"

"Sure, be glad to. Good luck, and let me know how it all turns out, okay? Feel free to call back anytime."

"Will do. Thanks. Bye."

I hang up the phone, elated. I've carried it off! I've finally made a connection which could help Carrie. Someone who really knows about her disease. And according to her, I've not been crazy in my disagreement with what Carrie's doctors are doing. The trick now is, how to convey the essence of my talk with Dr. Connelley to Carrie's doctors without offending them. Good about listening to me as they are, very few physicians take advice well, especially if it disagrees with what they believe. Tact would be crucial in order to even get a fair hearing tomorrow. And tact is rapidly becoming a quality I don't have.

THURSDAY, NOVEMBER 3, 9:00 A.M.

Radiology report.

Clinical data: NEC, Candida sepsis, newborn.
Chest, portable, 0900 hours: The central line has been removed. There are no pulmonary infiltrates and no significant internal change since 10/22.

THURSDAY, NOVEMBER 3, 10:30 A.M.

Nurse's note.

Neuro: When awake: alert, fair-good muscle tone, fair grasp, good suck. Responds appropriately to tactile stimuli. Not much spontaneous movement.
Resp: On CPAP 5 centimeters, 22% oxygen. Chest movement symmetrical. Bilaterally equal, clear breath sounds.

GI: NPO. Abdomen soft, nondistended. #5 oral gastric tube for decompression. Positive bowel sounds.

Skin: pale, warm and dry. Abdominal incision intact, no sign of infection. Genital rash warm to touch.

The next morning, I arrive at the hospital early to arrange a meeting with Carrie's doctors. First I read over their morning notes, then I head downstairs to the lounge armed with my articles and a summary of Dr. Connelley's words.

We all sit down at a round metal table in the corner and I do my best to communicate what I've learned without getting their noses out of joint. They seem to listen attentively, but as I look around the table watching them nod almost in unison I wonder if it is more than cursory politeness to a fellow professional. I swallow hard wanting to rant and rave as Carrie's father. But I'm positive that would get me even less of a hearing than I've gotten now. The opinions of fathers are meaningless here.

Thanking them, I hand out the papers I've so painstakingly gathered and leave.

Later, sitting near Carrie, I sit and ponder how little I can do even though I now feel that Carrie's treatment is not the only, and perhaps not the best, course of action. The average parent would believe everything is being handled absolutely correctly; I know this isn't the case, and that as a result my daughter will be given one of the most toxic medicines known, for at least two more weeks—medicine that could well cripple or kill her. This I find hard to take. But, nevertheless, I take it. I have no choice.

THURSDAY, NOVEMBER 3, 12:00 P.M.

Resident's note.

Feeding/nutrition: Weight up 110 grams. Will decrease amount of hyperal since will only be able to receive for 18 hours (amphotericin for 6 hours).

Resp: on CPAP 5 cm; still with periodic breathing, apnea, and bradycardia, but no prolonged episodes requiring manual ventilation today.

Infectious disease: Day #3 gentamicin/nafcillin/clindamycin— all discontinued today in view of all cultures (blood, urine, CSF) negative for bacteria. Central and peripheral line cultures at 48 hours show Candida; urine and CSF cultures show no growth at 48 hours. Central line removed, tip sent for culture. Receiving 0.4 mg/kg amphotericin today, up to 0.5 mg/kg tomorrow.

Hematology: Platelets 64,000, repeat 96,000. Will follow in view of earlier platelet problem.

Ophthalmology: Dr. Wilson to perform ophthalmological evaluation today.

At least something has come of my research and phone-call. Someone is going to examine Carrie's eyes carefully.

THURSDAY, NOVEMBER 3, 1:00 P.M.

Ophthalmology consultation.

Clinical data: 3 week old with Candida sepsis, history prematurity with oxygen supplementation, rule out Candida endophthalmitis.

Impression: No evidence Candida endophthalmitis; no evidence retrolental fibroplasia.

Good news and bad news. The good is if Carrie recovers, at least her eyes will be able to see. The bad news is that doesn't mean *she* will! Seeing requires a lot of intact brain pathways to produce vision, but at least all the oxygen and respiratory therapy hasn't given her retrolental fibroplasia [RLF], a disastrous accompaniment of oxygen oversupply to the premature baby's retina which causes blindness.

The question of whether Carrie has Candida sepsis still gnaws at me, if no one else, but nonetheless it is great news to find her eyes uninvolved. It really cheers Judy and me up.

However, Carrie herself doesn't cheer us up much. She is still lethargic, obviously very sick. The amphotericin? Who knows, at this point. Anything from now on can be either a result of sepsis or a side effect of the drug. At least the antibiotics have been discontinued. With no evidence of bacterial growth in any culture, there is no need to provide this kind of heavy, multiple drug antibiotic coverage, which can only encourage growth of Candida and resistant bacteria.

It is a funny thing, though. In my opinion getting the positive reports on those two blood cultures on Monday, has obliterated any sense of perspective on Carrie's doctors' part.

So intent and grateful are they for something concrete, something definitive to treat that whether or not there is anything really there or not seems irrelevant to them, at least as I see it. If the blood cultures had not grown Candida, you can bet that Carrie would have remained on all three antibiotics for weeks to come. And even though I have a different opinion, maybe that would have been the right thing to do. That's the problem I wrestle with. There is no such thing as a definitive answer; maybe we should toss a coin. Who knows? Certainly her recovery had collapsed one day after she had been taken off her antibiotics. I sigh heavily. So much of medicine in the end is guesswork, intuition added to emotion, a little "feel" thrown in for good measure, and maybe the phase of the moon taken into account as well.

Anyway, Carrie's central line has come out, though whether through efforts of my own it is hard to know. Certainly, no one has seemed convinced by my articles and tactful mention of my conversation with Dr. Connelley to stop the amphotericin; rather, it is being bumped right up, the dose doubled from yesterday. However, they have listened to my opinion about feeding Carrie. Here I feel on solid ground after all, if her nutritional status has to be compromised by the amphotericin, we should give her as much help as we can.

Hal Davis, the attending, makes what seems to me a valid point as to why he is against starting Carrie on oral feedings right now, even though her bowels are actively working. "Her breathing," he says, "remains irregular, and food and swallowing is very apt to cause even more in the way of breathing difficulties, the two mechanisms being controlled by closely allied areas of the brain. I would hate," he muses, "for her to aspirate, that is, inhale her food into her lungs, which could lead easily to pneumonia, a complication she really doesn't need right now."

This I accept, but what about the presence of the feeding tube which currently goes into her stomach through her mouth, and is being used to keep her decompressed? Couldn't she be fed through this tube? Doesn't the tube itself predispose to breathing irregularities? I recall that Jerry Green-bach, her previous attending physician had told me last month that tube feeding Carrie back then was dangerous until her breathing problems were corrected, for just this reason.

"Yes," he replies, "the tube passing through her mouth and throat doesn't help her breathing certainly, but it does let us keep gas from accumulating in her stomach from the CPAP. The positive airway pressure causes a tendency to swallow and accumulate gas, which we try to remove." This seems reasonable to me. Too reasonable to argue with. Thus, a nice, tidy, circular argument is closed. She can't eat because she isn't breathing right, and when she is, she can eat. Of course, maybe she is too weak and malnourished to breathe, but that's the way it goes.

So poor are Carrie's peripheral veins that as a last resort, they have to try to scalp veins now that the central line has been removed. In order to do it they'd fastened to her head a protective shield out of a small upside-down Dixie cup with the bottom cut out so they could see what was going on at the IV site. Most of the other preemies have them too. It looks hilarious, in a bizarre way, the array of tiny premature babies in this nursery all wearing upside down Dixie cups on their heads. It looks like a party with a lot of guests from another planet.

Then out comes the razor again, to begin the systematic head shaving that hallmarks the ICU baby. Carrie's hair, so pretty and dark at birth, had been shaved off when her NEC struck.

And Carrie's hair has just started to come back in spots, a dark fuzz, when the shaving begins again. Me, I am for taking it all off at once, stop the fooling around trying to save some hair here or there. She looks like a ragamuffin, a tuft sticking out the side, another on the top. "Take it all off," I say to the nurses.

They look at me as if I am joking, which I am not, but I do have a stupid grin on my face so I guess they think I am.

Lately I've noticed I often have a grin on my face, and
chuckle at inane things even though I am basically miserable
and depressed about this whole damn thing.

And never am I more unhappy than when I watch the
shaving of poor Carrie's fuzz off. I think once again of taking
a picture or two of her just as a sort of a reminder of how it
was for when she recovers. The problem is I doubt she will.
And then such a reminder will just be another sign of our past
agony. There is no sign of a happy ending here. The chronicle
of disasters just go on and on.

I remember when my friend Dick told me as Carrie was
recovering from her NEC and her operation that there'd be
three more serious problems before she left the hospital.

"Three more?" I'd said at the time. "I can't take any
more!"

"Well, you better get used to the idea. She's gonna have
three more crises," he'd answered.

Our remarks ring in my ears.

"How do you know? Why three?" I'd asked. "It makes
no sense."

"I just know, Joe. That's just the way it always is. Carrie
will have three more setbacks before she's well."

"You mean you think she's going to get well?"

"Absolutely. No doubt in my mind. But it won't just be
some smooth recovery from point A to point B. No way.
She'll make three detours. That's just the way it is."

Dick was intuitive, with as good a "feel" and judgment
as any physician I've ever known. It's a gift, which he'd been
born with. Plenty of doctors were as smart or smarter than he
was, but few could match his instinctive ability to make the
right decision time after time. A magical man. Little did I
know how prescient he was to be, as Carrie reeled from the
effects of her "Candida" sepsis and amphotericin therapy, the
first two of her crises. I winced, thinking if Dick was right
there'd be one more. At the time I'd thought I couldn't take it.
Now I hoped that was all I'd have to take.

I stand at Carrie's bedside holding the one foot of her

four extremities that is free of wires, tubes and tape. Her foot is cold and dry, very pale, and shaped just like Judy's, down to the broad, flat forefoot and olive-shaped big toe that Judy had been mercilessly teased about growing up in Jamaica. "Yamfoot" had been her nickname, and she'd always blamed it on bad shoes. Not likely, I think looking at Carrie's feet, wondering if she'd ever get the chance to try them out. The thought that she might not is agony. I bend down to kiss her little toes and feel one of my own hot tears fall upon it.

FRIDAY, NOVEMBER 4, 10:30 A.M.

Nurse's note.

Caroline had three episodes of apnea and bradycardia last night, each requiring bag and mask ventilation. During each episode head was unaligned with torso. Absence of apnea and bradycardia noted with towel role under neck to maintain accurate airway position. Tolerating room air with satisfactory blood gases.

   Infant needs continued close observation of respiratory status, as well as maintenance of perfect airway positioning with aid of neck role.

This note reflects so sophisticated a level of care as to make me marvel. The nurse, realizing that Carrie's windpipe, or trachea, was bent due to her head position each time she stopped breathing, solved the problem: she simply braced Carrie's neck with a small rolled up towel, such that Carrie's windpipe remains perfectly straight. The diameter of Carrie's trachea is approximately 3 millimeters, or 1/8 of an inch. Also, unlike an adult's windpipe, which is relatively stiff like bamboo, a baby's is soft and flexible, like India rubber. Any tension or bend on it makes it flex and kink, and the lumen is so tiny it can be easily pinched off. Somehow the nurse either knew all this or sensed it and stopped another crisis from occurring.

The level of nursing sophistication and observation going on in the ICU is making the difference for Carrie, keeping her alive when she is barely able to keep going. Whether that is to her advantage isn't certain.

On my way out of the ICU that morning I see Dick making his way in. In his diffident, quiet manner, he is keeping close tabs on Carrie, even though she isn't his patient, nor are we that close. Studying him I think he is a kindred spirit in many ways, although on the surface he seems totally the opposite.

Raised in a close, religious Minnesota home, family ties binding so strongly he might never shake free of them, he represented a different way of life from my upbringing as a several times institutionalized, troublemaking and troubled child who'd had only himself to look out for. I had never gone in for people telling me what to do, and now, frozen in this hospital limbo, at the mercy of a system I am part of but now have no control over, I am constantly enraged.

"She looks dreadful," I say. "Still not breathing right and her color's terrible. She looks dehydrated and she's comatose again, going back downhill. I'd take her off everything and see what happens."

"No, you don't want to do that," Dick objects. "She's sick, but she's got a chance."

"What chance? I can't believe her brain is still intact after all this shit, and who knows what else is wrong? If it were up to me I'd take her home and so would Judy. If she dies, so be it. I just can't stand the idea of continuing to flog her. She's a piece of meat, man, dead meat!"

"I disagree. I wouldn't let you take her out of here," Dick says adamantly.

"How could you stop me?" I ask. "I am not serious, but

if I was, if you know what I mean." If we could have just signed a form that said I'm aware of the risks and dangers of prematurely leaving the hospital, etc., etc., we'd have gone AMA. It was just too much, and both Judy and I had had it. The trouble was, no one else felt our pain the way we did, and no one else would have to live with what was left of Carrie, so it was easy for them to say, "Oh, no, you can't leave the hospital."

"I'd get a court order." Dick looks at me, his face troubled, "If I had to."

I turn away thinking. This man seemed to be my friend. I frown while troubled thoughts crowd my mind. Joe, you don't have any friends. The only person you can count on is Judy. If nothing else, this whole episode is teaching us just how life boils down to basic survival when all the politeness and manners are shucked off. Things haven't changed a bit as I see the world: no one gives a shit the way you do, and you are fooling yourself if you think any differently.

"You really would, wouldn't you?" I ask him, more in wonder than in anger.

He nods.

"You know," I say not caring any more about the impression my words make, "if Judy ever gets pregnant again, we're going to go to Canada for the delivery. At least there I think we'd have some say in the care of our child, if she is really a mess. I can't believe how everyone else but us decides what will be done to our child here."

"I don't think it's that different in Canada," says Dick.

"Well, then we'll go to Jamaica. Judy is a dual citizen of both Canada and Jamaica, and could live in either country. In Jamaica babies like Carrie don't last long, because there is no ICU anywhere on the island even remotely approaching the level of care she is getting here. Babies with NEC die, and die quickly. Survival of the fittest means just that, and the number of crippled, brain-damaged children who make it out of the hospital is a fraction of that here in the United States. The country can't possibly care for such children: Who would do it, and who would pay for it?

"I've chided Judy for years about the backwardness of Jamaica and how lucky we were not to have a baby being born there, under such primitive conditions. Now I see there is another side to this heartbreaking issue, and that thousands of families in Jamaica every year avoid the pain and terror we're enduring having a critically ill baby who is subjected to every procedure a hospital can think of and doesn't get any better, just hangs on—one continuing nightmare that doesn't end once you awake in the morning."

Dick watches me apprehensively, "Joe you're pretty much on the ragged edge," he speaks quietly.

"Damn right I am. Who wouldn't be." I spit out the words.

"You have to try to get hold of yourself for the baby's sake," he says.

"That sounds very sensible," I answer. "I used to sound that way too. It's easy to talk sensibly when it's not your child who is being tortured or your heart that is being broken."

Dick bites his lip. "I'll stop in again to see her."

"You do that," I answer bitterly. "See what you're all doing to her." I walk quickly away and decide I can't take anymore that day. I go home.

SATURDAY, NOVEMBER 5, 8:00 A.M.

Nurse's note.

Neuro: Good muscle tone, good suck, grasp and cry. Awake and alert.

Resp: Spontaneous, unlabored breathing, no apnea or bradycardia past two shifts.

> Skin: Warm, dry, pale pink/jaundiced. Left leg reddened, swollen.

When I return the next morning and see this note I rush in to see Carrie and am amazed. She is suddenly better. She is out of her coma, looking around and moving vigorously. She's had three days of amphotericin, not enough to clear a Candida sepsis, so perhaps she hasn't been septic after all, and just taking out the central catheter seems to have done the trick. The trouble is her doctors are now irrevocably committed to continuing the amphotericin. Their opinion is she's been septic, she is getting better, so keep on with the therapy. Don't stop when things start going your way, just keep up whatever you're doing. In Carrie's case, this means another week or two of amphotericin, which could become toxic at any time.

I disagree with her doctor's diagnosis and feel the treatment they've imposed could be potentially worse than the disease. Which one of us is right? Of course, I think I am. But I am only one person. How the hell can I be sure? Anyway there are more of them. They have the authority to do whatever they damn please. They are writing in the chart and I'm not, so I shut up. There is no point in grousing over what is obviously a *fait accompli* and completely alienating myself from Carrie's doctors. I button up my mouth. A hard thing to do. Especially since I know how arbitrary much of her care and, indeed anyone's, is dependent on mood and the individual physician's bent: I tell myself I'll subtly persuade them later. Am I deluding myself, rationalizing away the fact that I think they are taking a frightful chance, maybe killing or crippling my child, and that I can do nothing about it but watch? Probably, but delusions are all I have.

Despite her good news about Carrie, the nurse has noted Carrie is jaundiced, an observation not repeated until later that night by another nurse. Not until the next day, the 6th,

will Carrie's doctors act on this new information and take
blood tests for liver function. The nurse also notes, again an
observation not to be repeated by any of the doctors, that
Carrie's left leg is reddened and swollen around the site of
her IV infusion, through which the amphotericin runs.

Gently I examine Carrie. That afternoon the nurses have
removed the catheter, replacing it with one in the front of her
left elbow, a dangerous site since if it "blew," the catheter
could easily move into the nerve sheath running directly adjacent to the vein, and cause extensive damage to the nerves
running to the arm and hand. Also, the arm has to be kept
perfectly stiff and straight so that the catheter doesn't puncture the vein when the arm bends. There is so much "potential" space in the front of the arm that fluid could run there
for hours before being noticed.

I sit at her side and watch. Carrie's leg gets worse and
worse throughout the day. It continues to swell, and the redness moves up above the knee. "Great," I mumble, now she
can slough her foot and leg, and we can spend the months
after she recovers from whatever she's got now coming back
to the hospital for plastic surgery to repair the loss of skin,
nerve, muscle, and blood vessels in her leg before they ampu-
tate it.

It has taken three days to get into the first serious
amphotericin complication. Because it almost certainly is the
amphotericin, a highly toxic, potentially tissue-destructive
drug, with, as the Physician's Desk Reference warning states,
commonly observed ". . . local venous pain at the injection
site with phlebitis and thrombophlebitis. Extravasation may
cause chemical irritation."

"Now," you might say, "he tends to exaggerate, no one
has that serious a reaction to a drug; it goes away." You
wouldn't be alone saying so either, because most physicians
who should know better say the same thing. But what is particularly dangerous in medicine, even more so than in life in
general, is confusing what you wish for with what you know,
and believing the wish is the reality. Most of the time, drug

reactions are minor, and resolve with only a trace. But every so often, they don't.

Then there are horrendous complications. These are the ones we see in the operating room, weeks after the patient has recovered from whatever it is he'd needed the toxic drug for. We don't just see them once, either, but over and over again, as a painstaking, multistage series of operations is required to first, remove the rotten, infected tissue from the site, as well as a margin of healthy tissue to ensure healing, and then take bone, muscle, fat, and skin grafts as needed from other unaffected areas of the body to cover the defect. Sometimes the procedures work as well as they can be expected to, and other times amputation has to be performed, if the blood supply to the affected hand or foot is irrevocably compromised. Either way, to my way of thinking, it is a tragedy, an error in treatment at some point which has allowed a drug to flow where it shouldn't for too long.

Thus, I am especially sensitized to what is happening to Carrie's swollen left leg, puffy and edematous as it is. I've seen the dreadful possibilities which, if not personally witnessed, simply couldn't be imagined. I know, though I wish I didn't, that she is in a minefield, disguised as an ICU, of potential complications and is dodging bullets from a fierce crossfire as well.

The nurses keep applying hot, wet compresses to Carrie's leg throughout the day, trying to increase the circulation and carry away as much of the amphotericin as possible. To her physicians, this is a problem not even worth remarking on, as they keep their vision fixed on a more distant goal: recovery from Candida sepsis. The rest could take care of itself. I suppose this is a reasonable point of view from their perspective; after all, they don't have twenty-four hours a day to think about one patient, nor do they care the way I do. They go home and forget Carrie's troubles every afternoon, while I go home taking her problems with me until I get to sleep and then I awake at night with fears and thoughts I quickly write down on a bedside tablet.

SATURDAY, NOVEMBER 5, 3:00 P.M.

Resident's note.

    Feeding/nutrition: Weight down 20 grams, K 5.6 (heelstick), creatinine 0.6, BUN 17.

    Respiratory: Stable arterial gases, decreased apnea and bradycardia, less periodic breathing.

    Candida sepsis: All cultures remain negative except those from IV (positive for Candida). Urine, CSF negative, follow-up blood cultures performed last night. Day #5 amphotericin, 0.5 mg/kg/day.

    Hematology: Hematocrit 35, platelets 129,000.

    Plan: Will resume oral feeding if periodic breathing much decreased.

So, Carrie is holding her own, even improving. Maybe Dr. Connelley's advice to feed the baby and my advocacy of her advice has filtered down into the general team consciousness, because it seems like they'll soon let her start eating again. Lost in the whole mass of complications and problems, it seems to me, is the fact that here is a still tiny four and one-half pound premature baby, who by all rights should still have two more weeks in the womb, and whose ninth month of gestation normally would have been a period of explosive physical and brain growth, weight usually doubling in utero during the ninth month.

Instead, she weighs just what she did at birth, having gained no weight during a critical period when even a premature baby would normally be eating voraciously, trying to fuel the growth that had been denied by early birth. What damage is being done, I wonder, to the vital, delicate centers in her brain as she exists week after week on a regimen of sugar water, electrolyte fluids, antibiotics, and artificial amino acid supplements? Can she ever recover the lost ground?

My only hope is that somehow her developing higher brain centers are "shut down" while she is sick, simply delaying their development, until such time, if ever, as her body as a whole perceives itself to be once again a functioning unit. Perhaps then normal development will resume.

It seems to me that if Carrie's brain and central nervous system attempt to form under their present circumstances, they will be hopelessly, irretrievably damaged, a mass of half-formed, ill-conceived tissue with sharply limited functions and potential. But the thing is, you never know. As one of the interns in the film, *Young Doctors in Love* said on rounds after a debate about the nature of a patient's illness, "We won't know until the autopsy." With Carrie I am afraid we won't know what is left until it is too late to do anything but live with it.

SUNDAY, NOVEMBER 6, 8:00 A.M.

Nurse's note.

Neuro: Awake, crying, very active. Very strong suck, grasp, good muscle tone.

Resp. Continues on room air. Bilaterally equal breath sounds, symmetrical chest expansion, good, deep respiratory motion. No apnea or bradycardia, no periodic breathing.

My dark thoughts are instantaneously washed away by one sudden burst of light. Carrie is coming back. At 12:00 noon she received her first oral feeding (of electrolyte solution) since November 1st, and after that she started receiving half-strength breast milk from a bottle every three hours. Funny, she is exactly where she'd been six days ago, receiving exactly the same feedings on the same schedule, except now she is on amphotericin and we are all a week older, although I figure this last week has been worth at least, oh, twenty years on my internal aging system.

MONDAY, NOVEMBER 7, 12:00 P.M.

Resident's note.

Weight continues down slightly, but feeding well, half strength breast milk every three hours. Will change to full strength slowly, advancing as tolerated.

Respiratory: Second day stable on room air, without apnea or bradycardia.

Infectious disease: All cultures continue negative except blood cultures November 1, positive for Candida. Catheter tip from central line positive for Candida. Amphotericin 0.5 mg/kg/day continues, doing well. Plan to go on 7–10 days beyond first negative blood culture.

Hematology: Hematocrit 36, platelets 374,000, bilirubin 7.3. Plan: check liver enzymes, may move away from hyperal soon.

MONDAY, NOVEMBER 7, 2:00 *P.M.*

Nurse's note.

Moved to full strength breast milk, 15 ml every three hours. Tolerating well, and is vigorous feeder.
   Appears jaundiced, eyes yellow.

MONDAY, NOVEMBER 7, 4:00 *P.M.*

Radiology report.

   Clinical data: Four weeks old, status/post NEC, status/post Candida sepsis, with lethargy.
   Head sonogram: The ventricles are normal in size. There is no evidence of intracranial hemorrhage.
   Impression: Normal head sonogram.

MONDAY, NOVEMBER 7, 6:00 *P.M.*

Nurse's transfusion note.

Thirty ml packed red blood cells given over three hours. No apparent reaction.

Blood is still being drawn several times a day, every day, and the well is running dry. So, Carrie is given another blood transfusion. One more exposure to possible hepatitis, AIDS, and whatever else blood carries, as well as the risk of an immediate transfusion reaction.

Carrie's jaundice is now very evident, as her level of bilirubin, the liver product responsible for causing the yellow color, had risen to 7.3, six times the upper limit of normal. She is acting fine, eating, getting stronger, but when you look at her, you think your eyes have gone bad, or you've had a mild stroke. Her skin has a greenish-yellow tinge, and her eyes are bright yellow.

Will it ever end? I wonder. One thing after another. On the surface (no pun intended) jaundice isn't a problem, at least not until the bilirubin level is in the teens, when it begins to deposit in the brain and cause permanent brain damage. At the level it is in Carrie, though, it is still a bad sign, an indicator that somewhere, somehow, something in her body has gone wrong, once again.

For her doctors, it is a wonderful problem as opposed to her sudden collapse a week earlier and the frantic search for a cause for the apparent sepsis. First of all, it isn't acute so there is time to talk about the possible causes without rushing into anything. Also, chances are it will not suddenly become an acute problem. The bilirubin has increased in an almost indolent, unnoticed fashion for a week, no one even bothering to check it until yesterday, when Carrie was obviously lemon-yellow.

Second, there are a number of eminently plausible reasons that explain very reasonably why Carrie has jaundice. The amphotericin is one likely cause—abnormal liver function tests are one of the hazards of amphotericin therapy, and the detailed drug information sheet stated "therapy should be discontinued if liver function test results (bilirubin) are abnormal." Acute liver failure is also associated with amphotericin.

Hyperalimentation is another likely cause for Carrie's

jaundice, which in fact is now being termed hepatitis, since the first of the additional liver function test results has come back grossly abnormal.

That isn't all: The repeated blood transfusions have given Carrie's immature liver a huge load of red blood cell breakdown products, primarily hemoglobin, and this has broken down to bilirubin as well. For some reason, Carrie's liver is failing.

Now hard decisions need to be made: stop the amphotericin? A lot has been invested in the diagnosis of Candida sepsis, a lot of ego and self, the positive Candida growth from the culture of the central line catheter tip was even more evidence of Candida sepsis, viewed in the terms Carrie's doctors look at the problem. To me, the tip culture growth indicates even more strongly that her problem simply has been an infected central line, and removing it has solved her problem. The amphotericin is just window dressing that has so far caused a toxic local reaction in her foot and is now a likely cause for Carrie getting a potentially overwhelming, life-threatening problem.

No one ever recovers from acute liver failure. Don't let any doctor or specialist or surgeon tell you about all the therapies that are available. It's an ugly, disgusting death, the patient becomes delirious and disoriented, and as the end approaches, shunted into a side room at the end of an unused hallway.

"Who's fooling whom?" I used to wonder as an intern or medical student helping take care of such a patient. They were always on a myriad of drugs at the end, drugs to support the blood pressure, regulate heartbeat, bind the liver toxins, lessen the inflammatory reactions to the poisons their bodies spewed forth. Countless IVs, catheters and monitoring devices surround them, the forest of high-tech medicine, when everyone concerned knew they were goners.

Why doesn't someone discontinue all the drips and lines, give the patients as much morphine as they need, and just let the family sit quietly at the bedside with them, instead of whipping the family into a frenzy of hope, willing to sign and try anything because, "It can't hurt, and it might help."

Again there are no answers. I push these idle thoughts away and begin to dwell on Carrie problems again. That there is bacteria on the catheter tip is no surprise. Obviously, if you draw blood through a catheter and the blood culture is positive, everything it touched would like be positive also. Especially if the catheter is the source of the cultured organism. The whole circular argument just reinforces itself no matter how you looked at it—their way or mine. And because it does, it becomes easier to see why there is very little that is absolutely right or wrong in medicine. Someone somewhere is doing something that seems bizarre, even malpractice, and yet it's perfectly reasonable and internally consistent looked at it another way. I think I am beginning to hate the whole thing. And no wonder. Look how it is inflicting torture on my child.

The head ultrasound exam is the second one Carrie has had, the first coming when she was eight days old—three days after her bowel resection. This one has been ordered for the same reason as the other. Basically, trying to evaluate a comatose premature baby always gives rise to the question, "Was there anything that happened upstairs?" Thus a head ultrasound is ordered. Carrie is too sick to move down to the CAT scan room on another floor, and besides trying to keep tiny babies like Carrie still enough for a CAT scan means anesthetizing them. The ultrasound is a poor man's CAT scan that can often detect evidence of intracranial hemorrhage, a frequent accompaniment of critical illness in premature babies. So fragile are their blood vessels that bleeding can occur from almost any cause.

We get the results; Judy and I breathe a sign of relief. There is no visible or obvious evidence of bleeding into Carrie's brain. She looks alright clinically. Of course, we both know that often intracranial hemorrhage doesn't manifest itself right away, the first signs appearing years later when you think your baby is a survivor, an escapee from the ravages of

ICU complications. Only then do the seizures begin, the first subtle signs of developmental delay and mental retardation appear, and your heart breaks all over again.

As the night wears on, Carrie is advanced to full-strength breast milk, 15 milliliters every three hours. Two-thirds of her fluid intake is still IV, the hyperal and electrolyte solutions. The amphotericin continues. More liver enzyme tests are ordered. More bad news. Things are status quo for now, but something will have to be done. Carrie is looking stronger every day but she is yellow. On the other hand, her bowel, what is left of it, seems to be working well. One saving grace about bowel surgery in babies is that their intestines seem to have the ability to regenerate, like a salamander's tail. Thus, although Carrie has had about sixteen inches of her intestine removed, out of the total of perhaps eighty inches (although this average length varies tremendously between babies), chances are she will regrow bowel to replace the lost length, provided she doesn't continue to get complication after complication, as she seems to be doing.

Judy is pumping her breasts frantically now, because Carrie is starting to make inroads in the supply of frozen milk we've built up. It had seemed endless, the stack of frozen cups in the refrigerator piling up and cascading out every time we opened the door, but if Carrie is to get all her nutrition from milk, she'll need plenty, forty-five milliliters or so every three hours (an ounce is thirty milliliters). That means twelve ounces a day, nearly a pint! Considering the milk still just dribbles out, though Judy pumps and pumps that is a lot of dribbles. Judy's nipples are sore and cracked, in spite of all the salves and creams she's tried, but she presses on. She daydreams outloud that perhaps the baby actually sucking her breast, at long last, will open up the floodgates. After all, it has only been a month on the calendar since Carrie was born. Though it is the longest month we've ever lived through.

TUESDAY, NOVEMBER 8, 11:00 A.M.

Laboratory report.

Liver enzymes: Alkaline phosphatase 331 (normal 20–95); LDH 894 (normal 100–350).

TUESDAY, NOVEMBER 8, 1:00 P.M.

Nurse's note.

IV's infiltrated on each of past two shifts; sites changed. Left foot appears less red and swollen.

TUESDAY, NOVEMBER 8, 3:00 P.M.

Resident's note.

Feeding/electrolytes/nutrition: Weight up 50 grams; feeds increased to 24 ml breast milk every 3 hours; may start breast feeding and take rest from bottle. Plan to move to full oral feedings over next two days.

Infectious Disease: White cell count now 35,000, steady rise from 13,100 on November 1 to 18,100, 26,400, 31,300 over past week. Child appears clinically well; possibly leukocytosis secondary to amphotericin. Amphotericin now day #8, 0.5 mg/kg/day; all cultures but initial remain negative. Will repeat bladder tap today.

Hematology: Hematocrit 37, platelets 486,000; bilirubin up to 8.5 today, alk phos 331, LDH 894; possible hyperal related, thus will try to discontinue hyperal today, provided child tolerates p.o. feedings well. Will send blood for hepatitis B and S antigens to try and pinpoint cause of hepatitis.

Carrie's liver function continues to deteriorate. She is more yellow, and all of her numbers are heading up instead of down. Now is a crucial transition. If she can tolerate oral feedings and absorb them, the hyperal, a likely cause of her hepatitis, can be stopped and she'll still get the nutrition she so desperately needs. If her damaged bowel hasn't healed or she hasn't enough bowel left, anything can happen. It might rupture or she might simply pour out everything she ate into her ostomy bag. If this sad occurrence happens it is the beginning of Carrie being a "bowel cripple" who'll never be normal, but will require a bag and IV hyperal her entire life. And make no mistake, it will be a tortured one punctuated by infections, frequent re-operations, lack of growth, and pain, constant, never ending pain.

If Carrie can eat, absorb, and gain weight, on the other hand, she may yet make it out of the hospital intact. She looks strong and alert, and apart from her yellow tinge, better than she's ever been.

However, there is another case where looks can be deceiving, and no one knows it better than Judy and I; so we are glad that the hyperal is being stopped too: Carrie is running out of veins. With the amphotericin and the hyperal chewing away at her blood vessels, she is being eaten up; every shift a new IV has to be started because the last one had just "blown."

Carrie's white cell count is very high now, more than three times normal, probably a sign of amphotericin toxicity.

Since she is doing so well clinically it is unlikely she is still (if she ever was) septic. Doubt about whether or not she should even be on the amphotericin still lurks among Carrie's doctors; so they inflict another possibly necessary, possibly not, suprapubic bladder tap for urine to culture to look for Candida.

It is to us bitterly ironic that everything that remains wrong with Carrie is caused by her treatment rather than her disease. The liver failure, jaundice, and hepatitis are probably due to hyperal, possibly to blood transfusion (hence the tests for hepatitis antigens, markers of transfusion-associated hepatitis), or amphotericin toxicity. The elevated white cell count is probably a result of amphotericin. Carrie is a living testimonial to modern ICU medicine, in which the cures are often as bad as the disease.

At 9:00 A.M. Judy and I come in to feed Carrie, her first attempt ever at breast-feeding. We are both excited by the fact she's gotten to this point, but also frightened.

We watch as Sally, the morning nurse disconnects Carrie from her electrocardiogram electrodes, then carefully removes her from her isolette and carries her to the scale. I wheel the IV pole holding the hyperal bottle right behind her. Then the four of us, Judy, I, Carrie, and the nurse, clumsily make our way out of Carrie's ICU alcove to a little storage room across the hallway that has the only private space in the ICU. As we walk the IV pole wheels lock ground. The pole tips and sways precariously. With each step Judy and I panic more, afraid our whole caravan will crash to the ground, baby and all.

Then we stop, everyone waits at the door while I shove chairs, tables, old ventilators, and broken equipment out of the way, and drag two rocking chairs out of the ICU proper into the little clearing in the center of the room, which is lit like a skyscraper by eight banks of harsh white fluorescent light highlighting the green paint peeling off the walls.

In this miserable atmosphere, so different from our romantic illusions of what Judy breast-feeding our baby would be like, Judy sits down in one chair and takes Carrie, while I move the IV pole close to her. Then the nurse calls out, "Okay, now you're all set. Call me if you need any help," and leaves. I sit down next to Judy and we cast a long desperate look at each other. Judy's face wrinkles up like she is going to cry.

She unbuttons her blouse and puts Carrie to her nipple. Carrie not understanding the urgency we feel just turns her head and looks quizzically at us. Obviously it will take a while for her to learn how to breast-feed, especially since she's been getting used to a bottle. But to us it seems urgent that she eat now. It is a precious and tenuous moment where she has finally arrived at a point she can feed. A moment, we thought many times, we would not see. A little taste of what it's like to have a baby. Even though it is our greatest fear that it will soon end and she will become critically ill once again. The hospital's patient instead of our daughter.

Agitated, Judy presses Carrie to her breast and almost gags her. "Honey take it easy now," I plead.

Judy sighs and puts Carrie down again. Then she tries again and Carrie just lies there. Judy pushes her nipple into Carrie's mouth, and Carrie begins to choke. "Honey wait," I say and I bend down to suck the other breast, trying to show Carrie how it is done. Sweet milk pours into my mouth! I lick my lips to indicate to Carrie it's not bad stuff. Carrie looks at me, expressionless.

Judy begins to giggle, "Hey, stop that. What if somebody comes in?"

"They'll leave in a hurry," I say and begin to bend down again.

"Don't," Judy says, serious now.

I jump up and go to the door which has a deadbolt lock on the inside and lock it.

"Don't, Joe. Unlock the door. People will think something funny's going on in here," Judy insists.

"They'd be right," I answer grinning.

"Unlock that door right now, Joe," Judy orders.

I do meekly. I think though, what the hell. Why shouldn't we have a semblance of privacy amidst this shambles? Who cares what anybody thinks?

My initiative is gone though. We sit there wordlessly for about twenty minutes, Carrie, mostly looking at us, probably wondering what the hell is going on. After all, this is the first time she's ever felt Judy's skin against hers. Looking at them, my two girls, I smile. Stark as the conditions are, at last we are alone, the three of us. I daydream of what might have been had none of this happened.

After a while we get up and make our way back to Carrie's room rejoining the real world. Suddenly the thought comes to me, "What if we just take her home now?" I say to Judy. "We could bottle feed her if she didn't like breastfeeding, she'd be fine. No more hyperal, no more IVs, no more amphotericin, no more needle sticks. We'd have to change her ostomy bag, but you could do that with no problem." Judy doesn't look convinced. But I press on. "We'd keep her at home until it's time for her next operation to connect her intestine, and things will be great."

Judy interrupts, "Unless she has diarrhea, and won't eat, and becomes septic and comatose again." Miserable, I nod. So we don't do it.

All hope of Carrie's coming home between operations has been abandoned. It is obvious she's not going to be free of complications and problems, at least not in the foreseeable future. We'll just have to ride it out to the bitter end in the hospital. At this point, the end seems invisible. I just can't imagine ever getting through it all.

Everything is such an effort. Now as we watch apprehensively the nurse weighs Carrie after she's finished feeding. Her weight is unchanged. She's taken in nothing according to the scale. Judy sighs heavily and picks up a bottle. She feeds Carrie with it. The two of us are quiet. Judy doesn't like people to see how she feels but I see the tears in her eyes. The pressure is overwhelming to feed her daughter herself. True, it is self-induced pressure, but guilt has a way of doing that, and I suspect, of making it awfully hard to produce milk.

"It's all new to Carrie," I say, and Judy, her lips pressed together, tries to hold back the tears. I put my arm around her and we sit there facing the wall, lost in our private sorrows. I ask myself, how is all this affecting our relationship?

It is the sort of thing that could do anything to a marriage, I suspect. Probably some people grow closer, their relationship strengthened by the shared adversity, while others just grow to dislike and then hate each other, seeing their comfortable, predictable existence shattered by an unforeseen force, this immense rupture of the fabric of everyday life, the contrast to what they thought having a child would be.

For us, it is a strange time. I feel closer to Judy in that she is the only friend I have, and the only person who can really help get me through the agony. Even my best friends haven't had this child and don't feel it is part of themselves being constantly threatened.

On the sexual side though, it is a disaster. I have a hard time getting an erection knowing Carrie is lying there in the ICU—it seems sometimes as if she is right there beside us in bed. We'll be necking, and all of a sudden my thoughts turn to Carrie. All the excitement fades. The kissing and fondling stops, and we just lie there inert. On the rare occasions something doesn't happen to me, Judy sort of loses interest halfway through our love making.

I'll be going down on her, and we begin moving together almost in unison. Then suddenly her hips sort of slow down, and her legs fall apart. Or she'll be giving me head and I lose my erection, or we sort of just stop in the middle of fucking and lie there, holding hands. Unable or not wanting to continue, it keeps happening. We don't talk about it, but as the weeks pass by we have sex less and less often. Instead, we go to bed holding each other tightly for comfort and leave it at that. I have no desire for anyone else. In fact, I don't have much desire for anything. As long as Carrie is sick, we're depressed and sex doesn't seem that important. It is just one more thing to shrug our shoulders about.

At 6:00 we come back to the hospital and Judy once again attempts to breast-feed Carrie. A bit more success. This time Carrie weighs twenty grams more after feeding, which means she's taken twenty milliliters of milk (one gram weighs one milliliter). A funny thought strikes me as we both intently watch the scale. What if Carrie weighs less after feeding? Not as foolish as it might seem, since how she is weighed is so arbitrary anyhow. She has so much equipment attached to her that is or isn't included in the weighing, who can remember how it was last done? In fact, a couple of times Carrie does weigh less after feeding, but this is quickly discounted, as if the nurses want to keep us safe from such a mind-poisoning occurrence.

WEDNESDAY, NOVEMBER 9, 7:00 A.M.

Nurse's note.

Objective: Caroline is still taking P.O. feeds well. She is up to 25 ml breast milk every three hours and tolerates them well. She breast fed this afternoon with mom and did fairly well. She took 20 ml via breast and was supplemented with the rest to equal 25 ml. She takes the bottle feeds in about 5–10 minutes and burps well afterwards. Her abdomen is soft and not distended. She has active bowel sounds. Her ostomy site is pink and draining liquid yellow stool. Her mucous fistula and incision site are pink and left open to air. Caroline's weight is steadily increasing and at present is at 2080 grams. Receiving hyperal (last day) at 5.7 ml/hour, total fluids = 14 ml/hour.

Assessment: Tolerating P.O. feeds well with steady weight gain.

Plan: Increase feeds as tolerated, encourage mom to breast-feed as much as possible. Accurate I & O (intake and output),

guaiac and clinitest ostomy stool [test for blood and sugar], monitor GI status frequently, notify house officer if any changes.

Finally Carrie is chugging along, gaining weight in spite
of everything else. Even though the hyperal is not considered
the cause of her hepatitis, it is being continued for the rest of
the day anyway. No one wants to seem too hasty, after all.
This is like getting a flat tire on the way to work and deciding,
"Oh well, I guess I'll just drive on it the rest of the day and
change it tomorrow morning." Hard to believe, but it happens all the time in medicine.

Carrie's stools, such as they are, are constantly tested for
blood and sugar, the blood to indicate possible bleeding into
her gut, heralding a recurrence of NEC, the presence or absence of sugar indicating how well Carrie's remaining gut is
digesting its food. If sugar content in her ostomy drainage is
high, she isn't metabolizing her food well, and is not absorbing the nutrients she needs to live and grow satisfactorily.
Plenty of children who've had NEC are on lifelong injection
and hyperal regimens because of just such a problem. Of
course, the fact that Carrie is gaining weight is the bottom
line, regardless of what the tests reveal. That's always the way
it is in medicine: you use the tests that agreed with what you
see, and disbelieve or disregard the rest. That is the nature of
medical judgment and wisdom, such as it is.

WEDNESDAY, NOVEMBER 9, 12:00 P.M.

Resident's note.

Feeding/nutrition/electrolytes: Weight 2070, down 10 grams.
Potassium 6.2 (heelstick). Will increase feeds as tolerated, to full

feeds tomorrow. Hyperal discontinued now secondary to elevated liver enzymes.

Infectious Disease: White count 39,000, still increasing. All
cultures negative, including yesterday's bladder tap. Day #9
amphotericin.

Hematology: Hematocrit 39, platelets 146,000. Stable.

Liver function: Bilirubin still increasing, now 9.2. Feel that
hepatitis is most likely secondary to hyperal, which is now discontinued. To assess other causes will obtain: (1) Hepatitis B and
S antigen; (2) ultrasound of liver: assess liver and search for fungus balls/evidence of dilated ducts; (3) will check bilirubin and
liver enzymes frequently over ensuing days.

The amphotericin continues on, and the white count
continues to rise. So do Carrie's liver enzymes as her color
becomes an even more intense yellow. However, since the
hyperal has been decreed as the cause of her hepatitis, it is
now believed by one and all of her doctors that the amphotericin can have nothing to do with it, and so no mention of
amphotericin hepatitis is made. Carrie's doctors are committed to the amphotericin on the basis of those lovely cultures
nine days ago, and, by God, they believe them to be indicators
of Candida sepsis no matter what. So do fact and belief and
emotion intertwine to produce Carrie's treatment.

The liver ultrasound is just something to do, another routine test. They feel it is highly unlikely Carrie's liver is infected
with fungus balls while she recovers, gains weight, eats, and
continues to produce negative fungus cultures. I hope they're
right. But I know how many times they've been wrong.

WEDNESDAY, NOVEMBER 9, 6:00 P.M.

Nurse's note.

Ileostomy draining light yellow fluid that has the appearance of undigested breast milk.

Seeing this note my fear level begins rising again. This is what can turn things around and stop Carrie's recovery cold —failure to absorb her food. Her damaged and shortened bowel doesn't have the normal capacity to absorb, can't; but what everyone hopes for is that it still functions well enough for her to live.

THURSDAY, NOVEMBER 10, 8:00 A.M.

Nurse's note.

Ileostomy bag draining most of breast milk feed given—basically undigested.

Here it is, panicsville again. It has taken four days for Carrie to begin having significant problems.

THURSDAY, NOVEMBER 10, 10:30 A.M.

Nurse's note.

Stooling watery yellow liquid that resembles breast milk. Weight 2030 g (down 40 grams).

A continuing saga.

THURSDAY, NOVEMBER 10, 3:00 P.M.

Resident's note.

Feeding/electrolytes/nutrition: Weight down 40 grams. Patient taking breast milk from breast and bottle. Began having abundant output from ostomy immediately after feeding 35 ml every 3 hours. Now attempting smaller, more frequent feeds—10 ml/hour with hourly feeds and only 5 ml has appeared in ostomy over past 4 hours.

Plan: Continue for now as above. If more problems and much out through ostomy, will attempt continuous nasogastric tube feeds. If that fails, will begin elemental formula.

Infectious disease: Day #10 amphotericin. White count 30,000, down from 39,200. Will recheck WBC in AM, if unchanged or down and patient stable, will consider discontinuing amphotericin. All cultures except initial still negative.

Hepatitis: Bilirubin 8.8, essentially unchanged. Patient deeply jaundiced. Hepatitis S Antigen: Negative; Hepatitis C Antibody: Positive; Hepatitis S Antibody: Positive. Suspect this profile most

> consistent with transfusion of blood with positive antibody and not indicative of a hepatitis B viral infection in this patient.

Maybe now they will discontinue amphotericin, now that Carrie's diarrhea has become a threat to her well-being. Another possible side effect is loss of appetite, but luckily she hasn't yet had that one. The circular dance goes on: The amphotericin can cause an increased white count, yet it won't be stopped unless the white count decreases. Still an elevated white count normally indicates response to infection, but there is absolutely no evidence of ongoing infection: all the cultures since the first questionable pair are steadily negative, and Carrie is gaining in strength in spite of the myriad of complications assaulting her. It is as if she is determined to get out of this thing alive no matter what anyone does to her. Hold on little one, I silently pray. Keep on playing their game. Please win.

But all of a sudden the rules change. "No more breast-feeding," is the new rule, as now Carrie will get a precise, limited amount of milk every hour, around the clock. The thinking behind this is, if a smaller amount, or "load," is presented to her healing bowel, it can more easily metabolize it than a large, overwhelming meal.

All the same, it is heartbreaking to Judy. She's just started getting comfortable breast-feeding Carrie, and just as important, Carrie has just started getting good at it, taking almost everything she needs from Judy whenever she comes in to feed her, and needing no bottle supplement. She receives a bottle when Judy isn't there, but she seems happiest with the real thing, a triumph in three days after two months of IVs and NG tubes and bottles. Better yet, the milk is now gushing out at home when Judy uses the pump, more than ever, and their threatened shortfall has been averted. Bottles are piling up.

So much milk is flowing, Judy isn't sleeping well at

night, the sheets get so wet over and under her as her engorged breasts pour it out.

"Well, you always wanted big tits," I say to her, "and
now you've got 'em."

She laughs, "Anything for Carrie." Finally we think we
are getting a break.

It didn't last long. How long this new hourly feeding
schedule will go on is anybody's guess. If Carrie's gut doesn't
slow down, she'll be back to the NG tube again, or even on
the hyperal. All we can do is cross our fingers and hope.

She is still on amphotericin, still has hepatitis which was
getting worse every day, and now her belly has gone sour.
The small problems are compounding, adding onto each
other. I don't tell Judy but I am traumatized that something
will go drastically wrong, and the nightmare will begin once
again.

THURSDAY, NOVEMBER 10, 4:00 P.M.

X-ray report.

Abdominal ultrasound clinical data: 4 week old with NEC and
Candidemia, looking for source of sepsis.

Abdominal ultrasound: The liver, spleen and kidneys appear
normal. The gallbladder and biliary tree also appear normal.

Impression: Normal abdomen.

FRIDAY, NOVEMBER 11, 12:00 A.M.

Nurse's note.

Receiving P.O. feeds (with natural nipple) of breast milk 10 ml every hour. Appears to be absorbing these feeds well; only scant amount thin yellow secretions in ostomy bag. Consistency actually appears thicker than yesterday; they are no longer liquid/runny.

FRIDAY, NOVEMBER 11, 3:00 P.M.

Resident's note.

Feeding/electrolytes/nutrition: Weight 2060, up 30 g. K 5.8 (heelstick). Patient had much improvement when feedings changed to 10 ml hourly feeds. Increased to 12 ml/hour, then to 14 ml/hour today. Hyperal discontinued, IV out.

Infectious disease: Culture from Nov. 4 negative at 7 days. Has had 10 days amphotericin, amphotericin DC'd today. White count 29,900.

Hepatitis: Bilirubin up from 8.8, now 10.0. Alkaline phosphatase up from 331 to 499 last 3 days, SGOT 281 then, now 226. SGPT 195 (normal 4–30), LDH 894 then, 701 now. Patient still icteric with yellow skin.

Plan: Follow enzymes every 3–4 days, follow clinical status.

So—no more amphotericin, at long last, and on top of that, no more IV! Carrie is on her own for the first time since

October 14, when at age two days everything had gone to hell. We can't fully rejoice though. Her liver function continues to deteriorate, which can only be ominous, both from an immediate, practical point of view, since people with liver failure tend to lose their appetite and become nauseous, which would be disaster for Carrie right now, and in a more profound, long-term sense, as the bilirubin levels rise to a point that the material deposits itself in her brain, causing irreversible damage. Both are frightening possibilities, and both are not remote, unlikely happenings. They can well occur.

FRIDAY, NOVEMBER 11, 4:30 P.M.

Nurse's transfer note.

Condition stable, vital signs stable. Tolerating P.O. feedings well —14 ml breast milk every hour. Heart and lungs stable. Ileostomy draining small amounts clear white secretions. Voiding urine spontaneously. Good parental interaction. Moved to NIN.

Carrie is being transferred once again, out of the ICU and back to the NIN, where she'd been at the time of each of the two previous life-threatening events that had left her comatose and on death's doorstep. "Personally," I tell her attending physician, "I'd rather she'd stayed in the ICU until she leaves the hospital because the NIN just doesn't seem to agree with her." He smiles when I suggest this, but I'm certain he thinks I've gone around the bend. "Too involved," I suppose they'd term it, "Letting his emotions get in the way of the facts."

The ICU is for critically ill, unstable patients, and Carrie doesn't even have an IV any more, nor is she on any medication. Still, I like the fanatically close observation she'd been getting around the clock in the ICU—the intermediate nursery couldn't come close to this level of care, because each nurse had many more babies to care for. But I accept their decision, mostly because I have no choice.

Carrie is now back where she'd started, literally. The same room, the same nurses, the same routine, trying to eat and gain some weight. She is now a month old, lemon-yellow with bright yellow eyes, her body criss-crossed with surgical scars, a plastic bag stuck to her abdomen, and she weighs almost exactly what she had the day she'd been born.

Now comes the waiting game, as we just sit and see what happens. No more drugs, just her and her hourly bottle. Since she'd gotten used to breast-feeding, she'd been switched to a so-called "natural" nipple, one of those internal contradictions, in an effort to keep her used to the same sort of "feel" in her mouth as Judy's breast. Whether or not Judy would ever breast-feed her again is totally unclear, and the rich flow of milk is already drying up though Judy pumps religiously. A person can only take so much.

Now, any time we come in, it is almost time to feed Carrie and conversely, whenever we leave, there is less than an hour until the next one. It could have been a real strain and guilt-inducing pattern, leaving her while she was on these hourly feeds. Somehow, though, it wasn't so tough. Maybe we'd gotten thicker skinned, or maybe we weren't convinced it mattered who held the bottle. All we are sure of is she knows her nurses a hell of a lot better than she knows us. And that is agony enough.

We hold her, and she starts crying frantically. Give her to a nurse, and she quiets down. "Makes you feel great," Judy says miserably. But it is to be expected, I suppose, given the amount of time we spend with Carrie, even visiting three times a day, versus the constant presence of the nurses. In the intermediate unit, the difference would grow even more pronounced, as the nurses there often carry her around as they do their business.

On the one hand we are grateful for this. At least Carrie will get some human contact beyond being forcibly restrained while blood is drawn. Maybe it will balance all the pain she had to associate with being touched. In the ICU, in contrast, where she'd been attached to monitors and IV tubing, picking her up had been a big deal, and essentially the only time it happened was when we visited. It was just too busy and difficult, and the nurses there had too much to do. But on the other hand, it is another sign that we can't parent our own child.

FRIDAY, NOVEMBER 11, 6:00 P.M.

Nurse's NIN acceptance note.

Caroline received in no apparent distress. Review of systems essentially negative except GI, ostomy bag draining small amount thin white secretions, and skin, jaundiced with yellow sclerae.

Assessment: Stable infant.

Plan: Care as ordered; begin discharge teaching when appropriate.

Amazing! Someone had actually written the word discharge in Carrie's chart. Could it really happen? It doesn't seem possible. It has been this way for so long, so fixed has our routine become, that we believe it will never change. We just don't see how.

"Acceptance notes" interest me. I have yet to see a "rejection note."

SATURDAY, NOVEMBER 12, 2:00 P.M.

Resident's progress note.

Feeding/nutrition: Taking 14 ml hourly breast milk feeds. Total in past 24 hours: 320 ml. Total out: 98 ml. Continue with this feeding regimen. Will get abdominal x-ray.

Infectious disease: Patient with stable vital signs, abdomen soft, patient alert, active. Amphotericin discontinued 2 days ago; will follow clinical course carefully.

Hepatitis: Will recheck enzymes in 2–4 days; will carefully follow patient's status.

Nothing to do now but wait and watch, watch and wait. One thing about instability in illness—it never persists. That is, Carrie's inability to tolerate feedings except on an almost continuous, hourly basis, is temporary; either she'll stop tolerating them at all, or she'll begin absorbing better and return to a more sporadic, widely-spaced schedule. Likewise, any acute problem like angina pectoris (chest pain due to insufficient oxygen supply to the heart); it either stops or it continues until you have a heart attack.

SUNDAY, NOVEMBER 13, 1:00 P.M.

Resident's progress note.

Feed/nutrition: Intake past 24 hours: 320 ml, output into ostomy 151 ml. Seems to be having increased output from ostomy.
Had some sugar + output today, reflecting poor absorption/diges-
tion. Abdominal film results pending (taken this A.M.). Receiving
breast milk and formula since running out of stored breast milk.
Will consider basic elemental feeding if necessary.

Hepatitis: Recheck enzymes tomorrow.

The situation is deteriorating. Carrie's gut just can't
seem to take the load of food it needs to digest, and is starting
to pour it right through and out. Is it simply that her shortened intestine can't physically absorb the food, or is there
something else going on? We just don't know.

However, the death knell for breast-feeding is sounding.
Carrie is now receiving formula as well as breast milk since
Judy can't supply enough. One saving grace, though, is that at
least Carrie's problems with digestion have occurred while
she is receiving nothing but breast milk. Had they begun after
she'd been switched to formula, it would have been all too
easy for Judy to blame the formula and, indirectly, herself for
not being able to give Carrie the breast milk her doctors said
was so superior to formula.

Judy decides to keep using the breast pump anyway for
now, on the slim chance Carrie will turn around and be able
to resume breast feeding. However, Sunday evening three out
of Carrie's first seven feedings, she receives formula, and this
is the last of the breast milk available. She is getting 320 milli-

liters a day and Judy is bringing in fifty. We are out of luck. Since Carrie has stopped actually breast feeding, Judy has dried up once again, and not any of the perverse maneuvers and techniques I've invented can make it start. We know when we're beaten and finally give up.

SUNDAY, NOVEMBER 13, 3:00 P.M.

Radiology report.

Clinical Data: 1 month old, post ileal resection for NEC. There is a small amount of air within the small bowel. No pneumatosis is seen. No sign of free intraperitoneal air is noted.

An up. Carrie hasn't perforated. That is, there is no hole in her intestine that can be producing her problems, nor is there any evidence she is developing NEC. We go home and wait for the down side.

MONDAY, NOVEMBER 14, 2:00 P.M.

Nurse's note.

Caroline has lost 160 grams since yesterday. Weight now 1860, down from 2020 grams. On evening shift she put out 125 ml of stool in ostomy (total past 24 hours 265 out). Total in over the same 24 hours–336 ml. Patient's anterior fontanel [the space between the yet-to-close infant cranial bones, whose fullness indicates the general state of hydration] slightly sunken, poor skin turgor, dry mucous membranes. Sunken eyes.

At 12 midnight IV started in left arm, 18 ml/hour. Infant made NPO at 2:00 A.M. after she excreted 60 ml of liquid stool between midnight and 2:00 A.M. During the night she has started to look better, i.e., improved skin turgor, mucous membranes moist, eyes not as sunken.

Assessment: Dehydration due to excessive stooling via ostomy.
Plan: Continue on IVs
NPO continue
Blood tests as ordered
Frequent vital signs and weights
Accurate I & O (intake and output recordings).

By the next morning it arrives. Carrie has really "turned to stool," as we doctors say. In her case literally. Her gut has finally told us, "no more" by simply pouring out not only what she takes in but her own circulating fluid volume as well, dehydrating her in the process.

By immediately recognizing what was happening, Carrie's nurse quickly had taken steps to stop her deterioration. It is the difference between life and death. Had she been allowed to continue on through the night until her own doctors arrived back in Monday morning around 8:00 A.M. the damage might well have been irretrievable. Brain, kidney, heart and liver damage in premature infants very commonly follows severe, prolonged episodes of dehydration.

I clasp Judy's hand and we begin another vigil.

MONDAY, NOVEMBER 14, 3:00 P.M.

Resident's note.

Feeding/nutrition: At 11:00 P.M. last night patient's weight down 160 grams, noted skin tenting, decreased turgor, increased ostomy output. Tried both last of breast milk and clear electrolyte solution to control diarrhea, without success.

We decided patient was about 5–10% dehydrated and began rehydration. Will keep her NPO for now, but may try to resume feeds later in the day.

Infectious Disease: patient fairly stable except for feeding problem. White count = 21,000, vital signs stable. White count is actually down from last week. Will recheck white count tomorrow.

Hepatitis: Liver functions continue to deteriorate. Bilirubin now up to 17.0 (previously 9.0 November 9), alk phos 725 (was 499, normal 20–95), SGPT 250 (was 196, normal 4–30); SGOT 350 (was 226, normal 4–30), LDH 623 (was 701, normal less than 350). Will discuss further workup of hepatitis with attending today. Also, will request STAT GI [Gastroenterology] consult today re feeding management and hepatitis.

Carrie is really going sour. Her diarrhea has stopped for now, but she is no longer eating. Since she has no hyperal to sustain her, she is metabolizing her own body, of which very little remains.

Her hepatitis is now out of control. The resident can do nothing but ask for other opinions and watch, and treat the complications. Once bilirubin hits fifteen, it can begin to deposit in the brain, with devastating permanent results.

Gastroenterology consult.

Clinical data: 1 month old white female, status post NEC age 2 days with resection 30–40 cm of ileum (with preservation of ileocecal valve) at 6 days of age. Also status post Candida sepsis 2 weeks ago. Had begun PO feeds, but started stooling out. On hyperal most of life, now with elevated bilirubin and liver enzymes. (Father is attending anesthesiologist at Univ. of Virginia, mother is an ICU nurse). Please evaluate.

Report: History as above. Has obvious undigested breast milk with feedings, increased liver enzymes and bilirubin, Hepatitis S antibody positive. Was on hyperal; abdominal ultrasound and x-rays negative.

Physical exam: Liver 2–3 cm below costal [rib] margin, soft edge. Exam complicated by ostomy. Green-tinged ileostomy output. Spleen not palpable.

Impression:

1. Probable hyperal-associated jaundice

2. Rule out obstruction (doubt in view of color of drainage)

3. Malnutrition

4. Rule out gastroenteritis

5. Possible stone/sludge in gall bladder

Advise:

1. Trial at restart feeds, slow continuous NG tube breast milk; if fail, change to predigested formula

2. Check ph [acidity] of ostomy (fresh); if acid consider cimetidine

3. Stool leukocyte count and smear

4. Urinalysis/urine culture

5. Phenobarbital 5 mg/kg/day divided, twice a day

6. Consider reoperation to hook back up; liver biopsy

7. Blood clotting studies (PT, PTT)

8. Serum phosphorus

9. Consider sweat test.

Consults are interesting things. You get a consult for many reasons: maybe you're not sure of a diagnosis or planned treatment, and want a confirming "expert" opinion; maybe you have no idea what the fuck is going on, and just want to know what to do; or maybe you just want to be complete, to "cover yourself," should someone further down the line ask "Did you get a blah-blah consult?" House staff, that is, interns and residents, do a lot of the latter.

The nature of a consult differs depending on what sort of hospital you're in. In a private hospital, when an internist asks for a neurology consult, a fully-trained neurologist does the consult, taking the history and performing an examination, then writing his opinion and recommendations.

In a university hospital such as the one Carrie is in, a whole different system exists. The consult slips are stacked up each morning, then divided amongst the "fellows" and residents on that particular elective that month. Thus allocated, admittedly each patient is seen in detail by a physician, but one whose expertise and experience is often negligible compared to a fully trained specialist. Each resident takes a careful history and performs a physical exam, then returns to the attending and tells him the whole story.

The attending listens, then, depending on the expertise of the resident, the difficulty of the consult or the nature of the patient, does or doesn't go with the resident as well as the other residents on the service and the usual assortment of medical students, nursing students, and other hangers-on, to the patient's bedside, where he may chat with the patient or even examine him himself, in rare circumstances.

Then everyone leaves the room, trooping out like a herd of albinos, all clad in various white trappings, coats, dresses, pants, shirts, shoes, to the corridor, where the attending holds forth on "the truth," that is, what he feels is wrong with the patient, and makes recommendations. The resident then goes back to the chart room after rounds are over and writes out his consult note, which is then countersigned by the attending, usually under the words "Agree with above."

The consult note at a university hospital is often a source of derision and amusement to the residents and interns on the service. The very nature of a consult almost requires that it offer rare diseases as possible diagnoses and then demand exotic, esoteric testing to confirm or rule out these possibilities.

If a consult offers nothing new, it serves no function and the consultant is useless. Just as your car, taken to a different station, always needs something done to it that the previous mechanic never mentioned, the consultant must generate more possibilities—it is his or her *raison d'etre*.

Thus Carrie's GI consult Gary Richards produces new ideas. Cimetidine, an anti-ulcer medication with myriad side effects, is recommended for decreasing the acidity of her diarrhea, if it is acid. Phenobarbital, a barbiturate with as yet unknown effects on immature brain development, is recommended to slow down the diarrhea itself. Since she isn't absorbing anything anymore anyway, the GI consultant poses an interesting idea amongst the esoteric: Consider hooking her intestine back together, and see what happens.

The colon, which is now being bypassed in favor of the ostomy bag, is a very efficient absorber of water. Perhaps with it back in line Carrie can slow down her output a bit. Since she wouldn't be allowed any food for days after the operation, until her bowel is active once again (anesthesia and surgery, especially bowel surgery, stop bowel function dead in its tracks), this would give her upper intestine a chance to rest as well.

As long as they are in the belly, the surgeons can get a

piece of liver for biopsy and perhaps that will help in the diagnosis of Carrie's hepatitis. Liver biopsies are often done with needles through the skin, so called "percutaneous biopsies," but they are not nearly as useful as a chunk taken out under direct vision.

With the needle, you basically pray you don't hit a major blood vessel, because there is no way to stop the bleeding without opening up the patient, and bleeding inside the liver is hard to diagnose from the outside. Also, you can't pick your spot since you are essentially "blind," and you can potentially hit anything with that big hollow-core needle, especially if you are a resident doing your first one.

As a medical student, I did one liver biopsy. I was very pleased with myself, and the attending congratulated me on my nice technique. Unfortunately, the pathology report the next day came back "Intercostal muscle—no liver parenchyma identified." So much for my career as a GI consultant.

Carrie's consultant's last suggestion about testing for serum phosphorus is another shot in the dark. We usually refer to such tests as "serum porcelain levels." "Consider sweat test" is a cryptic way of saying maybe this baby has cystic fibrosis, the sweat test being a diagnostic tool for cystic fibrosis. Diarrhea is common in cystic fibrosis; so it is at least a rational diagnosis, but approaches the vanishing point in likelihood.

I wonder, considering all these possible and mostly improbable suggestions, which ones they'll experiment with on my child. I wonder, and my heart breaks once again.

MONDAY, NOVEMBER 14, 7:00 P.M.

Resident's note (addendum).

Discussed patient with surgeon who feels reanastomosis this week might be best option. Will discuss this with attending. Appreciate GI consult and recommendations. Will begin slow NG feeds and draw labs suggested.

Well now we know. Carrie will be getting put back together sooner than we expected, and for the wrong reason. It isn't that she is ready, gaining weight and thriving, but she is simply doing so poorly she can't do any worse with her bowel intact, and might do better.

Besides, she is getting dehydrated and malnourished, and without the hyperal she'll only be in worse shape for reoperation the longer the surgeon waits. I sigh heavily. Few things in medicine work out the way you plan them. Now it is back to tube feedings, reminiscent of her very first feedings a month ago. Then she was too weak to eat, but her bowels were fine; now she is eager to eat, and strong, but her guts are betraying her.

MONDAY, NOVEMBER 14, 8:30 P.M.

Nurse's note.

NG tube inserted; restarted continuous NG feeds of Pregestimil at 3 ml/hour.

When we come in that evening, Carrie is lying in her box, a tube up her nose attached to a syringe with formula. It is a sad sight, her ostomy bag completing the picture, food flowing in from a plastic syringe through a plastic tube and then right back out again into a plastic bag. Carrie seems sort of a way station, an outpost on her food's brief journey through her scarred, diseased body.

So we hold and rock her, talking to her, to each other and the nurses. They tell us the date of Carrie's planned re-anastomosis, the first we've heard about it. We are at once irritated to be finding out they've set a date this way, in passing, yet we are excited. Terrible as she is doing, she can't ever go home for good until she's been hooked back up, so this is, if it succeeds, one more step out the door. Still, we don't really imagine, nor can we, that she'll ever leave. Too much seems possible still, too many unknowns persist. We imagine every horrible scenario. In one her operation will go fine and then she'll get infected, or die of progressive liver failure. That would be something, to have her gut repaired and functioning only to get back the report of the liver biopsy from pathology saying she has cirrhosis, fibrosis, and scarring, a death sentence.

Moreover, that still won't be the end of it. There is one

more possibility, one of ultimate risk: a liver transplant. Performed at only a handful of hospitals in the world, and in children at only two, this operation offers one last hope. To Judy and I though, it is the cruelest of hopes. What Carrie has gone through up to now is nothing compared to the ordeal of a liver transplant victim.

Drugs, procedures, and complications are at their zenith here, and very few survive. Of those who do, most require another transplant, as the new liver progressively malfunctions and fails. Yet people still sign the consent form, while on television and in the newspapers and magazines parents plead for donors for their children. Maybe we are crazy in our adamant refusal to even consider such a thing, should the need and possibility arise. Me, I care too much for our baby to do that to her. Or so I think. Some might say I don't care enough, I suppose.

TUESDAY, NOVEMBER 15, 2:00 P.M.

Resident's progress note.

Feeding/electrolytes/nutrition: Weight up 120 grams. Has tolerated continuous feedings well, ostomy output down from yesterday. Will continue this regimen.

Hepatitis: Bilirubin 12.8, down from 17 yesterday. Appreciate GI consult, agree hyperal-induced hepatitis most likely.

GI: Will arrange radiographic studies tomorrow; plan reanastomosis Thursday.

The x-ray studies are crucial, because they let the surgeon know before he operates if there are any narrow, constricted, scarred areas of intestine which might have to be excised. Whether or not Carrie's large bowel, or colon, has been damaged by the NEC or its complications over the past month is unknown. The colon has been inoperative, its end simply opening into Carrie's abdominal wall, until it is reconnected.

As with everything else Carrie has to endure, the x-rays also carry a risk. Carrie will be given a barium mixture to swallow. Then the course of the barium will be traced down her intestine all the way out into her ostomy bag. There is a risk of rupture of either the small bowel, if it is still weak or thin-walled from the NEC, or the large bowel, from a barium enema which is part of the examination. Bowel rupture during x-ray studies means an emergency abdominal exploration to remove the barium.

WEDNESDAY, NOVEMBER 16, 1:00 P.M.

Radiology report.

Clinical data: One month old female, status post NEC, rule out stricture.

Barium enema, upper GI, and small bowel follow through: Barium was placed into the colon through a small red rubber catheter. The rectum and sigmoid are normal in caliber. The colon is normal in its course, until it reaches the junction of the splenic flexure and descending colon. At this point, a narrowed segment, several centimeters in length is present. There was no dilation of the colon proximal to this level and barium passed easily. Nonetheless, no change in caliber was seen over the period of observation. The more proximal colon to the mucous fistula appears normal.

Impression: Persistently narrowed segment of colon at the junction of the splenic flexure and descending colon.

An upper GI and small bowel follow-through was then performed. The child drank hesitantly. The esophagus is normal, though no large boluses of barium traverse the esophagus. The

---

remaining 30 cc of barium were placed into the stomach through
a nasogastric tube. The stomach was felt to be normal in caliber,
and there is no evidence of obstruction of outflow from the stomach. The position of the duodenum and the ligament of Treitz is
normal. Barium then flows into the small bowel which is diminished in amount. The caliber of the small bowel may be slightly
larger than normal, but no massive dilatation is seen, and no
obstruction to outflow is present. No strictured areas can be seen
in the small bowel.

Impression: Normal upper GI. Grossly normal small bowel
with perhaps slight dilation of the small bowel itself.

So, the x-rays have unearthed a possible area of damage
in Carrie's colon. If the segment appears irreversibly narrowed at surgery, it will have to be excised, which would
appreciably increase the risk of postoperative complications,
since the ends of the excised portion will have to be rejoined,
as well as the ends of the small and large bowel which had
been separated during the first operation a month ago. The
repair could later leak, or rupture, causing peritonitis, sepsis,
and death, so the more surgery, the greater the risk.

The rest of Carrie's studies are better. It looks like her
first surgeon has gotten all the damaged area during the first
operation, a result of skill and some luck, since often some
areas which appear normal at operation later become
scarred and damaged.

Pier Zender will be the surgeon this time. We talk with
him at length. He is a quiet, modest sort of man, with a wick-
edly sarcastic sense of humor who pokes fun at himself instead of others. "Joe and Judy," he says, "let me worry for
both of you. I'm used to it," he winks. "In addition to recon-
necting Carrie's gut and taking a liver biopsy, I am going to
insert another central line for easier venous access and a
feeding tube running directly from inside the stomach
through Carrie's abdominal wall and out. I feel that venous
access is critical to Carrie's recovery, especially should she

need drugs, and that the feeding tube will be easier to manage than the NG tubes Carrie has had most of her life." He pauses a moment, "Be optimistic, Carrie and I will try not to disappoint you."

I shake my head wearily. It is easy for him to be upbeat, but all we see ahead is trouble. The first central line, with its attendant Candida and subsequent amphotericin therapy, has been devastating, and we see it all starting again, since Carrie will be on antibiotics after this surgery just like before.

"Does she really need another central line?" I ask sighing.

"I think its best for her. I really do," Pier says as he runs his long tapered fingers through his thick gray hair thoughtfully.

"What about the feeding tube? Why not just use NG tubes if she needs tube feedings?"

"Well," he says, "the feeding tube makes it a lot easier to manage her intake; it doesn't need to be repositioned or kink like the NG tubes. Besides, she can go home with it," he pauses, strokes his chin and winks again, "which is nice in case she comes back in for any reason, say if she doesn't eat well or has diarrhea. That way we don't have to take her to surgery to put one in, but we can just manage her via the tube. It's a lot easier to do now, as long as we're going to be in there, than later."

The idea that Carrie would have to come back in has never really occurred to us, probably because the idea of her ever leaving is so hard to comprehend. All I see is another tube, another scar, and above all, a baby who isn't normal or right or whole coming home with a tube sticking out of her abdominal wall. I hate the idea. I'd rather she come back in and get the tube put in if she needs it. I want Carrie to be done with all the medical manipulations and just have a try at being a regular baby.

Wearily I trudge down to the operating room and find the chief pediatric anesthesiologist. "The operation is definitely on for tomorrow morning, first."

He nods, "That's fine, we'll take good care of her."

I murmur, "Thanks."

"Joe, try to relax. I like to do people's kids. Shows they have confidence in me."

I sigh. He is a savvy, skilled clinician. Carrie will be in good hands—I hope.

WEDNESDAY, NOVEMBER 16, 6:00 P.M.

Surgical pre-op note.

For resection of splenic flexure of colon and takedown of ileostomy, gastrostomy [feeding tube], central line placement, and liver biopsy. Elevated liver function tests, otherwise normal lab values. Orders written, permit signed. Blood for type and cross not sent, only enough specimen for type specific blood to be available. Type O negative will be available.

So, they plan to take the narrowed piece of large bowel as well. I wince. The resident has screwed up in sending blood to the blood bank, so they haven't enough blood to cross match Carrie completely. Thus, if she needs blood, it won't be the best possible match, but as close as they can get, which means her chance of a potentially lethal transfusion reaction is increased. I try to reassure myself but don't get very far. It doesn't happen often, but it does happen. Just this sort of thing is why I'll never rest easy until Carrie is out of the damned hospital. I smile at myself. Somewhere deep inside somehow I must fantasize that she's going to make it. If only that idealized wish becomes reality. I try not to think of how slim the chance of this really is.

WEDNESDAY, NOVEMBER 16, 9:00 P.M.

Our last visit with Carrie before surgery tomorrow morning. Judy and I decide not to come in the next day at 6:00 A.M. before she goes to the operating room. Both of us have seen the flurry of activity surrounding a patient who is about to go to the O.R.—the checklists, the last minute tests, and the rest, and we want our last look at her, if that's what this is to be, quiet and unhurried, without interruptions.

We just want to sit and rock her as she sleeps, unknowing, and talk about all that has happened to get her to this point, and about what may yet come. I've told the surgeon we'll wait out the operation at home, and asked him to call us when he has something to tell us. Once again, the ringing telephone will carry fateful news. Once again we will sit there, our hearts pounding, afraid to pick the phone up.

Most people spend the period immediately before and during an operation on a loved one at the hospital, usually in a waiting room designated for such a purpose. It's usually a crowded, uncomfortable place, smoky and poorly ventilated, with a lot of anxious people waiting for news. I've never understood why anybody would wait in one. They are the most depressing places in the world. There is no privacy. So that when the phone rings for a patient's family, they have to carry on a conversation about what happened in the operating room in full earshot of every other person in the room, each of whom listens acutely.

I suppose my antipathy toward organized, ritualized environments is why I have repeatedly said I would never willingly let myself, or anyone dear, die a painful, lingering death in a hospital. I want to be in my own home, comfortable and quiet, with family, not strangers, around me.

Yet twice I've watched Carrie fail in the last month, twice I've seen her near death in an ICU, with tubes everywhere, tests and blood being drawn and the whole wild beast of mod-

ern medicine running amok over her. Why haven't we taken
her out of the hospital?

We can't, is the answer. The nature of medicine in the
United States has altered in recent years, and parents are no
longer in charge, not when a sick child is concerned. Mandatory treatment can now be instituted if a physician feels it
might help, even if parents are opposed. That is, if a physician
feels a child might have a chance, no matter how small, and
no matter how dangerous the treatment, he or she can now,
with full legal backing, institute such treatment, in spite of
parents' wishes that their child be left in peace.

As a member of Congress involved in creating the legis-
lation decreeing such care stated, "No one has the right to
play God with the lives of these babies, except God himself."
Would that this legislator could see the gods in white in action
on the hospital wards.

Silent now. Judy and I sit at Carrie's bedside, each lost in
thought. Perhaps this is the last we'll see of Carrie. Even in
the best of hands, even setting aside the question of risks,
strange things happen in the operating room. We doctors understand some things about the human organism, but probably very little in relation to the real nature of ourselves, whose
essence we continue to seek nevertheless. Thus, occasionally
hearts stop beating for no apparent reason, and don't start
again, breathing ceases and won't resume, and kidneys fail,
never to function again.

As physicians, we seek all possible logical reasons for
these events, and in fact do find explanations of sorts for all of
them, but doubt lingers. Is an explanation the "why" or the
"what"? It is not difficult, given decent training, to concoct a
reasonable case explaining "what" happens in almost any
circumstance. The "why," however, while usually attribut-
able to some human or mechanical failing, sometimes can't
be pinned down. These are the places where our current
knowledge and theories come up against the vast panorama
of our ignorance.

Perhaps instead of frantically trying to build a logical

structure from shards of reason, we should look again at our ignorance, highlight it, instead of trying to pretend it's not there.

I think about this as I watch Judy rock our infant child in the midst of these strangers who have become our most intimate relations, because in their hands lies our child's fate.

THURSDAY, NOVEMBER 17, 6:00 A.M.

Nurse's note.

Neuro: Good tone, reflexes symmetrical throughout. Sleeping but responds appropriately to stimuli. Good suck and grasp.

Cardiovasc: On cardiac monitor. Heart rate regular, no audible murmur noted. Brisk capillary refill. IV infiltrated; will restart.

Resp: Bilaterally equal breath sounds. Chest symmetrical. No apnea, distress, or cyanosis.

GI: Electrolyte solution 5 ml every hour via NG tube. NPO after 2:00 A.M. for surgery in A.M. Abdomen soft, not distended, no masses. Good bowel sounds.

Skin: Warm, dry, jaundiced.

Other: In isolette. Ready for surgery.

THURSDAY, NOVEMBER 17, 11:00 A.M.

Surgeon's operative report.

Pre-operative diagnosis: Post bowel resection for NEC.
Post-operative diagnosis: Same.
Operation: Exploratory laparotomy, takedown of ileostomy

and ileoileostomy, insertion of central venous catheter, liver biopsy.

Clinical summary: This newborn infant required a substantial
bowel resection for NEC with perforation. She had an ileostomy
performed and is now brought to the operating room for a takedown of her ileostomy.

Procedure: With the patient under suitable general anesthesia, a silastic central venous catheter was placed in the left exter-
nal jugular field. The abdomen was then prepared with Betadine
solution and draped as a sterile field. The previous right upper
quadrant incision was opened fully. The adhesions in the peritoneal cavity were dissected free with sharp dissection. The end
ileostomy was dissected free, as was the mucous fistula in the
right lower quadrant. The ends of the bowel were trimmed and
an end-to-end ileoileostomy was performed using interrupted 5-0
vicryl sutures. We were able to salvage approximately 1 inch of
terminal ileum and the entire colon. Surprisingly, the radio-
graphically narrowed area of colon at the splenic flexure appeared normal and was therefore not resected. The abdominal
cavity was irrigated copiously with saline. Because of preopera-
tive hyperbilirubinemia, the liver was examined, and found to be
soft and somewhat bile-stained. Two core biopsies were obtained
with a Travenol needle and hemostasis achieved with simple
pressure. The abdomen was then irrigated copiously and closed
with interrupted 5-0 wire sutures. The subcutaneous tissues were
closed with interrupted 5-0 vicryl and the skin with interrupted
5-0 nylon. It should be noted that a tube gastrostomy was inserted prior to closure of the abdomen. The patient tolerated the
procedure well and was taken to the recovery room in satisfactory condition.

At 10:15 A.M. our phone rings.

"Hello," I say.

"Joe, it's Pier Zender."

"Is it over?" I ask. My heart skips a beat.

"We're all finished, and Carrie did just fine."

"Great," I say giving Judy who's lying beside me, the
thumbs up sign. "What did you do?"

"We reconnected her as we'd planned, and managed to

preserve the ileocecal valve and terminal ilcum, so she'll be
able to absorb enough vitamin B-12 to avoid having to have
shots all her life. The area of large bowel that looked questionable on x-ray looked fine, so we didn't have to resect anything there. We put in another central line, a feeding tube into
her stomach, and got a liver biopsy. Her liver didn't seem
hard or fibrosed, but we'll see what pathology says."

"Sounds good to me," I say. "I don't know how to thank
you."

"You're very welcome. That's one tough little kid, I'll tell
you that. She's got 'The right stuff,' " he says.

"Yes she has," I reply humbly. "See you soon, and
thanks again." I wonder what I can ever do to tell him how
much. He's given Carrie back to us.

"Bye."

As soon as I hang up, Judy says, "Tell me everything."

I do, ending, "For once," I smile, "things have gone
right. No problems, no complications."

"I'm afraid to believe it," Judy says wistfully.

In my mind a refrain plays:

"All the King's horses
And all the King's men
Couldn't put Humpty Dumpty together again."

But Zender has done just that. Carrie is now in one
piece. Granted she has some pieces permanently missing, and
a lot of extra equipment still attached, stomach tubes, central
lines, and the like, but at least the idea is right. We thought it
would never happen. Now if only she eats, gains weight and
the hepatitis goes away, she'll recover and be done with the
hospital. So deceptively simple, so tantalizing, it seems to us,
needing to think it can happen. So plausible. Yet we've been
slapped silly so many times with the depressing reality of Carrie's complications, how can we possibly be optimistic? To do
it we must be crazy. It's the only explanation, I think, as Judy
and I begin to, once again, plan a life with Carrie.

Of course, we both know the down side. Now comes the post-operative period. Back to the ICU. Carrie will once again receive no food until the surgeon feels her bowel anastomosis is strong enough not to leak when it beings to function. Intravenous antibiotics, ampicillin and gentamicin, two old friends, again will be begun to prevent post-op abdominal infection. The central line will be used once again, with all its attendant risks. We'll just have to hope that somehow it will work out better than after the last operation.

Despite our entreaties to each other in the car not to expect miracles we rush to the ICU again. The familiar routine: wash hands, don gowns, look into the stainless steel door above the sinks as we scrub, see our reflections blurred by the satiny finish. Then hurry to see Carrie. She is still sluggish and sleepy from the anesthetic, but at least she is there. A minor miracle: no bag on her abdomen, just a gauze pad taped on. Of course, a large yellow rubber tube now emerges from the previously unscathed left side of her belly, and a central line from the left side of her chest. Murmuring that we love her, we stand next to her, stroking her tiny hands, as she sleeps.

FRIDAY, NOVEMBER 18, 1:00 P.M.

Surgery resident note.

Resting comfortably now—easily arousable. Temperature 37° axillary, heart rate 134, resp. rate 50, blood pressure 80/44.

Resp: Had 6 episodes of apnea and bradycardia last night, lasting up to 13 seconds, resolving with moderate stimulation. Lungs clear to auscultation. On room air.

Cardiovasc: Stable, regular heart rate and blood pressure. Good peripheral pulses. No murmur.

GI: No bowel sounds. Gastric tube draining minimally.

Fluids: In: 147 ml; out 61 ml; weight 2100 grams (up 10).
Nutrition: Starts hyperal today.
Infectious Disease: On ampicillin and gentamicin.
Overall: Stable post-op condition post-op day #1. Will continue close monitoring.

Carrie is still recovering from her anesthetic, and her periods of apnea and bradycardia are the result of the still disordered control centers deep in her brain. Although apparent recovery from anesthesia occurs pretty quickly, within hours, even in adults full recovery takes a day or two. For this reason patients who can tell you their name, where they are, and who's in first place in the recovery room, and complain of severe pain, will tell you the next day that the first thing they can recall after their operation is waking up in their room. It's as if all that happened in the recovery room never really occurred.

Babies, especially small, premature ones like Carrie, have very immature nervous systems, easily disturbed and prone to malfunction. Some feel this is the cause of crib death, or sudden infant death syndrome, which every year results in thousands of babies, usually under six months of age, being found dead in their cribs.

For Carrie, or any small baby, recovery from general anesthesia takes time. She has to be closely observed to detect irregularities in her breathing or heart rate. Once the anesthetic has been eliminated, her system will once again function well, unless some other cause for disorder, like infection sets in.

FRIDAY, NOVEMBER 18, 3:00 P.M.

Pediatric resident note.

Will start hyperal today. Bilirubin 12, down from 17 on November 14. Will follow.

A possible glitch. Post-operative wound healing depends on having fuel supplied by food, yet Carrie can't eat because of the delicate nature of her bowel surgery. The closure has to be strong and healed before being tested. In an adult, enough reserves exist in existing body fat and tissues to allow wound healing without any additional intake. Carrie is so small and undeveloped she has no such reserves. Thus hyperal, the very thing that has probably plunged her into liver failure, and perhaps led to her failure to absorb food and the resulting diarrhea in this "last resort" operation to try and stem her inability to retain anything, is all that is left to nourish her.

So, although Carrie's wounds will now have what it needs to heal, her recovering liver might again start to deteriorate as it did before on hyperal.

It is a gamble but one that seems to all concerned worth taking. Judy and I agree. We want to give her every chance.

FRIDAY, NOVEMBER 18, 5:00 P.M.

Pathology report.

Livery biopsy: Consists of three 0.1 cm in diameter fragments of deeply bile-stained liver measuring 2.2 cm in length total which are entirely submitted.

Results: Extramedullary erythropoiesis. Marked cholestatis. Periportal inflammation with neutrophils, eosinophils, and monocytes with slight cholangitis.

Carrie's liver is full of bile, due to the obstruction of the ducts which drain it, and this is secondary to marked inflammation of the liver, probably resulting from a reaction to the hyperal. There is no evidence of fibrous scarring of the liver, which accompanies liver failure and shutdown. Thus, Carrie's liver disease is reversible, if she can heal from her surgery fast enough to begin eating and get off the hyperal before it once again begins to cause her liver to fail. It is simply a race between her intestine and her liver. The winner will determine whether she lives or dies. We are once again helpless; none of us can do anything but watch and wait.

SATURDAY, NOVEMBER 19, 1:00 P.M.

Pediatric surgery note.

Post-op day #2. Lusty cry, vital signs stable.

    Resp: Lungs clear, no further apnea and bradycardia spells since yesterday morning.

    Cardiovasc: Rate 144, no murmur, pulses good.

    GI: Faint bowel sounds present. No bowel movement.

    Fluids and nutrition: Weight down 20 grams. Electrolytes normal. Restarted on hyperal.

    Overall: Satisfactory post-op course.

SUNDAY, NOVEMBER 20, 2:00 P.M.

Nurse's note.

    Blood transfusion: 15 ml packed red blood cells given 1–2 P.M. No apparent reaction noted.

    So much blood is continuing to be taken for tests, Carrie is anemic again, although only in a very mild, borderline way. When we go in to visit, we note the hanging unit of blood, I ask, "Why is Carrie getting it. Has she started bleeding, or is something happening?" When we find that it is simply to make her numbers look better, I explode. "Another exposure to hepatitis, AIDS and transfusion reaction, for what reason?" I yell at Amy the blond nurse on duty. "Page the chief surgical and pediatric residents immediately."

"As you wish, Dr. Stirt," she says sweetly.

When they call down to the unit, I grab the phone. "Carrie has been ordered to receive blood by the surgical intern but that doesn't make a hell of a lot of sense to me," I say angrily. "Do you think giving her blood just to create normal numbers for her lab tests is anything but a pile of shit?"

They agree to stop the transfusion. Later that afternoon her orders are changed, and the frequency of Carrie's blood tests is dropped from every day to every other day. After all, there is no reason for such frequent sampling, it is just habit.

Thus do things happen to people in hospitals. Carrie might have gone on for weeks being stuck every morning for useless tests and receiving blood transfusions every few days to replace the blood being withdrawn, if I hadn't raised a stink. No one else will look out for your interests in a hospital, believe me. You'd better do it yourself, or else you take your chances. Faith is misplaced here. It belongs in a church. A hospital must never be confused with a holy place, god-like as its denizens may act and appear in their robes of white.

MONDAY, NOVEMBER 21, 2:00 P.M.

Pediatric surgery note.

Post-operative day #4: Hungry and irritable. Yellow. Lung and heart function normal.

GI: No bowel sound heard today, but 1 bowel movement yesterday. Bowel function returning slowly. Bilirubin 8.7 yesterday, down from 12 on November 18.

Overall: Satisfactory post-op course. Bowel function slowly

> returning; will discuss when to begin feeding with GI consult.
> Liver function improving in spite of hyperal.

MONDAY, NOVEMBER 21, 3:00 P.M.

GI consult.

Would begin feeds as soon as possible from surgical standpoint.
Use lactose-free Pregestimil full strength but low volume as continuous gastric tube feeding. Please nipple along with feedings to
stimulate lingual lipase. Could also use breast milk, but need to
watch for fat-glucose malabsorption.

It is a funny thing. Try as we might to communicate with
Carrie's physicians, though being medical people ourselves,
Judy and I still seem unable to really keep the lines open. For
instance, how can Gary Richards, the GI consult, suggest trying breast milk for Carrie: Hasn't it been eminently clear that
we had given up that idea weeks ago when Judy's milk dried
up and the baby was given formula instead? If we have this
much trouble letting Carrie's doctors know how we feel and
what is happening with us, how much more confused and
ignorant must non-medical people be about everything that
goes on in hospitals? Would a person without a medical background have questioned Carrie's blood transfusions two days
ago, or simply accepted it as "necessary" because of her
"anemia"?

Gary again offers "off-the-wall" advice—the reason why
he is the consult. Stimulating Carrie's mouth enzymes with a
nipple while formula is piped into her stomach through a

tube seems to be unlikely to do much for her digestion, but it sounds good.

We'd talked to Carrie's surgeon, Piers Zender, earlier Monday about when she can start eating, and he'd said not for a while. He is very conservative in his approach to beginning feeding after bowel reconnection and for good reason: a leak due to premature feeding and poor healing means he'll have to operate again, Carrie will have a major setback, and all the waiting and healing will have to begin once again.

Thus, he plans a slow introduction of clear fluids through the feeding tube directly into Carrie's stomach rather than anything by mouth. This way he can gradually and steadily increase her intestinal workload instead of relying on intermittent large meals which might overstress her system.

TUESDAY, NOVEMBER 22, 3:00 P.M.

Surgery progress note.

Appears hungry and active. Will begin feedings soon per attending surgeon's orders. Wounds look good; no problems apparent. Doing very well. Continue labs every other day.

Carrie is hungry. We are thrilled as we give her a nipple to suck and she chews it furiously.

WEDNESDAY, NOVEMBER 23, 1:00 P.M.

Surgery progress note.

Post-operative day #6. Appears active, alert and hungry. Wounds look good, all vital signs stable. Will begin gastric tube feedings today, 5 ml/hour. Pedialyte (a clear electrolyte solution) by constant drip.

    Assessment: Doing very well. Advance feeds as tolerated.

Six days after surgery, fluids are to begin. This will be a crucial test. Can Carrie tolerate the feedings without rupture? The stimulating effect of fluids in her gut will make her bowels contract and stress the surgical repair. We will soon find out how well it holds up. Carrie is very irritable, crying constantly it seems. Nothing seems to be wrong with her, no infection or wound pain. Perhaps she is simply hungry as everyone assumes. I suppose when a baby cries and can't talk and isn't fed, hunger seems a rational explanation. "Maybe," Judy says, "she's just had enough of the hospital and wants out."

Again, the thought of taking her home arises in our minds and again, the fear of things going sour and having to bring her back keeps us from doing it. We have no idea of how to take care of even a normal baby, and the specter of Carrie at home has just begun to make us aware of how frightened we are with the idea of us, not the hospital, taking care of her. We've gotten used to three visits a day, and sleeping through the night. What will we do with her? How will we manage? The idea of trying to learn after we've checked her out of the hospital AMA and possibly facing another crisis seems too daunting. So, we just sit and watch her. Silently labeling ourselves cowards, we wait until everyone says it is time for Carrie to go home.

THURSDAY, NOVEMBER 24, 3:00 P.M.

Pediatric resident progress note.

Feeding: Now on hyperal IV, electrolyte solution via tube. Weight up 60 grams. Suggest maintain fluids at current level, try for 20 gram weight gain/day (20 grams is about 1/20th of a pound, less than an ounce). Consider starting feeds with breast milk or Pregestimil soon.

Hepatitis: Bilirubin now 8.3, down from 10.1 on November 20. Hepatitis appears to be resolving. Suggest monitoring liver enzymes once a week.

Infectious disease: Day #7 of postoperative antibiotics (ampicillin and gentamicin). Suggest antibiotics could probably be discontinued soon, unless there have been positive cultures.

THURSDAY, NOVEMBER 24, 4:00 P.M.

Surgery progress note.

Postoperative day #7: Resting comfortably. Lungs and heart clear. Having liquid green stools, on Lytren 5 ml/hour via tube. Will continue Lytren, but decrease to 4 ml/hour. Afebrile on day #7.

Antibiotics: Will stop Saturday.

Overall: Progressing slowly. Follow.

A difference of opinion is starting to develop between the surgeons and pediatricians, with Carrie's management the object of contention. The surgeons are going very, very slowly in advancing Carrie's feeding, even though she appears to be tolerating whatever is given her. After all, it is difficult to form a bowel movement when you get nothing but liquids. The surgery team has responded to Carrie's liquid stools by decreasing her tube fluid intake by one milliliter/hour, a truly insignificant gesture, almost a homeopathic response to her perceived problem.

The pediatricians, on the other hand, clearly want to up Carrie's intake and start giving her oral nutrition. She is irritated and crying constantly, chewing furiously on a pacifier she has in her isolette. Her nurses are unanimous in their assessment. They say, "This baby is hungry and wants to eat!" To my way of thinking, of all the individuals involved with Carrie, they are the ones with the best clinical judgment. The number of hours they spend in close contact with children dwarf those of doctors.

Judy and I are also in the "feeding" boat. More than anything we want our baby to eat so she will finally be able to leave the hospital. Talking with the nurses and pediatricians and learning they feel the same way only strengthens our urgency about getting Carrie normal nourishment. What is the difference whether she takes her four millileters of clear electrolyte solution by mouth or through a tube directly into her stomach? It will get there in either case, and would seem a lot more satisfying if she could drink it herself.

We don't want Carrie to be a machine nourished by a tube. We want her to be a baby and eat normally. It is almost impossible to sit back and watch her being tube fed for no more reason than that her intake can be precisely regulated, without getting angry. She is a person, not a machine. We feel we are fighting a system trying to organize her when in fact she could just as well, and much more naturally, organize herself.

THURSDAY, NOVEMBER 24, 11:30 P.M.

Nursing note.

Infant-Parent Bonding.

Subjective: "She is looking less yellow. She's starting to look more like she should."

Objective: Caroline's parents were in to visit this evening Mother held infant continuously and both mom and dad talked with Caroline and stroked her. Asking appropriate questions.

Assessment: Good parent-infant bonding.

Plan: Encourage visitation; encourage questions; keep parents informed of Caroline's condition at all times.

FRIDAY, NOVEMBER 25, 1:00 P.M.

Pediatric surgery.

Weight up to 150 grams (?) from yesterday. Resting comfortably, less icteric. Less diarrhea, more formed stools. Bilirubin down to 5.8.

Plan: Give 1/4 strength Pregestimil four ml/hour via stomach tube.

FRIDAY, NOVEMBER 25, 3:00 P.M.

Nurse's note.

Active and alert, irritable and crying most of time when awake.
Appears hungry.

We see what we want to see. The surgery resident saw
Carrie "resting comfortably," while to the rest of us she is
"irritable and crying most of time when awake."

The entries in Carrie's chart over the last few days are
cool and objective, documenting her slow progress, but what
the chart fails to reflect is the raging battle developing between ourselves and the house staff. The head surgeon, we
find out later, is out of town for the Thanksgiving weekend.
The rest of the pediatric surgery group are very unlikely to
make any decision affecting Carrie's care. Each day we check
the orders to see how far Carrie's feedings have been advanced, and then I page the chief pediatric surgery resident
to discuss them.

For the first time, I am becoming a real pain in the ass,
but there is one saving grace about it: I don't care. During
these weeks I have changed. My daughter means more to me
than the good will of my fellow physicians. After all, they'll be
gone soon, but Carrie, I pray, will be around a long time.

SATURDAY, NOVEMBER 26, 2:00 P.M.

Pediatric surgery.

Resting comfortably. Weight up 40 grams. Tolerating ¼ strength Pregestimil at four ml/hour; will increase to five ml/hour. No diarrhea. Liver function tests: alkaline phosphatase: 340; SGOT: 93; LDH: 382. All down, apparently tolerating hyperal well in spite of ongoing hyperal hepatitis at time of restarting hyperal November 18.

I look at it a little differently. To me, the unusual clearing of Carrie's "hyperal hepatitis" is very unexpected. The condition usually gets worse on a patient's second exposure to hyperal. It doesn't simply mean that Carrie is one of those rare people who don't have a worse reaction the second time around. To me it throws into question the original diagnosis and makes me wonder if the earlier rapid deterioration in her liver function is due to something other than hyperal.

Quickly I run through the dates in my mind. Carrie had gone into a coma on November 1, having been on hyperal for two weeks. Amphotericin had been started on the 2nd, and her liver functions hadn't started to deteriorate until the 6th, the hyperal being stopped on the 9th. Carrie's liver enzymes had continued to skyrocket even though the hyperal had been stopped and the amphotericin was stopped on the 11th. The liver enzymes peaked three days later, on the 14th, and then began coming steadily down, even though the hyperal was restarted on the 18th. "Hyperal hepatitis" did not necessarily seem to me to have been her problem, but the whole issue of her amphotericin treatment had been one of very questionable judgment, as you've seen.

In fact, Carrie's whole hospital course seems bizarre, from the sudden appearance of NEC at age two days to her rapid descent into shock and coma and near death, to her seeming recovery and its sudden reversal, with Carrie seemingly in septic shock from something still not, to me, well characterized. Along the way she's been treated with a myriad of powerful drugs, with a seemingly good outcome at this point, but still, I wonder, what really caused her NEC, or the disease that we describe as NEC? Why did she suddenly deteriorate as she was recovering so nicely? The labels and descriptions for what have happened to Carrie seem to me just that, labels and descriptions as inadequate as the ancients' humors.

As difficult as it is to understand Carrie's past, the reality of Carrie and the rest of her life is what really concerns me. No matter what the "cause" of her sickness, she will be ours forever if she ever recovers, yet I sense that no one in the hospital really cares what she will be like once she leaves. This isolation of Judy and me I'd sensed while Carrie was still gravely ill, and only, I suspect, because I'd felt so ultimately unconcerned about my sick patients when acting as their physician.

All you want to do, as a doctor or nurse, is get the patient out of your care. That is the definition of success, and an appropriate one, because how could one possibly use long-term outcome as a criteria for good medical results? There's simply no way to keep track of the thousands of patients you care for only relatively briefly in their total lifespan, so by necessity you keep your goals immediate and concrete.

What this does, though, is render you impotent at seeing the big picture. Only a patient, or his or her family, has the proper perspective to view illness as a personal and resonating force, with effects that echo powerfully throughout that individual's and their family's future. Thus, personal responsibility for your own health and that of your loved ones is not just something one ought to feel: it can and should have a direct bearing on the medical decisions that are made. No human being lives in a vacuum, and a family must make it clear that they are as affected by illness and health as the individual who is sick. No one else really cares, not the way you do. You shouldn't expect them to, after all, if family and blood and love are to have real meaning.

SUNDAY, NOVEMBER 27, 2:00 P.M.

Pediatric surgery.

Hematocrit this afternoon 33—will transfuse.

SUNDAY, NOVEMBER 27, 3:00 P.M.

Nurse's note.

Caroline was transfused with 23 ml packed red blood cells because of a hematocrit of 33%. Vital signs stable throughout transfusion.

Yet another transfusion. Judy and I cringe. Carrie's hematocrit of thirty-three means that 33 percent of her circulating blood volume is made up of red blood cells, the rest being plasma. Normal range for a baby is in the forties, but Carrie has a good, non-pathologic reason for being somewhat anemic. Her blood is being systematically removed for tests faster than she can replace it. She is, considering everything, doing well. Giving her blood will not help her heal faster, but it will though, once again, expose her to all the very real, and in this case unnecessary, hazards associated with blood transfusion.

Hepatitis, AIDS, bacterial infections, others as yet unknown to be blood-borne, this is the exposure Carrie has once again, in my opinion, received unnecessarily. For what? To make a number look "more normal"? This is a fundamental problem in medicine, the drive to make the numbers normal. I can't begin to recall how many times as a medical student I watched frantically prepared infusions and medications get rushed into dying patients with "electrolyte imbalance." "Who cared?" I thought to myself. "Why are we doing this?" Then, when the patient died, there was a smug air of self-congratulation among the house staff as if to say, "Well, we did everything we could; she died with normal lab values."

Carrie doesn't need a higher hematocrit; she needs to be allowed to recover. The fact that her hematocrit *after* this transfusion is still thirty-three doesn't indicate she is bleeding, but simply that one of the hematocrit determinations was improperly performed. Nevertheless, another transfusion is given, the numbers recorded, and now the surgical resident can consider this particular problem "solved."

Is it just our imagination or has Carrie's transfusion been begun just after we've left Saturday afternoon and completed before we come back that night? Maybe it is easier for everyone that way.

SUNDAY, NOVEMBER 27, 4:00 P.M.

Pediatric surgery.

No apparent distress, resting comfortably. Physical exam unremarkable, lungs clear, appears well-hydrated. Abdomen with
good bowel sounds, no diarrhea; will increase feeds to six ml/
hour via G tube. Off antibiotics past 24 hours, remains afebrile.
Bilirubin down to 7.0. Doing well. Will advance feedings as tolerated.

SUNDAY, NOVEMBER 27, 6:00 P.M.

Nurse's note.

Very fretful and irritable, appears hungry. Chewing on pacifier
when held in mouth. Otherwise, appears less jaundiced, no other
evidence of distress.

Is this the same child? Carrie is howling almost constantly now, her feedings still going in through a tube directly
to her stomach. Hunger is a powerful, primitive, yet complicated reflex, and is satisfied as much by what passes through
the mouth as what enters the stomach.

When we come in to visit we find a bottle with a little
formula next to Carrie's isolette. No one says anything, but I

saunter up to Amy and ask "Is this Carrie's?" She nods reddening. I pat her on the back. Judy whispers "Thank you."

We know the nurses caring for Carrie recognize that just filling her stomach is not doing the job. They have, on their own, begun giving Carrie a little of her dilute formula by bottle, letting her drink it. Now as we watch, Amy pops the bottle in her mouth. Carrie gulps it hurriedly, as if she knows somehow she is a conspirator involved in something illicit.

Judy and I look at each other frowning. Judy had been a real activist as a neurosurgical ICU nurse, and knew just how flimsy and precarious was the reasoning behind much of the care she was ordered to give. When she thought that an intern or resident was doing the wrong thing, or had missed something, rather than get into a useless argument, she'd simply taken care of it as she knew best. She didn't give drugs when they were ordered out of habit but shouldn't have been, and her decisions were usually the right ones. Interestingly, though, this was rarely acknowledged by the house staff whose asses she'd saved on many occasions. They'd simply stand there on rounds as the attending neurosurgeon reviewed the chart and agreed with management they'd never thought to initiate. The nurses in Carrie's unit were equally competent and experienced, and we trusted their judgment.

She and I both feel that what Carrie needs is not to have her G tube feeding increased by one milliliter an hour, but to be allowed to eat. It is apparent to everyone, even the surgery resident, but herein lies the bind. The attending surgeon is away; Carrie's regular resident is off today; the other resident "covering" the service is simply there as a stopgap and knows nothing about Carrie's complicated course, and the chief resident, who is going into plastic surgery in New York City in six months is simply putting in her time. No real harm would accrue if Carrie continues as she is for another day until the attending surgeon returned, and no one wants to take the responsibility for initiating feeding. So it remains, the orders skirted, and the frustration on our part immense.

MONDAY, NOVEMBER 28, 10:00 A.M.

G.I. consult.

As long as there is no problem with gastric emptying, there is no reason to provide G tube feedings as dilute formula. I would decrease volume and increase calories by a factor of 4. This way you have only one variable to deal with. I would pay relatively little attention to stool consistency as long as intake and output are adequate. If we wait for firm stools, we have a long wait indeed, and a long time on hyperal with a sick liver. Would begin regular oral feedings immediately.

"Finally," I say to Judy who clasps my hand.

MONDAY, NOVEMBER 28, 11:00 P.M.

Nurse's note.

Neuro: Good suck, gasp, and cry. Very fussy and hungry, fretful, painful cry.

Cardiac: Regular rate and rhythm, no murmur.

Resp: Even rate, clear breath sounds.

Skin: Slight jaundice.

GI: Good bowel sounds. G tube site red and swollen. Doctor removed suture from site.

Overall: Taking oral feedings well every 2 hours; still crying intermittently; perhaps secondary to painful G tube site.

There is no doubt, Carrie is ready to eat and eat she does. The G tube is now nonfunctional, clamped off so that the food she eats doesn't simply run out of her stomach. "What's wrong?" Judy says miserably to Sally, Carrie's night nurse. She walks over to Carrie and motions to us. Then she lifts the edge of a protective rubber collar around the G tube site which keeps it anchored in place. The whole area is red and inflamed.

"Dammit," I cry out. "The tube isn't being used, it is hurting Carrie, and it will only continue to do so. Why not pull it out?"

"I'll mention it again to the surgeons on rounds tomorrow morning," Sally says frowning.

"I'll do more than mention it if something isn't done by the time we come in," I angrily retort.

The next day, Tuesday, November 29th, an event occurs in the operating room which no one else finds especially remarkable, but which plunges me into a meditative, thoughtful state for the rest of the day. Even now, years later, it occasionally stills my awareness of my immediate circumstances and plunges me back in time.

An emergency case is posted, a one-week old baby with suspected NEC for an exploratory laparotomy. Piers Zender, Carrie's surgeon, will operate on this child also. I stare at the entry in the emergency book, imagining just how bleak and devastated the parents of this poor child must feel, and the agony yet to come, no matter what the outcome.

I have a strong urge to go up to the ICU and talk to the parents, reassure them that we will take good care of their baby and tell them that I know how they feel. But I don't, because they won't believe me if I tell them I really understand how they are feeling unless I tell them about Carrie; and if I tell them that Carrie is recovering, if they are anything like me, they will simply feel jealous and even more hurt. No one likes to be told how great things will be eventually, not when they're miserable.

An hour later the infant comes down to our operating

room, IVs and tubes everywhere. Scrawny and blue, belly bloated and tense, she looks just like Carrie had. My heart pounds as I stare at her; my ears start to ring faintly.

She is comatose, so little anesthesia is necessary. I watch intently, standing next to the resident, behind the drapes, as Zender makes his incision. So this is what it had been like for Carrie. She'd been operated on in this same room, on the same table, twice.

The abdominal wall parts as the incision lengthens, and bowel, shiny, black, gangrenous, necrotic bowel, oozes out of the wound. The room is silent as the surgeon gently unwinds the length of intestine, foot after foot of black, swollen bowel, with occasional holes where the wall has burst and the contents emptied into the peritoneal cavity.

"We'll just close her back up," Zender says quietly, shaking his head. "There's nothing salvageable here."

I feel like I am going to faint. This is the baby's death sentence. She will be dead of overwhelming infection within forty-eight hours. The alternative would be to remove all of her intestines, rendering her without any digestive capacity at all. She might live, but only in a stunted, painful, probably retarded, excruciatingly uncomfortable way, and only for a short while. The surgeon has no interest in prolonging the agony of either the child or the parents.

I watch, mesmerized, as he gently replaces the intestine inside the abdomen and begins to close the wound. This is the other side of Carrie's fate, the one we haven't experienced. Someone else has suffered it instead. Them, and not us. Yet their pain is as great as ours would have been. I feel it myself. Yet I will sleep tonight, and not them. I will forget about it, or so I think (I obviously haven't) in a day or two. The amount of agony, pain and joy in the world seems to me, I think sadly, a single total, which simply is allotted here and there. An individual or family just happens to be at the right or wrong place at the right (or wrong) time.

TUESDAY, NOVEMBER 29, 3:30 P.M.

Nurse's note.

Parent-Infant Separation:
   Objective: Parents both in today. Mother touched, held and fed patient at 12:00 noon; father touched, held and fed at 2:00 P.M.
   Assessment: Bonding progressing well.
   Plan: Continue as ordered; report any changes. Evaluate continuously bonding.

Carrie's chart is replete with notes like this, a symptom of the "new, human" approach to pediatric nursing and medicine since the "revolutionary" discovery in the 60s and 70s that human interaction with high risk babies significantly improves their ultimate outcome. It doesn't take much sense to figure that a small child deprived of human contact and placed in a plastic box for months on end just after birth will not be as well off as one who isn't, but it wasn't until controlled studies proved this to be so that parents were allowed and encouraged to visit their hospitalized, sick children as often as they wanted.

WEDNESDAY, NOVEMBER 30, 2:00 P.M.

Surgery resident off-service note.

Caroline was the 2030 gram product of a 34–35 week pregnancy, delivered prematurely 10/12/83. Problems include NEC with bowel resection, since reconnected, Candida sepsis, and hyperal hepatitis, both adequately treated. Patient flunked breastmilk feeds and is now tolerating Pregestimil. She has done well recently and we are advancing oral feedings as tolerated. She will soon no longer need central line.

Physical exam: Unremarkable except for G-tube site, which looks mildly erythematous but okay.

Patient is on 1/2 strength Pregestimil, also on hyperal-not receiving adequate calories with this regimen but will advance as fast as possible. Afebrile off antibiotics.

Labs: All WNL except bilirubin, now 6.4 (down from 7.0).

Assessment: Doing well but baby is very hungry.

Plan: Continue current management. Dad is an anesthesiology attending here; Mom is an ICU nurse; they visit several times a day and have many questions and concerns.

Translated, this means "They're a pain in the butt, so watch out." I decide I've never liked this resident anyway. "Flunked breastmilk feeds," my ass. Judy had knocked herself out to try to breast-feed Carrie, but just couldn't hold on through the weeks of waiting and pumping her breasts. I suppose, though, from his point of view, we had flunked and Carrie had flunked. She hadn't gone on to breast-feeding for whatever reason, so she'd failed.

According to him the G-tube site problem is no problem. At least, he doesn't have to worry about it any longer. How the hell you explain away an obvious inflammation mystifies me.

Nevertheless, in spite of, or due to, everything that is happening, Carrie continues to rebound, eating everything. Her liver function tests are returning to normal, her jaundice fading. Is it possible? Would she really recover enough to go home? I feel like not only crossing my fingers but everything else as Judy and I begin for the first time to experience real hope.

THURSDAY, DECEMBER 1, 1:00 P.M.

Nurse's note.

Central line site slightly reddened around insertion site. No sign of displacement.

G-tube in place and clamped. Site red and raised.

Carrie is still "hooked up" to two things—her central line and her G-tube. The central line is now being used for clear fluids only, as her hyperal has been stopped since she is eating well and getting all the calories she needs from three-quarter strength formula. The G-tube hasn't been used in four days, but remains clamped off. Both sites are becoming irritated and inflamed, a prelude to infection—the last central line had started out the same way, finally growing out Candida and leading to the amphotericin infusion.

Why, I wonder, don't Carrie's doctors just go ahead and pull both lines? Why the delay?

SATURDAY, DECEMBER 3, 10:00 P.M.

Nurse's note.

G-tube site red, swollen, area raised, tender; dried, crusted material around it. Note some pus-filled areas around it. Infant screams and writhes when area cleaned.

Somewhere, someone's signals are getting crossed. The surgeons who intended to keep the tube in, no matter what, evidently are pretending to themselves and everyone else that the site is normal, and just needs good care. The nurses, who cared for children with these tubes routinely, know that the site is infected. Judy and I, who have experience with wounds, know too that Carrie has a purulent abscess developing around the tube, and that the only way to clear an infection caused by a foreign body is to remove the foreign body.

What frightens me is that very soon the surgeons will have to recognize the inevitable and put Carrie on antibiotics once again to clear the infection. This can only mean trouble, raising the risk of superinfection. I see the complications starting yet again, when Carrie is so tantalizingly close to getting out. I just can't let this happen. I have to do something, but what?

SUNDAY, DECEMBER 4, 12:00 P.M.

Nurse's note.

G-tube site draining copious pale green/yellow pus. Inflamed, red, raised and swollen. Caroline continues to be irritable when site cleaned, often remaining fussy for hours, crying self to sleep.

I can't take it any more. The veneer of trying to be the quiet, good doctor/father has worn off. I tell Amy, Carrie's nurse, to page Mike Haskell, the junior surgical resident.

She gives me her usual answer, "As you wish, Dr. Stirt."

I don't wait for him to introduce himself. I don't make small talk. Immediately I get to the point. "What do you make of Carrie's G-tube site? Come over here and check it with me."

He adjusts his horn rimmed glasses and peers into Carrie's box. "Well, it's a little red and swollen, but it's not too bad," he answers looking at the irritation with me.

"Not too bad? It's infected! What do you call the yellow-green stuff oozing out along the sides?"

He fingers his glasses, looking uncomfortable. "No, it's not really infected, it's just little irritated. We could put some antibiotic ointment around it. That might help."

"The only thing that will help is taking the damn thing out," I loudly retort. "Go across the room and look at that baby's G-tube," I say. "It's been in longer than Carrie's and doesn't look anything like this. That's the way it's supposed to look."

"Well, I can't pull out the tube." He still hems and hahs. "She's supposed to go home with it."

"The hell she will," I say definitively.

The attending surgeon is out of town; so the service is in the hands of the chief resident. I page her. Helen Young is going into plastic surgery in a few months. She is just marking time until she leaves. She doesn't want to be in the middle of this, but then, neither do I. Tough luck.

She is at home, so we will have to wait until she arrives. Amy offers to page Judy and I when Dr. Young comes so we can go have lunch, but I nix the idea "I'm not about to leave and miss her through some mixup."

When Young, a dark piquant-faced woman arrives an hour or so later she looks as if the junior surgical resident has talked to her and prepared her for my onslaught.

I dispense with trivialities. "Carrie's G-tube site looks terrible, and it's getting worse every time we come in. I want to see what you think."

"Let's see," she says. I know she knows exactly how the site looks, because she'd made rounds earlier that morning. She is just trying to get through the weekend until the attending surgeon returns, and then let him bear the brunt of the problem. But I'm not about to let that happen, not if I can help it. The attending surgeon is adamant about keeping the tube in. He always sends kids home with tubes, and will probably put Carrie back on antibiotics in an effort to keep the infection under control.

I know that once the tube comes out, it can't be reinserted, because the hole closes over and begins to heal very fast. The nurses have told me this, so I am prepared. I also know that if I lean hard enough, today is the day that damned tube will come out.

Dr. Young stands looking at the tube site, crusted over with dried pus, angry and swollen. The tube itself is awash in pus draining out of the hole around it. The room is silent, the nurse, Judy, myself, the chief resident, and junior surgical resident all stand around Carrie's bassinet. It seems to go on for a long time, this still-life freeze frame.

"Give me a syringe," Young finally says to Carrie's nurse.

She takes it and deflates the cuff holding the tube in place. The tube pops out of Carrie's abdominal wall, trailing a gush of yellow/white fluid down her abdomen.

"Jesus Christ," I exclaim, startled. "What's that?"

"That's just her stomach contents," Dr. Young says matter-of-factly.

I feel foolish. The chief resident tapes a gauze bandage over the hole, looks at me, and says "All right?"

"Thanks," I reply and she leaves. I know what it has taken for her to do that. Possibly she would face immense anger from the attending surgeon tomorrow, but she has done what she knows is right. I sympathize a bit with Mike Haskell, the junior resident, who had been in no position to take it out, but I have no sympathy for his pretense that there was nothing wrong with the site. If I had been in his position, I would have said, "I agree, it's badly infected, but I'm not the one to decide to pull it." He'd made a fool of himself by pretending it wasn't so.

MONDAY, DECEMBER 5, 2:00 P.M.

Pediatric surgery resident.

Caroline's central line and G-tube were discontinued this weekend. Weight up 20 grams.

Central line site clean. G-tube site red, has greenish mucopurulent exudate on outside. Very little drainage.

Lungs clear.

Abdomen: benign.

Fluids: All oral feedings.

GI: Eating well, every 3–4 hours. Weight increasing. 2 stools/shift.

Impression: Doing well. Superficial infection of G-tube site.

Plan: Local skin care. Will probably discharge soon.

I wonder if I'd have just "accidentally" pulled the G-tube out yesterday if Young had not. I think so. Judy was just as upset as I was and ready to do it if I didn't. Boy, that would have truly been an event.

For the first time since she was born, Carrie is not connected to anything, and she is eating. Judy and I can hardly believe it. Can we actually come in anytime, lift her out of her bassinet, walk around and hold her, without any problem? We marvel that for most people who have babies this is the only way it has ever been. As I pick up Carrie I feel so free and easy with her, and she is still in the hospital. I can't even imagine how wonderful it would be to walk around the house, singing and talking nonsense. Incomprehensible. At the moment, here in the intermediate unit, along with the ICU the only place Carrie has ever been, life seems good enough.

Now we truly start to believe Carrie is coming home after all. Until the G-tube and central line had come out there'd been too many false starts and dashed hopes to let us really think seriously about it.

At home that afternoon we open the door to her room at last, and air it out. It looks as ready as it had two months earlier, a lifetime ago. We pretend she is home, and carry a teddy bear around the house, imagining holding her. She'll be there, always. No more kissing her good night at the hospital. If we wanted to go out we'd have to call a babysitter. Who could we trust with this little thing? We don't want to feel anything has happened because we haven't been around when we should have. It is hard to escape the feeling, deep down, that somehow in some unfathomable way, we are in some way responsible for the series of disasters that have befallen Carrie. After all, we created her, so we are somehow linked to all that has occurred.

That night when we come to visit, Carrie looks good to us, her jaundice is fading, her skin just the faintest tinge of yellow, eyes a little off-white still. The "hyperal hepatitis," or whatever the cause of her liver failure, is rapidly disappearing. It even appears she'll avoid a follow-up liver biopsy to pinpoint the cause of her hepatitis. We sigh with relief. We don't want to bring Carrie back in for another operation and hospitalization, no matter how "minor." To us, no hospitalization could ever be termed minor again. We are determined to do anything necessary or possible not to have Carrie go back in once she leaves. We look upon her leaving as a reprieve, a commuted sentence. We aren't about to give it up lightly.

Now, with the opportunity coming at long last to have total responsibility for her, we are both reluctant and ready. What other new parents felt right after birth, has been delayed for months, and the intervening time and horrors have made us more eager, yet also more frightened than most people ever have to be.

TUESDAY, DECEMBER 6, 3:00 P.M.

Pediatric surgery note.

Doing well, no problems. Weight unchanged. Eating ad lib. G-tube site much better today, infection clearing, orifice sealed over.

    Infectious Disease: G-tube site: staphloccus growth (normal skin flora) on culture. Central line tip: no growth.

Everything that remains in an infected body for more than a few days is "cultured," or sent for analysis of bacterial growth, on its removal. It's routine. I wonder if Carrie's central line site grows anything out, like Candida, will her surgeons begin amphotericin again? I'm not sure, which is why I want Carrie out of the hospital before something else goes wrong out of the blue.

We decide one thing: as soon as Carrie comes home, we are all heading down to Jamaica to visit Judy's parents. Since Carrie is getting nothing but formula, we can take all her food, and Judy's mother is dying to see her granddaughter, so moribund when she'd left her, once again. It is as if we want to say "She was sick, yes, but damned if we're going to treat her like a sick child from now on." To me Carrie's survival means one thing: we should be bold, and do what we want, never hesitating for fear she is too delicate or fragile. She's dodged a lot of bullets, and perhaps she is charmed, after all.

WEDNESDAY, DECEMBER 7, 11:00 A.M.

Pediatric surgery note.

Caroline appears well. Weight unchanged second straight day. Stooling normally. Follow.

The attending surgeon, when we'd seen him on rounds earlier Wednesday, had been pleased about Carrie's overall appearance, but suddenly is noncommittal about when she'll be discharged. He'd told us "Later in the week, say Thursday or Friday," on Monday when we'd asked, but now he is hedging. "I am worried," he says, "that Carrie isn't gaining weight as fast as she'd been." In fact, her weight hasn't changed in two days. This bothers me. He goes on, "It indicates she might be having difficulty absorbing her food, a problem I feel can be handled better in the hospital."

"I disagree," I say vehemently. "We want her out." In an

irrational, nonsensical, childish way, both Judy and I believe she'll do just fine if she can just get out of this place, and we can carry her around and sing to her all day.

"I'm aiming for the weekend. If Carrie starts to gain weight over the next couple days, she'll be discharged," the surgeon says definitively.

We sigh. Just when Judy and I have begun to relax and think that things might be all right after all, we start to feel tension in the air again. Now, every visit we try to cram as much formula into Carrie as we can. We now ask the nurses only how much Carrie has eaten and put out during the last shift, no longer concerned with how she's been in general. The morning weighing becomes the most important moment of the day, and we watch it as carefully as a customer in a butcher shop, making certain no one is fiddling the scale or screwing it up by letting Carrie's leg trail over the edge.

Once again, it is numbers that will decide things, not how Carrie looks or we feel. Unfortunately, weights in a baby are as unreliable as any other tests or numbers a hospital generates. We remember the day some weeks past when Carrie's weight was a half-pound off from the previous day's. The half-pound in a four pound premature baby was like twenty pounds in an adult, yet the resident had just shrugged and put a question mark after it. Now we are dealing in grams, and portions of an ounce, to decide if Carrie is ready to go home. A wet diaper, or any change in what Carrie has on, or use of a different scale, can throw her weight off twenty grams.

WEDNESDAY, DECEMBER 7, 1:00 P.M.

Audiology consultant.

Hearing screen performed in intermediate unit per discharge protocol.

Impression: Right ear: possible significant hearing loss suggested by absence of clear response at any frequency. Left ear: within normal limits for all frequency ranges.

So, Carrie might be deaf on one side. From what, who knows? Maybe she'd been born that way, but, more likely, some combination of drugs, infection, malnutrition, and her two overwhelming episodes of apparent sepsis and decompensation and coma have caused the delicate hearing apparatus on one side to shut down.

Babies hospitalized in an ICU after birth who survive to be discharged have a much higher than normal incidence of problems in later life, some caused by their underlying disorders, others by their treatment. Thus, deafness, or significant hearing loss, is present in about 15 percent of infants following ICU treatment, as opposed to less than a 1 percent incidence in normal babies not hospitalized in an ICU.

I am slightly upset, but not much. Considering what could have happened and hadn't, being deaf in one ear doesn't seem like much. In other circumstances, if someone had told me that my otherwise healthy, happy baby was deaf on one side, I'd have been crushed, angered, scared, and demanding to know exactly what could be done. Instead, I shrug off the news. Who cares?

When we get home that day, two letters from the hospital

are there. "Bills already?" I say to Judy taking a deep breath. But no. The first is a letter informing us that, because Caroline is considered a "high-risk infant due to her requirement for prolonged ICU care following birth, she will be followed regularly in the hospital's Special Problems Clinic."

They have even set up her first appointment, for two Saturdays from her discharge date. Maybe they haven't gotten the word that Carrie's weight isn't going up fast enough for her to leave yet.

"Even if she gets out, there is no way we are going to that appointment, or any others that aren't for Carrie's benefit," I tell Judy.

"Agreed," she says, "hasn't she been through enough?"

I shake my head. Why would we take her to some clinic only to wait two hours and then have medical students, interns and residents poke at her, prod her, and question us? And at our expense? They have to be kidding. Our goal is to stay away from hospitals, not keep returning. The way I see it, Carrie's only "special problem" now is getting the hell out before something else traumatic happens.

The other letter is even better, a nice form letter informing us that Carrie's T4, a test to evaluate thyroid function, is abnormal.

"Every newborn infant in the state of Virginia has several blood tests performed in the newborn nursery soon after birth. One of these tests is to evaluate the infant's thyroid function. The thyroid is a gland in the neck which produces a hormone that is important for normal growth and development. Children whose thyroid levels are below normal may have serious problems with both physical and mental development.

"Your baby's newborn blood thyroid screen was mildly abnormal. This is a frequent finding with premature infants and probably is not a significant problem for your child. We believe your child is normal, but this test must be repeated. Please take this with the enclosed forms for repeating the blood test to your local physician and have him or her perform the blood test and return it in the appropriate envelope."

Babies with low thyroid function become cretins, overweight and retarded. I've seen a number during my training and Carrie, for all else that she has wrong, isn't that. The letter says, they believe "your child is normal." Well I know she isn't normal but she isn't hypothyroid either. They want Carrie to get stuck once more, anyway. "Screw this shit," I murmur, and toss that letter in the trash too. I mean, is Carrie going to live as a person or a victim? We've all had enough.

THURSDAY, DECEMBER 8, 2:00 P.M.

Nurse's note.

Parent-infant separation. Subjective: "If Caroline is doing well clinically, why can't she come home today? It's not that we can't do for her what the nurses are doing for her here in the hospital. We could provide more care if she came home."

Objective: Mrs. Stirt is quite frustrated that Caroline will not be scheduled for discharge today. She relates that she feels competent enough to give Caroline the same, or better, care than Caroline is receiving in the NIN in respect to the continuity of the Stirts as caregivers, and the competence that comes from their experiences as medically oriented professionals.

Assessment: Frustrated parents, anxious to have Caroline at home.

Plan: Support and encourage parents to verbalize their feelings; tender loving care as per routine.

Nothing like a little psycho-babble to fill up a chart.

THURSDAY, DECEMBER 8, 4:00 P.M.

Pediatric surgical note.

Caroline doing well, but did not get fed for more than six hours
last night. Feeding ad lib. Weight: down 80 grams. Liver function:
Bili 6.7 (normal 0.2-1.2), alk phos 402 (normal 20-95), SGOT 93
(normal 4-30), LDH 339 (normal 110-350). Hepatitis improving.
Doing very well.
   Plans: Discharge this weekend.

"If she is doing very well, why is she losing instead of
gaining weight?" Judy agonizes. Well, I find out and go
through the roof. Simple enough, yesterday evening nobody
fed her. She is the healthiest of the babies in the intermediate
unit, on no medications, about to go home, and requires no
special care, unlike all the other babies there. So, when problems arise on the night shift, Carrie's cries can be ignored,
with no consequences. That's why we want her home.

Now though, her immediate discharge is no longer certain. If she doesn't gain weight, she can't go home, but if she
isn't fed, she can't gain weight. We know she'll be a lot more
likely to be fed when she is hungry at home, but she can't go
home. New Catch-22.

FRIDAY, DECEMBER 9, 4:00 P.M.

Pediatric surgery note.

Caroline doing well. Eating great. Weight unchanged. Will discharge home in AM tomorrow if weight gain.

"If weight gain?" We are determined to take care of that problem. Judy and I visit Carrie every three hours starting at 7:00 A.M. Friday. Each time we pick up a bottle and feed her, pushing every drop we can into her. It seems insane to me, this absolute necessity to record a weight gain on the scale before she can go home, when she is clinically doing so well. But, it has been this way all along, the reliance on tests and objectivity, so it shouldn't surprise me. It irritates the hell out of both Judy and I though.

The attending surgeon had decreed "if she's recorded a weight gain Saturday morning, she can go home." When we finally leave Friday night, we plead with the evening nurse to tell her successor on late nights to feed Carrie incessantly.

The next morning, at dawn, we wake up. We manage to wait until seven to call the hospital to find out if Carrie's gained weight or not. Trembling, I begin to dial. Judy sighs, watching as I make a mistake and have to dial again. She leans forward listening intently.

"Intermediate nursery," I sputter.

I manage to find my voice. "Hi, this is Joe Stirt, Caroline's father. Can I speak to her nurse, please?"

"Just a minute."

I hold on as the ward clerk goes to get Carrie's nurse.

"Hello," she says.

"Hi, this is Joe Stirt, Carrie's father," I take a deep breath. "I'm calling to see if she gained any weight or not at her weighing this morning."

The pause seems interminable. Finally she answers. "Yes, she's up sixty grams, and she can go home today."

"Up sixty grams? Great!" I shout. "We'll be there as soon as we can to get her. Thanks a lot."

Judy and I embrace, yelling and laughing and crying. "Let's go," I say.

"I'm ready" Judy says. "I've been ready for what seems like forever."

I nod, my eyes filling with tears.

Within minutes we throw on some clothes, run out to the car, and drive to the hospital. We'd taken in a pink dress, a lacy sweater and a pastel receiving blanket for Carrie to come home in earlier that week. Now we dress her for the first time. We are in a rush to get her out of there but we can't help stopping for a moment to admire Carrie, who looks like a tiny doll. Then out of the unit we go, taking the stairs two at a time and out the door of the hospital. It is a cold December 10th, brisk and clear. The three of us are together at last. Finally free.

$\mathcal{E}pilogue$

Fourteen months have passed since Carrie has been discharged from the hospital. Carrie is already talking a little and laughing a lot.

She hasn't had to be hospitalized for anything and for this small miracle, Judy and I are constantly grateful.

Carrie may well have major problems in the future. This we cannot know.

Already she appears to have some kind of a hearing deficit in one ear, but she wakes up awfully quickly if there's a sound. So we don't worry that the damage is extensive and though she's very small for her age and probably always will be, she appears to be developmentally normal. Of course, when a child, your child, has been through what Carrie has, you are always fearful, always vigilant.

We worry that her gut is missing a long portion of bowel and she might not ever absorb enough to grow to what would have been her ultimate size.

We worry that she has diarrhea once in a while and seems to have more frequent bowel movements than other kids her age, and maybe she always will.

On the other hand, she has been incredibly well and the

301

possibility of her ever having serious problems related to her bowel grows smaller the longer she stays well.

A recent study states that "long-term growth and neurodevelopmental studies of infants surviving necrotizing enterocolitis have been very encouraging. All studies demonstrate that morbidity is no higher than that due to prematurity, respiratory distress syndrome, or other problems present before the onset of necrotizing enterocolitis."

Despite our good fortune we know that for every child who emerges like Carrie, relatively unscathed from severe neonatal sickness, there are many more who exist, silently, victims along with their families of a system which cannot predict who will be well and who will never recover.

Our months of withdrawn silence while Carrie lay ill continue for years and lifetimes in tens of thousands of homes across the United States, families scattered and withdrawn into private pain and agony, because they haven't been as lucky as we are—and have a child severely physically deformed and mentally retarded.

Sandy Rovner, in the Washington Post, wrote: "Those who would most strongly advocate the so-called Baby Doe rules believe that even a breath of life demands the most heroic efforts to prolong it. The parents of a sixteen year old girl who is deaf, blind, and frozen at the intellectual level of a ten-week old infant believe that her smile is worth it all. As her father says at what has to be the most heartbreaking "Sweet 16" party ever televised, "It may not be the kind of life that would fulfill me . . . but she does sense love and sensitivity and warmth. When people say a life can only be (valuable) if it's productive, I can't accept it . . ."

"But the anonymous mother of a retarded five year old counters, "Our babies, when they are born, do need protection, and if we parents are taken out of the picture they are going to be at the mercy of modern medical gadgetry, condemned to go through procedure after procedure, operation after operation, and no one will be there to stand up on his behalf and say, "Let him alone . . . let him go . . ."

William McPherson wrote, "There are two kinds of truth, of course, the kind of truth in which the opposite is false and the kind in which the opposite is also true. Journalism sticks to the first; the rest is physics." I would submit: "Or medicine."

Judy and I well know the many pitfalls and heartbreaks which might have befallen Carrie and those which still might.

Through much of her hospitalization, Carrie was gravely ill; the effects of repeated episodes of coma can linger forever. If insufficient oxygen reaches the brain and nervous system during the period when development should have been at its most rapid, permanent deficits may result, which will only become apparent as a child grows and fails to be normal in one way or another. On the other hand, if an infant receives supplemental oxygen for weeks, blindness can result from an oversupply of oxygen to the developing retina. The long-term effects of high oxygen concentrations at a critical phase of development remain unknown.

Carrie received general anesthesia twice, with potent agents. The long-term effects of such drugs on children are unknown. She had a tube in her larynx twice, to aid her breathing. Scars and strictures of the windpipe occasionally follow such instrumentation, resulting in the need for major surgical procedures, usually inadequate, to produce a satisfactory airway. This possibility remains in Carrie's future.

While she has recovered from her underlying disease, it left scars. The possibility of adhesions (scar tissue from her operations which twists and constricts the intestine) forming is very real, and one which frightens Judy and me every time she doesn't eat well, especially if she vomits. In a normal child, these symptoms usually mean nothing serious; in Carrie, they might herald bowel obstruction and the need for an emergency abdominal operation to release the scars.

Her bowels may also not grow properly in some areas, due to scarring. This may not become apparent for some time. These areas may produce pain and obstruction in the future, requiring further operations.

Carrie's severe episode of hepatitis, apparently over, may leave its mark on the liver. A small percentage of children with apparently resolved hepatitis continue to harbor the active virus which may have caused or been associated with it. Only years later, when liver failure occurs, is this apparent, and terminal liver cancer, though rare, does occasionally occur.

Carrie received twenty-seven blood transfusions, with a risk of one to two percent per transfusion of contracting transfusion-related hepatitis. Results of tests to detect the presence of the carrier agents of infectious hepatitis are confusing and inaccurate at present, so we have to just wait and see.

Certainly, the possibility of Carrie's having picked up the causative agent of AIDS or any of a number of other possibly blood-borne diseases, such as leukemia, exists, and the latency, or quiescent, period of such diseases is many years long.

Finally, what of the truly long-term consequences of her hospitalization and treatment? Carrie received radiation of all sorts in the course of her diagnosis and treatment, starting even before birth.

While in Judy's uterus she received ultrasonic radiation to detect her developmental age. During her first episode of jaundice right after birth, constant ultraviolet bilirubin lights were focused on her head, and ultrasound examinations performed to look for hemorrhage and organ damage. When she appeared to have pneumonia scores of x-rays were taken to assess her NEC and lungs. Her ovaries were never shielded during any of these examinations.

Besides the potential carcinogenic and developmentally damaging effect of all these different forms of radiation, I fear what effect they had on the developing germ cells in her ovaries, all of which were present at the time this onslaught of radiation occurred.

A female's entire complement of ova, or eggs, is present at birth, and so a woman's gene pool, more than a man's, is exquisitely vulnerable to radiation from birth onward. Should I discuss this with Carrie when and if she gets old enough to have children of her own? Or should I say, "the hell with it," and see what happens? What if she has a deformed child? Do Judy and I bear responsibility for letting her think things are just fine?

Such are the things that make me less than blasé about the future. Still each time I see Carrie gurgling or hold her tight I reflect on the decision Judy and I made when she was struggling for life to ask the surgeon not to try to save Carrie if her entire bowel was dead. The decision seemed obvious and inevitable. Today, if we were to be in the identical situation with another infant, I'm not sure we might not make the opposite choice.

Afterword

Carrie is eight years old now, in the third grade. The only physical impairment yet discovered is that indeed she is deaf in one ear, as diagnosed by the hearing exam towards the end of her last stay in the NICU. She has compensated remarkably well, such that if I didn't tell her teachers, they'd never realize she had a hearing loss. Only a nearly imperceptible movement of her head to put her good left ear more in the field of sound hints at her disability.

Her speech is normal, although for a while we feared it would not be, so the hearing impairment is relatively benign. In fact, not only is her speech normal, but last semester she was chided by her teacher for being a "chatterbox"; so we probably don't need to worry about her hearing in the future. Carrie's also pointed out that by sticking a finger in her left ear as if she's scratching it, she can block out all sound without being obvious, a real boon, it seems, at recess when she's being teased or bothered by someone.

Most amazing to us is that in the years since she was discharged from the hospital, she's not ever had to return for any reason, and she's grown steadily to the point where although she's still rather scrawny at four feet two inches tall

306

and fifty-two pounds, she's about average height for her age. It's obvious that she has enough intact bowel to absorb what she needs to grow, because she gets nothing whatsoever in the way of dietary supplements or medication.

Equally surprising to me in view of what I see daily, is that she's not had any problems with adhesions or bowel obstructions as a result of the extensive surgery she had as an infant. We've been lucky, both in having highly skilled surgeons and in the results of their handiwork.

Of course, there are still the numerous scars crisscrossing Carrie's belly, but she's so blasé about them that she insists next summer we get her a "belly-shower" swimming suit with cutouts over the stomach and back.

"Carrie, my child, my dear child," I tell her with feelings whose depth she will never know, "if that's what you want, that's what you'll get."